Who would deny the opportunity to see God? Interestingly, the 'seers of truth' teach
(beyond this world) and immanent (perceivable in our immediate surroundings). Fo
remains only theoretical. How can we begin to tangibly perceive the Supreme Person i
book, Urmila Edith Best and Kamala-sita Dasi enrich us with philosophical insights an
to elevate our consciousness and bring us face-to-face with Divinity. The beautiful illus
ling complement the text and bring it to life. This is a welcome addition to any spiritual

– SB Kesava Swami: Speaker, Spiritual Advisor, Author of *Book Bhagavata: The Life Companion*, and *Tattva: See Inside Out*

I am very pleased to see Urmila Edith Best and Kamala-sita Dasi's Krishna Meditations: Finding the Divine in all Aspects of Life come to fruition. This book is a practical guide to a challenging issue: how to see Kṛṣṇa everywhere. The Lord Himself speaks in Bhagavad-gītā of the benefits of such vision:

yo māṁ paśyati sarvatra
sarvaṁ ca mayi paśyati
tasyāhaṁ na praṇaśyāmi
sa ca me na praṇaśyati

"For one who sees Me everywhere and sees everything in Me, I am never lost, nor is he ever lost to Me." (Bhagavad-gītā 6.30)

There are two levels of seeing Krishna everywhere. The first is to see Him with eyes coated with pure spiritual love like the cowherd girls of Vrindavan (Brahma-saṁhitā (5.38): premāñjana-cchurita-bhakti-vilocanena) and the second is to see Him in the opulence of His creation. He explains this second level of vision to Arjuna in the tenth chapter of Bhagavad-gītā:

śrī-bhagavān uvāca
hanta te kathayiṣyāmi
divyā hy ātma-vibhūtayaḥ
prādhānyataḥ kuru-śreṣṭha
nāsty anto vistarasya me

"The Supreme Personality of Godhead said: Yes, I will tell you of My splendorous manifestations, but only of those which are prominent, O Arjuna, for My opulence is limitless." (Bhagavad-gītā 10.19)

The first type of vision, seeing Kṛṣṇa everywhere with love like the gopīs, is not yet within our grasp, so in Krishna Meditations, Urmila and Kamala-sita utilize verses from the Bhagavad-gītā and Śrīmad-Bhāgavatam, as well as Kṛṣṇa's qualities, to see Him in the world around us.

We should not take their work as a curiosity as to how Kṛṣṇa appears to us in this way. Rather we should see it as an opportunity to increase our eagerness to see Him. Śrīla Prabhupāda writes: "We must be very, very eager to see Kṛṣṇa. Somehow or other you must develop this eagerness, this desire: 'I must see Kṛṣṇa.' Kṛṣṇa is looking for how eager you are to see Him." (Journey of Self Discovery, 2:2).

Having a genuine desire and eagerness to see Kṛṣṇa will automatically help us become detached from the illusions of this world and awaken our desire to see Him in His original form in Śrī Vṛndāvana-dhāma. That desire will help us call out to Him like the Six Gosvāmīs:

he rādhe vraja-devike ca lalite he nanda-sūno kutaḥ
śrī-govardhana-kalpa-pādapa-tale kālindī-vane kutaḥ

"Oh Queen of Vṛndāvana, Rādhārāṇī! O Lalitā! O son of Nanda Mahārāja! Where are you all now? Are you just on the hill of Govardhana, or are you under the trees on the bank of the Yamunā? Where are you?" (Śrīnivās Ācārya, Ṣaḍ-gosvāmy-aṣṭaka 8)

Urmila and Kamala-sita have done a great service in helping us reach that goal by appreciating Kṛṣṇa in forms we can see with our very eyes. Like all readers of this book, I am eager to see Kṛṣṇa. Thus, Krishna Meditations will be my constant companion for the rest of my life.

– Indradyuma Swami: Bhakti-yoga teacher, Author of *Diary of a Traveling Monk*

A beautifully written book that is perfect for anyone who wants to deepen their understanding of meditation upon Sri Kṛṣṇa. I was taught by the author, Urmila Edith Best, how to meditate on the Lord at a very young age, and this book is a perfect companion for anyone who wants to learn more about meditating on Kṛṣṇa. I am so excited for this book to be published! What a gem! This book will surely help expand your understanding of the Lord and His meditations.

– Gaura Mani devi dasi: Grammy Nominated Singer

What better gift to give a friend than such a delightful meditation to evoke their remembrance of Lord Sri Kṛṣṇa? Whose eye and heart would not be charmed by these uplifting essential messages illuminated in a Vrindavan mood of simplicity and beauty? Each of these inspirations in the *Krishna Meditations* book pulls us a few steps closer to awakening attraction to Sri Govinda, the beloved Lord of our hearts.

– Rukmini Walker: founder, The Urban Devi Collective

Krishna Meditations: Finding the Divine in all aspects of life offers the reader beautiful meditations and intentional remembrances to assist us in seeing our Lord in every atom of His creation, and in everyone's heart. I especially like reading the descriptions of Lord Krishna's 64 qualities, and reflecting how the Lord personally attracts and serves His devotees and reciprocates their love. Thank you, Urmila Edith Best, Kamala-sita Dasi, and artist Nadiya Mani Darling, for giving us a wonderful book to increase our daily Kṛṣṇa meditations.

– Kosarupa Dasi: award-winning author and artist

In 1971 I wrote Śrīla Prabhupāda asking what is more important, service or remembering Kṛṣṇa. I didn't think of Kṛṣṇa much when busily engaged in service, so I was wondering if I should slow down so I could remember Kṛṣṇa more.

"The first line of Prabhupāda's reply read, "The whole point of everything is to become absorbed in thoughts of Kṛṣṇa." My instinctive response was, "That's impossible." And then a feeling of guilt came across me as I thought, "I really don't think of Kṛṣṇa much."

But all Prabhupāda was telling me was what the Padma Purana teaches.

"Kṛṣṇa is the origin of Lord Viṣṇu. He should always be remembered and never forgotten at any time. All the rules and prohibitions mentioned in the *śāstras* should be the servants of these two principles."

Nanda Kumara Prabhu was in India with Prabhupāda in the early days and they would regularly go to the Yamunā to bathe and play in her waters. He told Prabhupāda that he gets into the enjoying spirit because the weather is perfect, the water is warm and the devotees are enjoying themselves together. So, he asked Prabhupāda how he could remember Kṛṣṇa in this environment.

Prabhupāda said Kṛṣṇa is the taste of water, the light of the sun, and the fragrance of the earth; so are you not seeing the sun, tasting the water, and smelling the earth? By noticing these aspects of Kṛṣṇa you will remember Him in any situation.

Those who help us remember Kṛṣṇa are our greatest benefactors. I would like to offer my appreciation to Urmila and Kamala-sita for showing us how to see Kṛṣṇa in everything and thus fulfill the goal of Kṛṣṇa consciousness to always remember Kṛṣṇa and never forget him.

And I love the illustrations. I'd like to see them all made into posters so I can wallpaper my room with them!

– Mahatma Dasa: Writer, Retreat Facilitator, Social Media Content Creator and Counselor. He focuses on teaching how to practically apply Kṛṣṇa consciousness in day-to-day life.

In 316 short reflections inspired by Bhagavad-gītā and Śrīmad-Bhāgavatam, *Krishna Meditations* invites us to daily contemplate, celebrate, and delight in all the ways Kṛṣṇa is present with us and calling us to him in love. With charming illustrations to aid our reflections, these meditations are a treasure trove of insights that lend a contemporary vision of Kṛṣṇa in the world to enrich our lives.

– Pranada Comtois: author of award-winning *Wise-Love*, *Bhakti Shakti*, and *Prema Kirtan*

The essence of all spiritual teachings is to always remember God and never forget Him. Urmila Edith Best and Kamala-sita Dasi offer us Kṛṣṇa Mediations to help us do exactly that – to remember Kṛṣṇa, the amazing Supreme Personality of Godhead, wherever we go, whatever we do and whatever we perceive. We are grateful for all the time, energy and thoughtfulness these Vaiṣṇavīs have put into the pages of *Krishna Meditations.*

– Visakha Dasi: author of *Five Years, Eleven Months and a lifetime of unexpected love* OurSpiritualJourney.com

It is my pleasure to see *Krishna Meditations* by Urmila Edith Best and Kamala-sita Dasi. *Krishna Meditations* is a different kind of literature than what many of us are accustomed to in the Kṛṣṇa consciousness movement. It is more a practical tool than a theoretical book. It is designed to assist devotees in their most essential and important activity – constant remembrance of Kṛṣṇa.

In his *Bhakti Sandarbha, anuccheda* 277, Śrīla Jiva Goswami quotes *Garuḍa Purāṇa* regarding the urgency of always remembering the Lord:

ekasminn apy atikrānte muhūrte dhyāna-varjite
dasyubhir muṣiteneva yuktam ākranditum bhṛśam

"If one moment passes without meditating on the Lord one should cry
out loudly as if something was stolen by thieves."

The real success of Śrīla Prabhupāda's movement is not in how many buildings are owned, in the amount of money collected, or in the external number of members. Śrīla Prabhupāda's purpose in coming to the West was not for making construction projects or bank accounts – it was to spread consciousness of Kṛṣṇa. In a Sunday feast lecture at the Atlanta temple in March of 1975 a devotee asked him, "What pleases you the most Śrīla Prabhupāda?" His simple answer: "If you love Kṛṣṇa."

Śrīla Bhaktisiddhanta Saraswati Thakur Prabhupāda made a similar comment in an article in the *Harmonist* in January of 1932:

> "It is of course, no proof of the real success of any religious movement that it has been enabled to secure the allegiance of a large number of professed followers. The actual teachings of no prophet are followed by more than a very small minority of his professed followers."

Urmila and Kamala-sita have compiled a practical guidebook that can help each of us to fulfill the most fundamental and important element in the mission of Śrīla Prabhupāda and Sri Caitanya Mahaprabhu which is to be absorbed constantly in *Krishna Meditations*. I'm hoping that by the blessings of my guru and the *vaiṣṇavas*, and this delightful book I may yet one day join this wonderful movement.

– Madhavananda Das: Director of GORA, the Gaudiya Odia Research Association. Jagannath Puri Odisha. Managing editor of Gopal Jiu Publications and Sri Kṛṣṇa Kathamrita Magazine.

There are two ways to become Kṛṣṇa conscious: to bring Kṛṣṇa into our consciousness and to take what is already in our consciousness toward Krishna. And one of the things that is usually present in our consciousness, and often prominently present at that, is nature and the many things that nature is filled with. Such things may be present in our consciousness due to their necessity, utility, beauty, majesty or mystery or a combination of these.

Contemplating such elements in this series of brief yet deep reflections, Urmila and Kamala masterfully demonstrate how we can drive our thoughts toward a deeper appreciation of Kṛṣṇa's presence, purpose, and power in our daily lives.

– Chaitanya Charan: the spiritual scientist, Author of more than 25 books on The Bhagavad-gita, Ramayana, and related topics.

Krishna Meditations

Finding the Divine in all aspects of life

Urmila Edith Best & Kamala-sita Dasi
Illustrations by Nadiya Mani Darling

GOLDEN AGE MEDIA
BACK TO CULTURE

ISBN: 978-0-6397-8288-1

Contact us:
Golden Age Media
Nandgopāl Jivan Dāsa
Mobile: +91-8506805060
E-mail: ngjd.gkg@gmail.com
Web: www.goldenagemedia.org

Dedication

To all who want lives saturated with a vision of the Divine and who seek to see Kṛṣṇa everywhere.

Acknowledgments

Thanks for editing to Vaikuṇṭhamūrti Dāsa, B.A. Asrama Swami, and Nirvana Kasopersad. Thanks to Mukundāṅghri Dāsa who managed the project, even rescuing it! Thank you to Anita Stander and Richard Jones for layout and design, including the cover design. Thanks to Jñānāñjana Dāsa for the painting of Kṛṣṇa on the cover, which originally appeared as part of a larger painting for verse three of Śrī Manaḥ-śikṣā. We appreciate the participants in our classes on these topics while the book was in production who gave us helpful feedback and encouragement. Nadiya Mani Darling's amazing artwork brings the text to life and we are very grateful for her creative expertise. Thanks to Rukmiṇī Devī Dāsī for the inspiration for meditation 13 in the section on the Lord's qualities. Most of all we thank A. C. Bhaktivedanta Swami Prabhupāda who translated and commented upon the scriptures that served as the basis and inspiration for these meditations. He urged us to see the Divine Śrī Kṛṣṇa everywhere, and we hope this work helps our readers to do precisely that.

"A devotee should not see anything as being separate from the Supreme Personality of Godhead, Kṛṣṇa. Ether, fire, air, water, earth, the sun and other luminaries, all living beings, the directions, trees and other plants, the rivers and oceans – whatever a devotee experiences he should consider to be an expansion of Kṛṣṇa. Thus, seeing everything that exists within creation as the body of the Supreme Lord, Hari, the devotee should offer his sincere respects to the entire expansion of the Lord's body."

– *Śrīmad-Bhāgavatam* 11.2.41

Table of Contents

Preface

Kṛṣṇa, the Supreme Lord, is both identical with and separate from His energies. By meditating on His energies, therefore, we can learn much about Kṛṣṇa and appreciate His presence. Kṛṣṇa recommends such meditation throughout the scriptures. For example, at Kurukṣetra He tells the cowherd girls of Vṛndāvana, His beloved devotees, to always feel His presence through His energies.

Śrīla Prabhupāda comments on the above in *Kṛṣṇa Book* (Chapter 82):

> This important instruction by Lord Kṛṣṇa to the *gopīs* can be utilized by all devotees engaged in Kṛṣṇa consciousness. . . The cosmic manifestation is nothing but a display of Kṛṣṇa's energy, and because the energy is not different from the energetic, nothing is different from Kṛṣṇa. When this absolute consciousness, Kṛṣṇa consciousness . . . is present, then we are not separated from Kṛṣṇa.

Introduction

Urmila Edith Best: This book started many years before its publication when I swam in an indoor pool in London in cold weather. I was there at the invitation of a friend. As I swam, I mentally chanted the Hare Kṛṣṇa *mahā-mantra*. I noticed how soft and yielding the water was, and at the same time I became aware of the water's strength. "Just like Kṛṣṇa," I thought, "soft yet strong." That brief yet joyful and satisfying experience opened a different kind of perception within me, and I started noticing how everything in the world could connect me to thoughts and awareness of Kṛṣṇa's presence. Often, we may feel that Kṛṣṇa is only transcendent to the world, and thus we feel disconnected from Him in our daily life. I wanted to share that fulfilling feeling of connectedness and thus started observing, meditating, and writing.

The first result was a series of articles in *Back to Godhead* magazine on perceiving Kṛṣṇa in the material elements. I also gave some talks and seminars on the topic. Several friends urged me to write more and produce a book. I worked for a while, using the various quotes in the *Bhagavad-Gītā* where Kṛṣṇa says "I am" various aspects of our experience.

While involved in that writing, I asked Kamala-sita to join as co-author, and she started writing on Kṛṣṇa's sixty-four qualities. We gradually started writing from descriptions of the universal form given in the *Śrīmad-Bhāgavatam*, and the book evolved into four distinct sections of meditations. For years, it was on the back burner, until Kamala-sita offered to meet with me in Germany. From then on, we worked on it nearly daily until it was done. We each wrote sections and edited each other's work until, we hoped, the book seemed to have been written by one author.

This book is meant to be a reference guide – any day or time a reader can choose one of the meditations. One could choose a meditation in order or at random, or one that is connected to where one is or what one is doing. The meditations are intended to stimulate a transformative spiritual experience of linking one's consciousness with Kṛṣṇa. They are designed to provide a spark of impetus to directly perceive that everything is spiritual, part of Kṛṣṇa, non-different from Kṛṣṇa as His energy, and the specific ways in which Kṛṣṇa Himself directs us to perceive Him in our ordinary life.

The meditations are not intended to be philosophical musings alone, nor were they written in that mood. In order to write each meditation, we entered a state of quiet receptivity and observation, requesting the mercy of Kṛṣṇa to reveal how He could be found in some specific way given in *śāstra*.

Readers can use the written meditations to try to connect with the authors' epiphanies and use them as indicators or models for their unique and individual insights. Perhaps some readers will want to start their own journal or other artistic expression – writing, painting, or singing their understandings – and delight as they discover the myriad, or most likely infinite, ways in which each element or *śāstric* statement brings them to connect with the Lord. Perhaps some of these journals will see their way to publication, and we will have dozens or hundreds of books filled with specific realizations so that "the whole world is filled with Kṛṣṇa's singing," as Śrīla Prabhupāda wrote. The artwork is intended to aid the process, both of connecting with the specific meditations in this book and providing a base for personal realizations. And while this book was written for those who already know of Kṛṣṇa, the *Bhagavad-Gītā,* and the *Śrīmad-Bhāgavatam,* we hope that similar books and art can be produced for those unfamiliar with the tradition.

Kamala-sita and I desire that readers gain at least as much delight from reading and pondering the meditations as we did in discovering them and putting our discoveries into print. We seek the blessings and good wishes of our spiritual masters and readers that someday the whole world will function in relation with the Supreme Personality of Godhead, Śrī Kṛṣṇa.

Kamala-sita Dasi: I met Urmila for the first time in 2013, and over the years our relationship grew to be one of the most important friendships of my life. Our friendship was traced out in our many letters to each other over the years. And without knowing it, I was already writing *Kṛṣṇa Meditations*.

One year, after I had written a birthday message to her, Urmila asked me to help her write a book that she was busy with. First, I studied Kṛṣṇa's sixty-four qualities as explained in *The Nectar of Devotion,* and then wrote meditations on how we can see them in the world around us, as part of our everyday lives.

During the writing process life happened. I got married, moved to a new country, had some ups and downs of all sorts, and the project was moved to the back burner. In 2018, however, we both found that we would be in the same country at the same time for the first time in a very long time.

So, we met in Goloka-dhāma, Germany, for our first intensive face-to-face work session to get the project going again. It took another session in 2019 to make more progress. Fast forward another few calendar years, and "Ta-da!" We give you *Kṛṣṇa Meditations.*

You may ask what exactly this book is for and how you should go about reading it. The foundational purpose driving this work was that we wanted to inspire people in seeing Kṛṣṇa everywhere by giving them examples of how *we* try to see Kṛṣṇa everywhere. In this book, we find sections from *The Nectar of Devotion*, the *Bhagavad-Gītā,* and *Śrīmad-Bhāgavatam* in which Kṛṣṇa Himself and the sages tell us how we can see Kṛṣṇa in the world.

This is not a book that has to be read from cover to cover in order to make sense. Rather, we may read the sections that inspire us at different times. These meditations can serve as an inspiration to use our imagination and our life experiences to see Kṛṣṇa. And the result, we hope, would be that we look at our computer screen, for example, and not only see the daily grind of work but perhaps see the light reflected from the screen and see how Kṛṣṇa is like the light.

We hope that this book brings as much illumination to your life as it did to ours.

Finding Kṛṣṇa in the Elements

Earth
GIVES US A
SENSE OF
BALANCE
harmony
AND
GROUNDING
WHEN WALKING
UPON
Her

Finding Kṛṣṇa in the Elements

This section takes us on a journey back to the original essentials of the world we live in. Everything on this earth is a combination of the five elements: earth, fire, water, air, and ether. *Everything.* So, whether we are walking through a park or on a busy city sidewalk, or even stuck in front of our screens more than we can care for, we can still see Kṛṣṇa.

Śrīla Prabhupāda says:

> *Tat-paratvena.* As soon as we are in Kṛṣṇa consciousness, our seeing, touching, smelling – everything become *nirmala*, purified. Then we can immediately see Kṛṣṇa. These eyes, so long it is not purified, we cannot see Kṛṣṇa. As soon as it is purified, you see Kṛṣṇa. As soon as it is purified, you see Kṛṣṇa, nothing but Kṛṣṇa.
>
> (Lecture on *The Nectar of Devotion*, Vṛndāvana. November 11, 1972)

So, to see Kṛṣṇa in the elements is to see Kṛṣṇa in the very ingredients that make up our world, natural or man-made. These meditations focus on how we could see Kṛṣṇa in the natural elements and thus become closer to Him in meditative love through what is found in our everyday lives.

Earth Meditations

The Planet Earth Reminds Us of the Lord

Meditation 1

The earth is solid and dependable, and Kṛṣṇa is so dependable that even demonic beings know that if they follow universal rules, the Lord will not harm them. Anyone can depend on Kṛṣṇa to accept offerings made with faith and devotion, regardless of a person's background or material qualifications.

Meditation 2

The earth is tolerant and continues to support us even though we abuse her by drilling for oil, strip-mining her body, and by spilling the blood of her children upon her in war. In a similar way, Kṛṣṇa continues to be the friend of all living beings, even those who blaspheme Him and try to cause Him pain.

Meditation 3

The solid nature of earth gives us a sense of balance, harmony, and grounding when we walk upon her. Similarly, anyone in touch with Kṛṣṇa can stay undisturbed in any situation.

Meditation 4

The earth can sometimes change her face from that of a benign solid object to one of sudden anger in the form of quakes and volcanoes. Similarly, Kṛṣṇa's face, normally graced with a sweet, gentle smile, can sometimes show loving anger, such as when His incarnation Balarāma caused an earthquake in ancient Delhi to bring the rulers there to their senses.

Meditation 5

Despite the occasional upheavals, the earth is the foundation and support of everything. Kṛṣṇa also tells us in the (*Bhagavad-Gītā* 7.7) that He is the support of all, holding everything as a string holds the pearls of a necklace.

Meditation 6

Mountains are towers of earth. Sometimes wearing hair of snow, their rocky peaks poke through the clouds. Huge, solid, beautiful, and majestic, they draw our eyes again and again. Mountains have been compared to the bones of the Lord's universal form, the framework of the cosmos (*Śrīmad-Bhāgavatam* 2.1.32, 8.7.28, 10.40.13-14).

Kṛṣṇa's Shelter and the Earth

Meditation 7

Shelter is one of our prime necessities. In the form of the materials that make up our homes, the earth is a source of shelter from the weather, intruders, and animal pests. Brick, cement, steel, wood – all are directly from the earth or grow from her. When looking around our shelter, we can remember how Kṛṣṇa is the ultimate shelter. He sustains and maintains all living beings. His love, wisdom, mercy, and kindness offer us the shelter of spiritual knowledge. When we attain that knowledge, we have no fear of heat, cold, rain, decay, or thieves. Rather, we know we are eternal spiritual beings who can never be touched by any material difficulty. Beyond that, one who knows Kṛṣṇa finds deep shelter in His all-good love, a love whose quality and quantity is millions of times greater than the love we feel when coming into our mother's arms in our childhood home.

Meditation 8

People feel a sense of shelter in the place where they were born or spent their childhood. This attachment to homeland brings enough pleasure for people to make great sacrifices to keep a connection with it. The attachment can be so strong that huge armies go to war for the sake of their homeland, risking death and lifelong injury. What price humans are willing to pay for attachment to a particular piece of the earth! Earth is simply part of Kṛṣṇa's material energy, representing a fragment of a fragment of His opulence and splendor. May we remember how attachment to the ultimate source of the earth, Kṛṣṇa Himself, gives unbounded and ever-expanding satisfaction. Those who taste a drop of attachment to Kṛṣṇa gladly surrender more than any soldier to deepen it; they will sacrifice anything and everything to increase it! Yet upon doing so, they still feel as if they have given nothing at all compared to what they are gaining.

All-attractive Kṛṣṇa and the Earth

Meditation 9

Our bodies, and indeed all physical objects, are drawn to the ground by gravity. We experience gravity at every moment. If we take a minute to feel how we are being pulled, anchored, attracted to the earth, we can think about how that attractive force is the energy of Kṛṣṇa's expansion, Balarāma or Śeṣa. God is actually the all-attractive, His attractive force partially functioning under the name of gravity.

Meditation 10

The earth attracts not only through gravity but also through magnetic energy. We can remember how the saint Prahlāda declared that his mind and heart were drawn to Kṛṣṇa as naturally as iron to a magnet. (*Śrīmad-Bhāgavatam* 7.5.14)

He
IS THE
support
OF ALL,
HOLDING
EVERYTHING
as a string
HOLDS THE
pearls
OF A
necklace

Kṛṣṇa's Divine Qualities and the Earth

Meditation 11

The planet earth is the largest object we directly touch daily. Her size can remind us of how Kṛṣṇa is the greatest, the largest – bigger than the biggest. Just as we cannot see beyond the horizon, so we can never know all of God and His unlimited, expanding qualities and activities.

Meditation 12

The Bible says that our bodies come from dust and return there as well. Our bodies are formed from the food we eat, which grows in the earth. And when we, the soul, leave our body at death, the body is buried or burned, returning to a state of mixing again with the earth. Dead bodies thus become the basis for the growth of new bodies. Similarly, Kṛṣṇa says that He is the beginning, middle, and end of all things (*Bhagavad-Gītā* 10.32); He is their origin and their dissolution. (*Bhagavad-Gītā* 7.6) Thus, His divine qualities can be seen in the earth.

Working with the Earth

Meditation 13

Working with dirt can be a deeply satisfying experience. Planting, weeding, watering, fertilizing – all may give a sense of peace and satisfaction rarely found in the concrete jungles of modern cities. Even city dwellers flock to parks where they can sit on rocks or grass and lean against trees. Walking barefoot in sand or soil and getting one's hands full of rich loam is a delight that has attracted children for millennia. When contacting soil, we can meditate on how fulfilling it is for the soul to connect with its ultimate source, the Absolute Truth, Śrī Kṛṣṇa.

Meditation 14

Satisfaction from handling soil comes in part from the fresh smell of the land. Kṛṣṇa says that He is the fragrance of the earth. (*Bhagavad-Gītā* 7.9) Whatever scent we find in flowers, fruits, vegetables, grasses – anything grown from the earth – reveals some part of Kṛṣṇa's divine fragrance. And what of malodorous smells originating from dirt? Even they represent Kṛṣṇa in His aspect as the eventual destroyer of the material world.

Meditation 15

Earth can be utilized as a medium for artistic expression. Paper or fabric on which we write or paint come from the earth's products. Materials of sculpture are generally taken from the earth. Mineral pigments abound in rocks, and brilliant hues are found in plants growing from the earth. Souls in human bodies who shape the earth and her products in artistic ways show how they, as tiny spiritual portions of Kṛṣṇa, can manifest creativity and beauty. Thus, whenever we see such products of artistic skill or when we engage in the creative process, we can remember how the ingredients and the ability are from Kṛṣṇa, whose own artistic skill we can glorify and only poorly imitate.

Kṛṣṇa and the Earth's Wealth

Meditation 16

The earth reminds us of Kṛṣṇa's unlimited wealth, as she is the source of our wealth in the material world. Land is always one of the greatest sources of wealth in all societies. We enhance the value of land with buildings that are made of materials coming directly or indirectly from the earth. Products of earth such as metals, gems, oil, coal, natural gas, and

Her
SIZE CAN
REMIND US HOW
Kṛṣṇa IS
THE GREATEST,
THE largest~
BIGGER
THAN THE
biggest

THE
Lord
PREFERS
NECKLACES
OF
berries
TO THOSE OF
diamonds

so forth are all major sources of wealth. Rukmiṇī Devī, Lord Kṛṣṇa's principal queen in Dvārakā, said that Kṛṣṇa can be described as not possessing wealth because He is Himself that very wealth. Kṛṣṇa is the earth and thus wealth itself. Whenever we deal with wealth, whether paper, metal, plastic, or any other form, we can easily recall that the wealth comes from earth and, ultimately, Kṛṣṇa. One who thinks like this uses all wealth in ways that please Kṛṣṇa and accepts whatever opulence Kṛṣṇa desires to give His servant as a merciful gift, called *prasādam.*

Kṛṣṇa's Transcendent Abode

Meditation 17

Walking through a forest or garden heavy with green, we can remember that Kṛṣṇa, the Lord of lords and king of kings, prefers His highest spiritual realm to be a simple pastoral setting. Certainly, Kṛṣṇa has innumerable transcendent residences, prototypes for the grand royal palaces and cities that have flourished over history on this planet. But in such a regal atmosphere Kṛṣṇa does not display His full range of intimate loving dealings with perfect souls. Rather, He likes to sport in exchanges of love surrounded by forests and rivers. In the supreme spiritual kingdom, Vṛndāvana, the Lord prefers necklaces of dried seeds and berries to those of diamonds. Flowers resembling pearls decorate His spiritual form. He is a village boy herding cows with His friends, using hard fruit as balls, and minerals as decorative body paint. The land in Kṛṣṇa's ultimate paradise is a fully conscious person. The ground is soft and made of varieties of colored jewels.

Kṛṣṇa's Pastimes Related to Earth

Meditation 18

Early in universal creation, the demon Hiraṇyākṣa caused the planet earth to fall out of orbit and sink into the Universal Ocean. Kṛṣṇa then assumed a gigantic form as a boar to rescue the earth. The Lord searched after the earth by smell and dove into the ocean, dividing it in two and causing two huge waves on each side. Upon finding the earth, He lifted it on the ends of His tusks and took it out of the water. The Lord then carefully placed the earth within His sight on the surface of the water and infused it with the potency to float. After this, He fought with and killed Hiraṇyākṣa.

Meditation 19

Five thousand years ago, when Kṛṣṇa appeared on this planet, some of His young cowherd friends accused Him of eating dirt. His mother looked into His mouth to verify if that was the case, and she saw not only some dirt but the entire planet earth! She also saw the sun, moon, stars, and the whole universe. Although astonished by seeing Kṛṣṇa's opulence and power, she retained her parental affection for her young child.

Meditation 20

In Kṛṣṇa's incarnation as Lord Caitanya, He ate dirt as a young boy. His mother scolded Him and asked why He would prefer dirt to sweets. The Lord replied that sweets are ultimately just a transformation of earth, so why discriminate? The Lord's mother, however, refuted this monistic philosophy by saying that although dirt and sweets are the same from one point of view, eating dirt directly will simply cause disease. Lord Caitanya was pleased to hear His devotee expounding the philosophy that Kṛṣṇa and His energies are simultaneously and inconceivably the same and different, a more nuanced view of reality than monism.

UPON FINDING THE
Earth
HE LIFTED IT
ONTO THE END OF HIS
tusks
AND TOOK IT OUT OF THE
water

Meditation 21

Although Kṛṣṇa is always earth in the general sense that His energies are simultaneously the same and different from Him, He is directly His earthly abode of Vṛndāvana. While devotees understand this point about Vṛndāvana in general, they worship in particular one place in Vṛndāvana as Kṛṣṇa: Govardhana Hill. That's because Kṛṣṇa, during His pastime of lifting Govardhana Hill, declared that He is the hill. In the form of rocks and dirt, Kṛṣṇa serves His own devotees. He gives His cows grass and water and provides His friends with caves, beautiful sporting places, and jewels and minerals for ornamentation. Out of love for His devotees, He takes this form as a servant of His own servants. Since each part of the Lord is also the complete Lord, even a tiny pebble from this hill is a full manifestation of Kṛṣṇa. Devotees therefore worship stones from Govardhana Hill on their altars just as they worship the Deity of Kṛṣṇa.

The Deity

Meditation 22

The Deity of Kṛṣṇa is another personal incarnation of the Lord, made of materials from the earth. He appears in the Deity form, usually of rock, metal, or wood, to accept worship from those whose vision allows them to see only gross matter. Because Kṛṣṇa and His form are absolute, a rendition of the Lord's form according to the descriptions of the scripture is the Lord Himself. Therefore, although neophytes in spiritual life think they're seeing a form of matter, the Deity incarnation of the Lord is spiritual. From Kṛṣṇa's perspective, matter and spirit are equally His energy. Conditioned souls see some of His energy as matter only because of selfish desire and contaminated consciousness. Those who serve the Deity under the direction of a spiritual master will gradually invoke Kṛṣṇa's mercy, and Kṛṣṇa will reveal how the Deity is none other than Himself.

Water Meditations

Water Reminds Us of the Lord

Meditation 1

Kṛṣṇa is the taste or the essence of water (*Bhagavad-Gītā* 7.8), the quality that quenches our thirst and brings satisfaction.

Meditation 2

When swimming, we can experience the softness or liquidity of water. One of Kṛṣṇa's qualities is His softness. His body is so soft that it changes color where it has been brushed by a leaf. His soft body stimulates, or inspires, His devotees' love for Him. The scriptures describe that the Lord and His form are the same, so both His body and His sentiments are soft. The liquidity of water reminds us of the flowing and melting quality of the Lord's love and kindness. Particularly when Kṛṣṇa takes the mood of His chief devotee and appears as Lord Caitanya, His heart melts with compassion for all living beings, and He freely gives love of God without considering the merit of the candidate. His heart is, therefore, like melted butter or flowing water, soft and fluid.

Meditation 3

Water is powerful, so much so that its swift flow can provide all the electricity for a city, or one huge wave can create tremendous destruction in a moment. The power of water reminds us that one of Kṛṣṇa's opulences is unlimited strength. He creates, maintains, and destroys countless universes effortlessly. He carries planets on His head with such

His heart is therefore like melted butter, soft and fluid

KṚṢṆA
assumes the form of a
GOLDEN FISH

nonchalance that He is hardly aware of their weight. If all the potential and kinetic power of the world's water were combined into one gigantic wave, it would not equal the tiniest fraction of Kṛṣṇa's strength. The dual nature of water – soft yet powerful – reminds us of how Kṛṣṇa, whose eternal spiritual form is that of a delicate sixteen-year-old boy, easily fought with and killed huge, muscular demons who were tormenting innocent citizens.

Kṛṣṇa's Water Pastimes

Meditation 4

When Kṛṣṇa creates the material world, He assumes an immeasurable form that lies in a sleep-like yogic trance on His incarnation, the serpent Śeṣa, who floats on the Causal Ocean, which is alive and spiritual. Uncountable universes, one of which we inhabit, come out of the Lord's body when He exhales.

Then the Lord enters each universe and from His perspiration creates an ocean that fills half the universal shell. He lies down in that water, and His consort the goddess of fortune massages His feet.

The Lord enjoys floating on this cosmic ocean with His consort. Because each of us is a small part of the Lord, we have His propensities to a minute degree. So, the common human desire to float on a boat, raft, or other device with one's beloved comes from the Supreme, the source of everything.

Meditation 5

In Vedic cosmology, planets are conscious persons. The planet earth once fell into the universal water when demonic persons disturbed her orbit by drilling for resources and upsetting her balance. Celestial beings, called *devas,* who control the universe in service to Kṛṣṇa, wanted the earth to be rescued. Responding to their desire, the Lord came to save her. He assumed the form of a splendid, gigantic boar (Varāha), dove to the bottom of the Universal Ocean, picked up the earth, and gently carried her on His tusks to the water's surface. As He did so, a great demon challenged Him. Lord Varāha then carefully placed fearful earth on the water and gave her the ability to float. A fight between the Lord and the demon ensued within the great ocean. After defeating the demon, Lord Varāha returned to the spiritual sky. The Lord thus both enjoyed fighting in the water and rescuing His beloved from harm in the water.

Meditation 6

Sometimes a flood devastates the universe, and Kṛṣṇa assumes the form of a golden fish to play in the water. Tied to a horn on His head is a boat carrying sages, Vedic knowledge, and seeds to replenish the world after the flood. During this pastime, Kṛṣṇa enjoys His play within the water as well as His loving relationship with the great sages.

Meditation 7

Kṛṣṇa in His original form often sports in water with His friends and beloveds. For His water pastimes He chooses rivers such as the Ganges and Yamunā, who are also goddesses purely in love for Him. Kṛṣṇa also plays in lakes and ponds filled with lotuses and swans and surrounded by jeweled pavilions. These bodies of water are persons, His devotees, and alive with love and bliss.

Fire Meditations

The Sustaining Power of Heat

Meditation 1

Heat outside and inside our bodies sustains us. The most basic bodily need after air is not food or water but correct temperature. We experience life-giving heat from the sun in two ways: directly on our skin and indirectly through digestion, which releases the sun's energy that had been transformed into our food through photosynthesis. For warm-blooded creatures like us humans, eighty percent of the food we eat is used to produce internal heat. That heat came from the sun, was stored in plants, and then freed by our digestive process. We may remember that heat is Kṛṣṇa's energy (*Bhagavad-Gītā* 7.9), and therefore it is Kṛṣṇa who sustains us with warmth. He also sustains us by His presence in our heart and in every atom around us. Kṛṣṇa sustains even those who entirely forget Him and do not acknowledge their dependence upon nor express any gratitude toward Him.

Meditation 2

Heat is, after all, invisible. To a conditioned soul, Kṛṣṇa is also invisible. The way heat sustains us – while still remaining invisible – again brings to mind the verse in the (*Bhagavad-Gītā* 7.7) in which Kṛṣṇa says that He is like a string upon which pearls rest. We know the string is there because the pearls hang in an orderly way, but the string itself hides in the pearls' core. We also know that heat is there when we feel the effects of fire. Similarly, although Kṛṣṇa is invisible to us, we can understand that He is behind the miracles of creation.

The Destructive Power of Heat

Meditation 3

We must handle fire with care and respect. A slight shift in temperature and, instead of life, there is death or severe injury. Even though we might huddle close to a bonfire on chilly days, we don't get too close. Similarly, unless we have pure love of God, we serve Kṛṣṇa according to the rules of worship and service to avoid getting burned by offenses.

Meditation 4

We can appreciate the destructive power of heat. Mitch Kahn, an experienced firefighter, writes: "A fire is like a living thing – a living engine of destruction, and each blaze has its own personality. There's a sound and smell to a wildfire that you never forget; burning brush and searing wind roaring like a jet engine, and the acrid odor of scorched earth."[1] The destructive power of heat brings to mind descriptions of periodic universal dissolution as described in the Vedas. At that time, the Lord, being unhappy at the conditioned souls' who work against their own spiritual self-interest, envelops the cosmos in heat more intense than numerous suns.

Meditation 5

The destructive burning of heat also purifies and cleanses. Farmers sometimes burn a field to remove weeds and their seeds, leaving the ashes to fertilize the soil. Scientists and medical doctors depend on the sanitizing action of heat's destructive force. Similarly, Kṛṣṇa tells us in the (*Bhagavad-Gītā* 4.19, 4.37) that transcendental knowledge of the soul and God burns up all ignorance and suffering.

---

1 (https://www.guideposts.org/faith-and-prayer/prayer-stories/answered-prayers/hope-and-faith-in-the-wildfire)

AT THAT TIME
THE
LORD
envelopes
THE COSMOS
IN HEAT
MORE INTENSE THAN
numerous
suns

Meditation 6

Just as seeds fried in high heat lose all power of germination, achieving loving union with Kṛṣṇa removes the potency of all material desires that bind us to karma and rebirth.

Meditation 7

When a devotee takes vows of commitment to serve the Lord, the initiation ceremony involves throwing seeds and grains into a sacrificial fire. The fire is understood to be Kṛṣṇa's tongue: He eats the grains and thus purifies the giver.

Kṛṣṇa as Heat

Meditation 8

Warmth is often associated with life itself, which can help us remember that the Lord is the Supreme living being, the source of all life. (*Bhagavad-Gītā* 9.18, 14.4) Warmth is also associated with love; we speak of a warm embrace or, conversely, of a cold glance. Kṛṣṇa's warmth is one manifestation of His encompassing love for all living beings. Whenever we feel the warmth of the sun, fire, or the furnaces in our buildings, we can feel both the life and the love of Kṛṣṇa.

The Transformative Power of Heat

Meditation 9

Heat transforms both the texture and the flavor of raw food, making hard vegetables swim in their own juices when flames lick the bottom of a pot. Similarly, a connection with Kṛṣṇa can release a flow of affection even from dry philosophers and melts even steel-like hearts into the flowing butter of love.

Meditation 10

Just as heat reveals a variety of flavors otherwise hidden in uncooked food, service to Kṛṣṇa manifests diverse and intense emotions of ecstasy.

Meditation 11

According to Āyurveda, the heat of digestion ultimately produces vitality and strength. The chemical fire in our body, with which Kṛṣṇa directly identifies Himself in the (*Bhagavad-Gītā* 15.14), distills food to its essence to nourish the body's organs and systems. In doing so, it separates value from waste. Similarly, in the final stages of purification through serving Kṛṣṇa, the soul is brought to its pure state of spiritual power, in which all unwanted things, such as identification with the material body and mind, are finished.

Meditation 12

Cooking with too much heat burns the outside of food while leaving the inside raw. Cooking at just the right temperature, with patience, gives us food that is tasty throughout. Similarly, under expert guidance we need to apply with care the process of connecting with Kṛṣṇa through chanting, hearing, and serving. Impatient *bhakti-yogīs* may take up extreme practices that leave them discouraged, with their heart barely touched. But those who have enthusiasm, confidence, and patience find that *bhakti-yoga* gradually transforms their thoughts and feelings, melting their hearts.

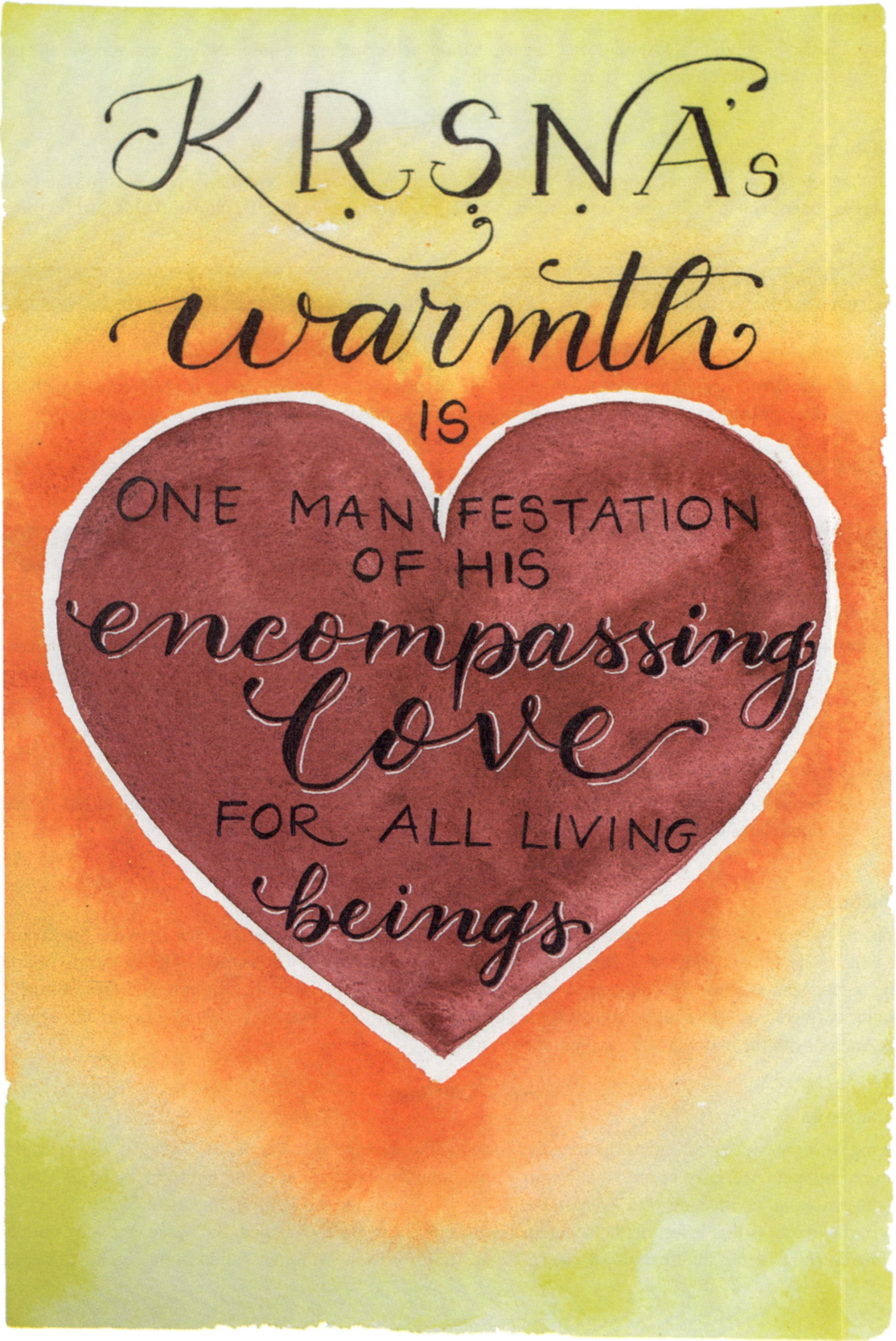
KṚṢṆA's
warmth
IS
ONE MANIFESTATION
OF HIS
encompassing
love
FOR ALL LIVING
beings

Meditation 13

Heat cooks our food by exciting molecules that crash into each other. In this way, heat can destroy a food's structure and create a new one. Heat also creates air currents upon which birds travel the skies. Heat from the sun pulls water vapor into clouds, thus starting the cycle that both purifies the water and distributes it around the world. Heat's effect of causing other things to move and flow reminds us that contact with Kṛṣṇa is stimulating. Even inanimate objects react to Him – rocks melt at the sound of His flute. Kṛṣṇa stirs the heart and mind of all who connect with Him.

Light and Kṛṣṇa's Love

Meditation 14

Just like warmth, light is closely associated with life and love. We speak of how people's eyes light up when they meet someone they love. A person full of life is often described as having a sunny disposition. Light thus reminds us that Kṛṣṇa is the life of all that lives and the most loving friend of all.

Light Delights and Welcomes

Meditation 15

Lighted candles, colored light bulbs, and fireworks often play a role when friends, families, and communities gather for holidays, festivities, and celebrations. Upon seeing such lights, we can meditate on how every day is a festival in the self-effulgent spiritual world. Kṛṣṇa, the reservoir of pleasure, delights in eternal varieties of transcendent parties.

Meditation 16

Whether we are visiting others for a party or entering our own home, light welcomes us. When the lights are on, we know that someone is home and awaiting our arrival. Greeting others with light is as ancient as humankind. Thus, we offer a flame to the Deity in the traditional *ārati* ceremony performed in Kṛṣṇa temples. As a famous prayer says, the devotee offers Kṛṣṇa *ārati* with the lamplight of love. Kṛṣṇa is also welcoming us with His light – His love – shining forth in all splendor to invite us back home.

Light and Knowledge

Meditation 17

Our ability to see requires light. Similarly, to clearly see both truth and illusion and thus choose to reunite with Kṛṣṇa requires that our hearts be illumined by the scriptures, which are the words of Kṛṣṇa and His representatives. Indeed, gaining such knowledge is often termed "enlightenment". Therefore, whenever we see light, we can remember how Kṛṣṇa is the source of knowledge on every level, both spiritual and material.

Meditation 18

To function, our eyes need light entering them, but Kṛṣṇa's eyes, which are the sun and the moon, emit light. Sunlight and moonlight, therefore, come from the eyes of the Lord. The sun is sometimes equated with Kṛṣṇa's weapon Sudarśana, which means "auspicious vision". We sometimes communicate with only our eyes, and Sudarśana is called "the master of speech", because when, by the merciful gaze of the Lord, we become filled with the light of knowledge, truth comes from our mouth.

KṚṢṆA
THE
reservoir
OF
pleasure
DELIGHTS IN ETERNAL
VARIETIES OF TRANSCENDENT
parties

BY THE
merciful
gaze
OF THE LORD
WE BECOME FILLED
WITH THE
light
OF
Knowledge

Light as Nourishment and Rejuvenation

Meditation 19

Light is the source of nourishment for the body. At the bottom of the food chain are plants that use photosynthesis to transform sunlight into sugars and starches. Through this process, transformed light is the food that nourishes the bodies of nearly every living being on earth. If we meditate on how our food is the sun's energy and that Kṛṣṇa is directly the light of the sun (*Bhagavad-Gītā* 7.8), we can easily feel a connection with Him with every bite.

Meditation 20

Besides the blazing light of the sun, there is soothing moonlight, which cools and refreshes us after a day of work. Coming to Kṛṣṇa's shelter is often compared to taking advantage of moonlight for relief and peace. Also, the moon inspires romantic love among ordinary people, but it can also remind a spiritual practitioner of Kṛṣṇa's pure love dance with the saintly milkmaids.

Fire and Kṛṣṇa's Beauty

Meditation 21

Fire is beautiful, full of majesty. Sunshine sparkling on the ripples of a lake on a clear day, an outdoor bonfire on a chilly night, clusters of stars in the heavens, glittering chandeliers, neon signs, blinking lights on Christmas trees, tiny flames on cotton wicks in little clay pots floating on the Ganges – all show how fire is certainly splendid. This can remind us that Kṛṣṇa, the source of all beauty, says He is the splendor of fire. (*Bhagavad-Gītā* 15.12)

Meditation 22

Not only is fire itself beautiful, but the beauty of anything exists only because the light of some fire illumines that object. Without light, the word *beauty* would have no meaning, as there would be no ability to behold it. Without fire there are no colors. If all beauty and brilliance depend on fire's light, we can hardly imagine the beauty of the Supreme Lord, who is the very source of all fire, warmth, and illumination. (*Bhagavad-Gītā* 15.12) How gorgeously brilliant His form must be! Sacred writings describe Kṛṣṇa's spiritual, eternal, ever-youthful form as effulgent and beautiful beyond material understanding. His cheeks are compared to sapphire mirrors upon which His swinging earrings are reflected. Kṛṣṇa's clothes glow like liquid gold, and His toenails are so brilliant that when He places His soft feet on jeweled footstools, the multi-colored jewels appear to be made of crystal.

Kṛṣṇa's Pastimes with Fire

Meditation 23

Once, after Kṛṣṇa had vanquished a serpent polluting the Yamunā River and the surrounding area, most of the inhabitants of Vṛndāvana village were resting near the river. Suddenly, a fire started, and as the flames threatened to burn everyone, Kṛṣṇa drank the fire.

Meditation 24

Another day, Kṛṣṇa and His friends had taken their herds of cows, goats, and buffalo across the Yamunā to a large banyan tree. Busy playing there, the boys did not notice that the animals had wandered away looking for succulent

HOW
gorgeously
brilliant
HIS FORM
MUST BE

grass. When they realized that they had been negligent and failed to protect their families' source of livelihood, they looked for the animals in vain. Finally, the boys found and followed the trail of eaten grass and trampled vegetation. Meanwhile, the animals had wandered far away and had encountered a forest fire. Fleeing, they became stuck in sugar cane. The sharp leaves and strong cane made it hard for them to extract themselves, and they cried in fear. Kṛṣṇa called each animal by name, and they called back to Him. Kṛṣṇa and the boys then traced the animals to the cane and rescued them. But as they all walked back to the banyan tree, great winds whipped the fire closer, surrounding them. The boys looked to Kṛṣṇa and begged Him to save them, His intimate friends. Through a loving look, Kṛṣṇa told them not to fear and to close their eyes. He had been thirsting for fire (perhaps as some people like spicy food), so He drank the huge fire like a cooling beverage. Gradually the boys and animals opened their eyes to find, much to their surprise, that not only was the fire gone, but they were back at their starting place near the tree, grateful to be close to the river, where after the heat of the fire they could drink to their full satisfaction.

Meditation 25

In the battle with Banasura, Kṛṣṇa summoned His weapon of utter cold to counteract Śiva's weapon of excessive heat. Those weapons were personalities. As the heat weapon gradually decreased in intensity, he cried for help to Lord Śiva, but Lord Śiva could not do anything against Kṛṣṇa's weapon. Eventually the heat weapon surrendered to Lord Kṛṣṇa and sought His shelter.

Meditation 26

While Kṛṣṇa spoke the *Bhagavad-Gītā* in His universal form, fire came from His mouth, burning the universe with its radiance. (*Bhagavad-Gītā* 11.19)

Air Meditations

Kṛṣṇa and Subtlety of Air

Meditation 1

One of the most significant qualities of air is its subtlety. Although air is all around us, pushing on our body with a pressure of fifteen pounds per square inch (one kilogram per square centimeter), we are practically oblivious of it. We usually breathe unconsciously too, so subtle is the air moving in and out of our lungs. We see air only through its effects, such as when it moves branches and straw or carries smoke and water vapor. Kṛṣṇa too is subtle. He is almost imperceptible to a materially conditioned soul, visible only by His effects. We see His handiwork in a flower's beauty or the predictability of the planets' movements, but we do not see Him. The natural laws on which we base our math and science imply a lawmaker. But much of the nature of that lawmaker stays unknown.

Meditation 2

Air, although subtle, can move things that seem far more substantial than it. Violent air in tornados and other storms can throw buildings afar and push wood splinters into metal. Similarly, with only the indiscernible movement of His will, Kṛṣṇa can move, shape, change, and scatter everything perceivable. On the spiritual plane, the gentle gust of a whisper of His name, heard or spoken with merely a shadow of affection for Him, can move Him to dismantle a steel-framed heart, turning anger and lust into spiritual love.

THE
gentle gust
OF A
whisper
OF HIS NAME
CAN MOVE HIM TO
DISMANTLE
a
STEEL-FRAMED
heart

WITHOUT A
conscious,
DELIBERATE
AND
loving
RELATIONSHIP WITH GOD
~NOTHING~
ELSE GIVES US FULL
satisfaction

Kṛṣṇa and Air Everywhere

Meditation 3

In our experience, air is everywhere, as is Kṛṣṇa. And just as air carries other substances without mixing with them, Kṛṣṇa stays aloof and unaffected even though He is in the heart of every living being and within every atom. Air is also neutral, carrying heavenly fragrances from flower gardens and putrid smells from rubbish heaps. Similarly, Kṛṣṇa remains unattached even though He responds to our desires and actions. If we act in violent and "rancid" ways, He carries us to lower planets. If we act in pious and "fragrant" ways, He carries us to heaven.

Kṛṣṇa and Air as the Essence of Life

Meditation 4

Of all the elements essential to life, air is the most fundamental. We simply cannot live without it for even the shortest time. Our other bodily needs – water, food, shelter, warmth – have no value if we have no air. We certainly cannot think of meeting our social, mental, emotional, and intellectual needs without a constant supply of air. How can we enjoy a delicious meal in the company of loving friends if we're suffocating? Similarly, our relationship with Kṛṣṇa is our primary need. Without a conscious, deliberate, and loving relationship with the Lord, nothing else gives us full satisfaction. Persons who entirely neglect their relationship with God or put that relationship as anything but a top priority, find that the good and pleasurable things in their lives fail to give them the satisfaction they expect. While such people often try to adjust what and how they enjoy, they rarely consider that the real solution is as basic as breathing. Furthermore, because Kṛṣṇa is complete, making one's relationship with Him the top priority brings automatic satisfaction of all other needs. One can then deal with the world from a position of inner peace and joy. A person in such a position has complete freedom, not dependent on anyone or anything for satisfaction.

Meditation 5

Air provides oxygen for our digestion, which brings nourishment and health to our cells. This reminds us of Kṛṣṇa's statement in the (*Bhagavad-Gītā* 15.14) that He joins with the outgoing and incoming air of life to digest our food. This movement of air is essential for digestion because it moves the food from our mouth to stomach, intestines, throughout the blood, and to all the cells in our body. Kṛṣṇa is there with the air, causing this movement of transformation and transportation of food.

Kṛṣṇa's Movements and Air

Meditation 6

The movement of air seems to make plants and trees dance and forms attractive patterns in water and sand. Blowing air also sculpts rock into works of art. We are reminded that Kṛṣṇa's movements are as graceful as a dance and He not only dances Himself but induces others to dance with Him. In fact, He likes to dress as if He is a dancing actor about to go on stage. His dancing with His pure devotees in the spiritual world is perfectly choreographed – more graceful, soothing, complex, exciting, and intricate than the swirling waves of a stream whipped by the wind.

His dancing
in the spiritual world
is more
graceful,
soothing,
complex,
exciting
and
intricate
than the
swirling waves
of a stream whipped
by the
wind

KRSNA's
breath
HAD FLOWED
THROUGH HIS
flute
AND
TRANSFORMED
INTO THE
Gayatri
mantra

Air in Kṛṣṇa's Activities

Meditation 7

In His form as Viṣṇu, Kṛṣṇa rides through the air standing on the back of the giant eagle Garuḍa. From there, He sometimes fights battles with demons, such as those in the great cosmic fight for a jug of nectar. (*Śrīmad-Bhāgavatam* 8.10)

Meditation 8

To create the material world, Kṛṣṇa expands Himself into the gigantic form of Mahā-Viṣṇu resting on the Causal Ocean. As the Lord breathes out, universes come from Him and gradually expand. When He breathes in, the universes gradually reenter His transcendent form. We are living in one of those universes, riding on the Lord's breath.

Meditation 9

When increasing materialism periodically covers spiritual knowledge, Kṛṣṇa comes in various incarnations to set things right. One incarnation, Hayagriva, has a golden humanlike form with the head of a horse. The air He breathes from His divine nostrils is the sweet sounds of Vedic wisdom, given to Brahmā, the first created being in the universe. Because any of Kṛṣṇa's senses can perform the action of any other sense, He can sing sweetly with puffs of air from His nose.

Meditation 10

At the beginning of the universe, Brahmā searched for knowledge of himself, his duty, and the nature of the cosmos. After meditating for thousands of years, he heard Kṛṣṇa breathe in his heart. Kṛṣṇa's breath had flowed through His flute and transformed into the Gāyatrī *mantra*, which then came out of Brahmā's mouth as Vedic knowledge.

Meditation 11

Everything in the spiritual world is conscious, including Lord Kṛṣṇa's flute, His constant companion and intimate devotee. Kṛṣṇa blows on His flute to herd His cows. The music bewilders even expert musicians on heavenly planets and induces a contrary nature – rivers flow backward, rocks melt, and animals and people become stunned in ecstasy. The great devotee Bhaktivinoda Ṭhākura, the father of Śrīla Prabhupāda's spiritual master, wrote in *Gītā-mālā 2.6* that Kṛṣṇa abducts the mind of His devotees with the enchanting songs of His flute as well by His sweet bodily fragrance, which are both blowing in relentless waves upon the wind.

Space Meditations

Qualities of Space

Meditation 1

The *Bhāgavatam* describes space as the element from which all other gross states of matter and energy evolve. Space is thus the foundation or source of everything, reminding us that Kṛṣṇa is the cause of all causes.

Meditation 2

One of the most peculiar aspects of space is the difficulty to describe, define, or perceive it by one's mind and senses. We often understand space more by what it is not than what it is. For example, we commonly define space as an area

KṚṢNA
IS
EVERY
THING,
AND IS
THE
essence
OF
EVERYTHING

without furniture, or a shelf without books. Similarly, those who rely exclusively on sense perception and logic struggle to define the Absolute Truth and resort to saying what it is not. In Sanskrit this process is referred to as *neti neti:* "Not this; not this."

Meditation 3

Despite its elusive definition, space is the main component of material reality. Modern science tells us that even the densest objects are mostly space, which pervades everything. Similarly, Kṛṣṇa is everything, and is the essence of everything.

Space Perception and Kṛṣṇa

Meditation 4

How a living being understands and defines space depends on that particular living entity's level of consciousness. For example, a bug on my windowsill cannot understand how the rooms in my house are connected or how the city in which I live relates to the country or the planet. Similarly, our ability to understand Kṛṣṇa and perceive how His energies connect throughout the universe depends on how much our consciousness is developed in spiritual realization.

Meditation 5

Generally, we focus our awareness on the stuff that exists within space rather than on space itself. Similarly, a materially conditioned soul generally absorbs the consciousness in Kṛṣṇa's material energy rather than in Kṛṣṇa Himself, within whom everything rests.

Meditation 6

When we notice space, it generally evokes positive, expansive emotions. We feel relief and satisfaction when there is room in a closet, drawer, or suitcase for the object we desire to keep. Similarly, as our hearts become freed from the clutter of material desires and ambitions, we free up space in our consciousness for our most valuable purpose, which is to revive our relationship with Kṛṣṇa. This experience brings us immense relief and satisfaction.

Meditation 7

Many spiritually inclined people reserve a part of their living area as a "sacred space" for worship, prayer, meditation, and renewal. The many places to which the faithful make pilgrimage to find meaning, peace, and joy are also sacred spaces. Ultimately, a sacred space is called *dhāma*, the form of the Lord Himself.

Meditation 8

Space around our body allows for stretching, health, movement, and expression, which bring us vigor and vitality. Spaces in artwork define objects and messages. When we wish to express deep joy, we surround our body with space – by jumping, dancing, diving, even parachuting. This nature of space as both an impetus for, and a way to express, joy and freedom reminds us that Kṛṣṇa's ultimate spiritual reality is full of freedom, joy, play, and sports. His service is not limited or stereotypical, and He exalts in a full expression of individuality.

WE
marvel
AT THE DISTANCES BEYOND
imagination
-SIMILARLY-
Kṛṣṇa IS
mysterious
dark, beautiful
AND GREAT
BEYOND OUR
imagination

Meditation 9

"Where do you live?" It's a question even a stranger feels comfortable asking. When we seek to understand something, we first want to "place" it. We want to determine its position in space. Similarly, we can evaluate something only when we know its relationship with Kṛṣṇa. Indeed, perceiving something without knowing where it stands in relation to the Absolute Truth is illusion and falsity.

Meditation 10

Sometimes we turn our attention from the space in our immediate surroundings of rooms, buildings, and cities to the vast expanse of the sky. The blue of the sunlit sky is a reflection of Kṛṣṇa's transcendental body and can remind us of Him. The night sky has fascinated humans since the dawn of time. We marvel at the distances beyond imagination, and at the beauty of the lights that hint at worlds we can only guess about. Similarly, Kṛṣṇa is mysterious, dark, beautiful, and great, beyond our imagination and inaccessible to our material senses.

Space and Kṛṣṇa's Opulence of Detachment

Meditation 11

Although space is both everywhere and the source of everything, it always retains its identity and doesn't mix with any other form of matter or energy. Kṛṣṇa Himself refers to this attribute of space as analogous to His own detachment and neutrality (*Bhagavad-Gītā* 9.5-6). As the Supersoul, or the soul of all souls, Kṛṣṇa is the well-wishing witness who, like a neutral judge, awards all living beings the pleasing or distressing results of their actions and desires. Nothing takes place without the sanction of the Supersoul, and He is the ultimate doer. But He claims no responsibility for the suffering and enjoyment of the willfully deluded.

Meditation 12

An essential part of Kṛṣṇa's deep love for all living beings is His completeness and His ability to independently satisfy all His needs and desires. An ordinary conditioned soul's "love" stems from possessiveness and thus easily turns to grief or anger. Genuine spiritual love is rooted in freedom and sacrifice. Kṛṣṇa loves without conditions, manipulation, or force. He loves simply to love. Even though the scriptures describe Kṛṣṇa as being controlled by His pure devotee, He's controlled not by fear of loss but by the devotee's freely given love. Space reminds us of full freedom to love, with no boundaries or conditions, like expansive space.

Meditation 13

The sky displays renunciation by not mixing with anything. Similarly, Kṛṣṇa shows His renunciation by disappearing from the pleasure dance with His dearest devotees, the milkmaids of Vṛndāvana village. Indeed, Kṛṣṇa is so detached and independent that He travels away from Vṛndāvana, His ultimate abode, where even the buildings and water are alive and full of devotion for Him. In His role as a warrior prince, He was so renounced that He casually walked away from battle with the evil Jarāsandha. He left to attend to a letter from His future wife, although no fighter would normally dare risk his reputation as a courageous hero by fleeing from combat.

A
U
M

Space and Sound

Meditation 14

India's sacred writings describe that each "element" has a corresponding sense and sense object that allow us to perceive it. We perceive space through hearing and sound. Many creatures, such as bats and whales, use sound to detect space. Blind people often become skilled at using sound to determine space and location, and to some extent all of us naturally use sound in this way. In addition, sound is vibration, which involves movement, and without space, nothing can move. Kṛṣṇa says that He is all sound carried in space. (*Bhagavad-Gītā*.7.8)

Although all sound is Kṛṣṇa, when the sound has a covering of ignorance or passion, Kṛṣṇa is not perceived. We can perceive Him through His *avatāra* of sound – certain sound combinations that are His own form. Kṛṣṇa's names are the sound forms of His personality. When the Vedic literature says that the Absolute Truth has no name, it means no name in the material sense – a limited designation separate from that which is designated and subject to change according to language and custom.

Probably the most well-known sound form of the Absolute is *oṁ*. *Om* is part of many mantras chanted by Kṛṣṇa's devotees, but the sound form of the Absolute Truth that forms the basis of the spiritual practice of the Hare Kṛṣṇa movement is Hare Kṛṣṇa, Hare Kṛṣṇa, Kṛṣṇa Kṛṣṇa, Hare Hare/ Hare Rāma, Hare Rāma, Rāma Rāma, Hare Hare. "The impersonal sound of Kṛṣṇa is *oṁ*," Śrīla Prabhupāda writes, "but the sound Hare Kṛṣṇa contains *oṁ*."[2] (*Bhagavad-Gītā* 8.13, purport)

Kṛṣṇa's Sportive Activities in Relation to Space

Meditation 15

Perhaps one of the best-known descriptions of Kṛṣṇa involving space is His display of His universal form to His devotee Arjuna, recounted in the (*Bhagavad-Gītā* 11.7, 11.13): Lord Kṛṣṇa says, "Everything – moving and non-moving – is here completely, in one place." And Sañjaya, the narrator, says, "At that time Arjuna could see in the universal form of the Lord the unlimited expansions of the universe situated in one place."

Meditation 16

Kṛṣṇa's mystic potency of having all of space within Him, in one place, was evident when, on two occasions, Mother Yaśodā looked into His mouth. She saw all of outer space within His spiritual body. She saw the stars, planets, sun, and moon. She was astonished to see all of material cosmic space as she asked Kṛṣṇa to open the apparently small enclave of His mouth. In this regard, Brahmā, the creator of this universe, prays, "Although You are now within this universe, the whole universal creation is within Your transcendental body – a fact You demonstrated by exhibiting the universe within Your abdomen before Your mother, Yaśodā." (*Śrīmad-Bhāgavatam* 10.14.16)

---

2 The saint and scholar Jīva Gosvāmī's explanation of *oṁ* clarifies Prabhupāda's statement. Jīva Gosvāmī writes that the two sounds that blend to become "o" – "a" and "u" (pronounced "uh" and "oo") – indicate the Absolute as masculine (Kṛṣṇa) and feminine (Rādhā) respectively, while the "ṁ" (*bindu*) indicates ourselves, the living beings. (See *Śrī Caitanya-caritāmṛta, Ādi-līlā* 7.128 referencing the *Bhāgavata-sandarbha*) Like the "a" in *oṁ* (*aum*), *Kṛṣṇa* and *Rāma* are the Absolute as masculine. And like the "u" in *oṁ, Hare* is the Absolute as feminine. The grammatical form of the mantra implies that someone is speaking to the Absolute Truth. That speaker is us, the living being, the "m" in *oṁ*. The Hare Kṛṣṇa *mahā-mantra* is therefore a conversation, a request for service, and an exchange of affection. It is not just a statement of the reality of divine loving reciprocation, but a full experience of that reality.

EVERYWHERE
ARE HIS
hands AND legs,
HIS EYES,
heads AND faces
AND HE HAS ears
EVERYWHERE

Meditation 17

In the *Brahma-saṁhitā 5.35* Brahmā explains, "All the universes exist in Him, and He is present in His fullness in every one of the atoms that are scattered throughout the universe, at one and the same time." We find it impossible to get a mental picture of this description of Kṛṣṇa's relation to space. How can the Lord be fully present in every atom while the whole universe is also present within Him?

Kṛṣṇa describes this fact in the *Bhagavad-Gītā 9.4–6*:

> By Me, in My unmanifested form, this entire universe is pervaded. All beings are in Me, but I am not in them. And yet everything that is created does not rest in Me. Behold My mystic opulence! Although I am the maintainer of all living entities and although I am everywhere, I am not a part of this cosmic manifestation, for My Self is the very source of creation. Understand that as the mighty wind, blowing everywhere, rests always in the sky [space], all created beings rest in Me.

Meditation 18

One of Kṛṣṇa's pastimes that show His inconceivable relationship with space occurred while He was staying in Dvārakā. When the Brahmā of this universe came to visit Kṛṣṇa, he saw that Brahmās from many other universes were also there. Each one was thinking that Kṛṣṇa was within his own universe, and none was able to see the others or interact with them. Kṛṣṇa exhibited a similar opulence when He sat in the middle of concentric circles of many cowherd boys and each perceived that Kṛṣṇa was facing him directly. One commentator says that this pastime of the Lord reminds us of the *Bhagavad-Gītā* verse (13.14): "Everywhere are His hands and legs, His eyes, heads, and faces, and He has ears everywhere."

Meditation 19

Although Kṛṣṇa is everywhere – in all space – at once and all places in space are within Him, He delights in traveling through outer space in a vehicle, as if He needs to move from one location to another. The Lord's vehicle is often a tremendous eagle-like divine being named Garuḍa. Kṛṣṇa also travelled at least once on a horse-drawn chariot that sped past the stars and galaxies. To assist His friend Arjuna, He went beyond material space, through the universal coverings to the Causal Spiritual Ocean.

Meditations from the Bhagavad-Gītā

I AM THE
taste
OF
water

Meditations from the *Bhagavad-Gītā*

In this section, we look at verses from chapters 7, 9, 10, 11, and 15 of the *Bhagavad-Gītā* in which Kṛṣṇa explains very clearly who and what He is in our daily lives. Some of these meditations might at first glance be similar to those in the section on Kṛṣṇa in the elements, but in this section the focus is different. We go deeply into the specific verses and examples from the *Bhagavad-Gītā* and how we could apply them in our own way of seeing the world.

Śrīla Prabhupāda explains this process eloquently in a letter to Kṛṣṇa Devī:

> Actually, there is nothing but Kṛṣṇa all around us. This is explained in the *Bhagavad-Gītā*. He is the taste of water, the light of the moon, the fragrance of the flower, the light of the sun, the sound of the sky, the power of the strong, and so on. So, one who is actually making progress in Kṛṣṇa Consciousness can see Kṛṣṇa everywhere. At every stage of life, who can avoid the sunlight, the moonlight, the fragrance of the flower, the taste of the water, the sound of the sky, and so on; but one has to learn it, that there is Kṛṣṇa in all these varieties of existence. Without Kṛṣṇa there is nothing. It is simply by the influence of Maya that we forget the relationship of Kṛṣṇa with everything that be.
>
> (Letter to Kṛṣṇa Devī, San Francisco. December 21, 1967)

Meditation 1: Taste of Water

I am the taste of water (*Gītā* 7.8)

On a scorching summer's day there's hardly anything that quenches our thirst like fresh, cool, pure water. It refreshes and cleanses us, and facilitates and lubricates all our bodily functions. Kṛṣṇa is the one who is removing our fatigue and bringing us relief even on a physical level. It is He, and He only, who spreads flowing life throughout our body and mind. Water in this world gives us a hint of how any touch with Kṛṣṇa gives relief and life. Kṛṣṇa quenches the thirst of our souls in this world where we have forgotten Him. Kṛṣṇa is truly the taste, or pleasure, we get from any liquid substance, and without liquidity none of our senses have any enjoyment. Our eyes need tears, our nose mucus, our ears wax, our tongue saliva, and our skin, oil. All come from the water we drink, and the "taste" or pleasure we experience through our senses from that water is Kṛṣṇa. Kṛṣṇa is, after all, the reservoir of all *rasa* and the form of *rasa* itself. Our bodily pleasures are but tiny indications of the supreme bliss He would like to share with all of us.

Meditation 2: The Radiant Sun

I am the light of the sun (7.8); of lights I am the radiant sun (10.21); the splendor of the sun,
which dissipates the darkness of this whole world, comes from Me. (*Gītā* 15.12)

When we think of our childhood, many of us will remember a time when we were afraid of the dark, maybe at bedtime. There is something inherently menacing about dark spaces. How frightening it is to walk in a dark alleyway or forest path at night! Perhaps we had to fetch something from a dark or dimly lit basement and then found ourselves running to the light as fast as we could. What relief we felt when dawn came or when we came to a lit area! Darkness brings fear and uncertainty or the feeling of being out of control. However, light brings relief and certainty. As dawn breaks and the sunlight begins to dissipate the darkness, we are no longer afraid. Sunlight not only helps us to assess our surroundings more accurately but also brings forth new life. In the same way, Kṛṣṇa is like sunlight, the Supreme Giver of life. He gives us clarity, certainty, and courage. We feel relief in sunlight because it is Kṛṣṇa.

Splendor
OF THE
sun
WHICH DISSIPATES THE
darkness
OF THIS WORLD

Meditation 3: The Splendor of the Moon

I am the light of the moon (7.8); among stars the moon; the splendor of the moon (*Gītā* 15.12); I become the moon and thereby supply the juice of life to all vegetables (*Gītā* 15.13)

The moon and its light have been part of mystery, intrigue, and magic for as long as people can remember. The moonlight fills us with a sense of wonder, and its silvery rays are in ways more soothing than the rays of the sun. In the same way, Kṛṣṇa is the ultimate source of mystery and allurement. We can see the moon as one of Kṛṣṇa's eyes, set on the dark expanse of the night sky, which is like Kṛṣṇa's skin. Sometimes Kṛṣṇa looks at us with the wide eye of the full moon and sometimes winks at us with the crescent moon.

Stars provide direction, beauty, and a reminder of the vast universe that we forget during the day. In magnificence and brilliance, the moon is the chief of the night's heavenly bodies and it rules the night sky. Like the moon, Kṛṣṇa is the leader of all who give light and understanding. In comparison to His brightness all others are simply stars. The moon surrounded with stars appear to be dancing in the night sky, as Kṛṣṇa dances surrounded by His many friends and associates.

The moonlight gives juice to vegetables, and some fruit juice brands also have a full moon harvest option because the moon gives more flavor. Indeed, many farmers time their harvest according to the moon's phases and astrological position. The crispy cucumber, the crunchy carrot, and the dripping tomato all receive subtle nectar from the moon, and the varieties of that liquid taste flow from Kṛṣṇa. How much taste there must be in the reservoir of all pleasure!

Meditation 4: The Splendor of Fire

the splendor of fire [is] also from Me. (*Gītā* 15.12)

Dancing, ever-changing flames captivate us so that our eyes are riveted to the sight. We thus remember Kṛṣṇa the all-attractive, who enchants the milkmaids to the extent that they hate the interruption of their blinking eyes that hinders their vision of Kṛṣṇa. Fire's grace reminds us of the Lord's dancing. Fire's light reminds us of Kṛṣṇa's effulgence. Fire's splendor and glory are part of many celebrations and decorations, from fireworks to neon signs to flickering-colored lights draped over buildings. How much more glorious is the source of all that light! Oh, if we could see Him, all the splendor of fire in one place, at one time, and in one person, how captivated we would be! Let us look beyond the glittering of the world to the glittering earrings of Kṛṣṇa, swaying as He dances and plays His flute.

Meditation 5: The Fire of Digestion

I am the fire of digestion in the bodies of all living entities (*Gītā* 15.14)

The *Cāraka Saṁhitā* (Chapter 28) explains how good digestion leads to health and bad digestion to illnesses of all kinds. Yet, digestion itself is somewhat mystical. How amazing it is that plants transform sunlight, water, and some minerals into leaves and fruit! And it is wondrous that, through the fire of digestion, our body takes those plants and transforms them into our skin, hair, nails, eyes, bone, muscles, and all our organs. This chemical burning process of digestion transform one form of energy into another. This mysterious process of transformation within our bodies is Kṛṣṇa creating our form anew from His own potencies of light, water, and earth. Thus, the energy, health, and growth we feel is our connection with Him.

When we suffer from bad digestion, our connection with Kṛṣṇa may appear to be interrupted. Since time immemorial our fire of connection with Kṛṣṇa may seem to our illusioned perception to have gone out, and thus we have to suffer the consequences of spiritual indigestion. Whether on a bodily or spiritual level, our remembrance of the Lord as our digestion, and our prayers to Him as digestive power, can restore us to health.

THE LIGHT OF THE
moon
FILLS US WITH A SENSE OF
wonder

SPLENDOR
of
fire

Meditation 6: Heat in Fire

I am the heat in fire (*Gītā* 7.9)

On a frosty winter morning, with everything enveloped in snow, the sunrays give gentle and welcoming heat to all that brave the cold. We feel the Lord's love and protection in that heat, even in the heat of our homes when we enter and gain relief from the miserable rain and wind. Without Kṛṣṇa's heat giving potency, we would be lost in this cold material world.

Kṛṣṇa is also directly involved in the cooking process as heat, whether the fire comes from wood, gas, electricity, or other fuel. As Kṛṣṇa in the moon rays gives the juice of life to vegetables, so Kṛṣṇa as fire's heat releases those juices and gives varieties of flavor and texture to the same vegetables, depending on the cooking method. Inversely, we can also meditate on our dependence on that fire whenever we run out of gas or have an unexpected power cut and can't cook.

Meditation 7: Sound in Ether

I am the sound in ether (*Gītā* 7.8)

The *Padma Purāṇa* states:

> If a devotee once utters the holy name of the Lord, or if it penetrates his mind or enters his ear, which is the channel of aural reception, that holy name will certainly deliver him from material bondage, whether vibrated properly or improperly, with correct or incorrect grammar, or properly joined or vibrated in separate parts.

Each syllable of the holy name is potent, and the name is the same as the Lord. As the Lord has infinite names, and each utterable syllable of sound is part of one of these names, the Lord is present in all sound vibrated through space. However, anyone who chants an authorized name of the Lord gets great spiritual benefit, whereas those speaking those same syllables not put together in words that are names of God do not find transcendental knowledge and bliss. At the same time, those who already realize that the Lord and His name are the same do, indeed, find that He is present in all sound and thus relish His presence everywhere.[3] Intentionally using sound and language to glorify Kṛṣṇa is the natural behavior of those with genuine realization.

Śrīla Prabhupāda explains:

> Sound is produced by the ether. So many sounds we are hearing. If you simply remember this *śloka* of *Bhāgavata*, that *śabda*, any sound . . . Hare Kṛṣṇa sound is transcendental. That's all right. But if you don't like Hare Kṛṣṇa sound, you take any sound, any sound is also . . . coming from the original sound; simply it is covered by *maya*. What is the difference between spiritual and material? Everything is spiritual. *Sarvaṁ khalv idaṁ brahma* [*Chāndogya Upaniṣad* 3.14.1]. But when it is covered by *maya*, it is material. That's all. And what is maya? Forgetfulness of Kṛṣṇa.
>
> (Lecture on *Bhagavad-Gītā* 7.8, Bombay. February 23, 1974)

Therefore, the roaring vehicles on the road, electric tools, or other repetitive sounds can remind us of instruments used to accompany the Lord's dancing. The birds' singing can remind us of birds in the Lord's abode who glorify Him and His associates. As all sound is ultimately spiritual, anything we hear can transport us to one of the pastimes in the spiritual world.

3 The sixth chapter of the Twelfth Canto of the Śrīmad-*Bhāgavatam* states that all sounds in material existence come from *oṁ*, which, in turn, came from the most subtle spiritual sound from Brahma's heart. *Oṁ* is described as the sound form of the Lord as pervasive energy, as the all-knowing Supreme Soul, and as the Personality of Godhead. Thus, whatever sound we hear is ultimately Kṛṣṇa Himself.

I
AM THE
sound
IN
ether

Meditation 8: Ability in Humans

I am the ability in humans (*Gītā* 7.8)[4]

What makes our nerves take signals to and from the brain, our muscles contract, and our brain to process? Where our ability comes from and how it is managed is a great mystery. Even when we study the mind and brain, we still do not know everything. We can lose any of our abilities instantly in an accident or illness, and our control over them is not absolute even in the best of situations. We are born with some natural talents, and others elude us despite years of training and effort. While our free will is, indeed, ours, and we can direct our abilities towards specific goals – though we cannot control achieving them or not – the abilities themselves do not come from our effort alone. As we meditate on any of our abilities, even the most mundane, such as the ability to sit without falling over, we can start to feel, to sense, that these abilities are the Lord Himself, going through us and within us, as He is the "self-sufficient philosopher who has been fulfilling everyone's desire since time immemorial." (*Śrī Īśopaniṣad* 8)

Meditation 9: Original Fragrance of Earth

I am the original fragrance of the earth (*Gītā* 7.9)

Such a large variety of smells come from earth – each kind of fragrant flower has its unique smell by growing from the same earth. What an amazing chemist the Lord is! From the earth, with sunshine and water, He produces the night-blooming jasmine, the ylang-ylang, gardenia, rose, plumeria, mogra, and an almost endless variety of fragrances. Each smell is different – sometimes subtly and sometimes obviously so. The earth itself has a faint smell that brings satisfaction to the gardener, farmer, or even one relaxing on a back porch. All these smells are Kṛṣṇa Himself. So, we can just imagine the scent of Kṛṣṇa! It is said that the pleasant scent of residents in higher planets spreads for eighty miles around. Here on earth, we sometimes smell flowers from a few blocks away. Kṛṣṇa's fragrance, however, pervades the spiritual world, and, indeed, all His creation. We can be aware of His smell, if we are in proper consciousness.

Of all the senses, smell most alerts us to what is pure or impure, so Kṛṣṇa in the form of smell guides us to what is binding and what is liberating. The sense of smell is also most likely linked to emotional memory and impressions, such that certain smells will trigger emotional responses in particular individuals according to their experiences. In a similar way, all smells can trigger our appreciation of Kṛṣṇa and remembrance of Him. And what of the bad smells? Even the bad smells remind us that Kṛṣṇa warns us of danger, impurity and disease if we care to pay attention. Bad smells also tell us of the cycle of destruction and creation – how from death and decay spring birth, growth, and life. All so-called bad is ultimately used for good in Kṛṣṇa's perfect creation.

Meditation 10: The Living Force

I am the life of all that lives (*Gītā* 7.9); in living beings I am the living force [consciousness] (*Gītā* 10.22)

The life force and where it comes from are a mystery that scientists have not yet been able to solve. How does a fern sapling push through solidified lava after a volcanic eruption has destroyed its habitat? How is it that spring, with new life, follows even the most severe winter? How is it that people suddenly pass away, regardless of their age? What is that essence that has passed away and has left an empty shell? As the living force of everyone, Kṛṣṇa is our consciousness, our self-awareness. He gives us infinite possibilities, spread over innumerable lives, to serve Him. Even when we are faced with death, Kṛṣṇa guides our living force into the next life, or back to Him.

4 In 7.8, Kṛṣṇa says that He is *pauruṣam* among the *nṛ*, which is a condensed form of *nara*. *Nṛ* means "human." So *nṛṣu* means "amongst humans." However, one can also understand the verse to be specifically about human males as follows: *pauruṣam*: neuter -- manhood, virility (opposite of *strītva* womanliness), manly strength or courage or deed, valor, heroism, *nṛ*: a man, hero, person; in the plural, often: mankind, people.

I AM THE
original
fragrance
OF THE
earth

Life
OF ALL
THAT Lives

Meditation 11: Penances of all Ascetics

I am the penances of all ascetics (*Gītā* 7.9)

To do penance is to right a wrong or to endeavor to restore balance to a relationship or situation after we did something to upset that balance. In other words, it's an attempt to fix something that we did or something in ourselves that caused pain or disturbance. Saying "I apologize" is an example of penance. Kṛṣṇa says that of penances He is the penance of all ascetics. We may ask, "What makes ascetics so special?" Ascetics from all religious traditions are those who offer their lives as one complete act of penance. They have realized their forgetfulness of God and want to repent to say, "We're sorry." Beyond apologizing, they live to restore the balance. Kṛṣṇa says that of all the ascetics' practices He is most present in their penances. Not only is He present, He is the actual penance.

How is this statement true if Kṛṣṇa is sinless and never has to apologize? We can meditate on how Kṛṣṇa comes to this material world whenever there is irreligiosity, such as when He came to save the Pāṇḍavas from the sinful sons of Dhṛtarāṣṭra, when He came as Lord Varāha to save Mother Bhumi and kill Hiraṇyākṣa, and when He came as Lord Rāmacandra to kill Rāvaṇa and save Sītā. These instances are all descriptions of imbalances that occurred within the material world. Since the material energy is a part of Kṛṣṇa, when He comes to the material world, He comes to restore balance within His own energy. Therefore, Kṛṣṇa is penance itself because He is the Ultimate Restorer of balance.

So, in our own lives, what does it mean to live a life of penance? In what ways do we try to restore the balance in our lives? By chanting the holy names of Kṛṣṇa, we perform penance in the sense that we try to remember Kṛṣṇa. When we perform devotional service, it is in the mood of serving Kṛṣṇa out of love, but also to remember Kṛṣṇa after forgetting Him for so many lifetimes. When we become ascetics, in the sense that our whole life is dedicated to righting the wrong of forgetting Kṛṣṇa, then Kṛṣṇa is present in our acts of penance, those acts by which we constantly and consistently try to rectify our wrong.

Meditation 12: Intelligence of the Intelligent

I am the intelligence of the intelligent (Gītā 7.10)

All bright ideas, no matter how big they are, come from Kṛṣṇa. He is the intelligence that creates works of art such as the Sistine Chapel, Gaudi's Sagrada Familia, the architecture of Notre Dame, etc. He is the intelligence that creates a perfectly constructed building, whether it be from wood, glass, or metal. He is the intelligence of anyone who audits financial reports, teaches mathematics, or solves the Rubik's cube. Kṛṣṇa is the intelligence of anyone who solves problems of pollution or invents water-saving techniques. He is the intelligence that gives a child the ability to walk and climb. We can feel Kṛṣṇa working in our ability of knowing, understanding, and being able to figure things out. Our admiration for the intelligence of others gives a tiny hint of the glory of Kṛṣṇa's brain.

Meditation 13: The Strength of the Strong

I am the prowess of the powerful (Gītā 7.10); I am the strength of strong (Gītā 10.36);
I am the strength of the strong, devoid of passion and desire (*Gītā* 7.11)

Kṛṣṇa is the strongest, carrying the planets on His heads without even noticing them. He effortlessly defeats great demons, whom even the demigods fear. Through His energies in nature, He smashes rocks in the roar of crashing ocean waves, sweeps the earth clean with windstorms, and burns the desert with a raging sun. Yet, Kṛṣṇa's form is delicate and youthful, such that when he entered the wrestling area of Kamsa, the audience felt it was unfair for muscular, professional wrestlers to compete with young, delicate boys, such as Kṛṣṇa and Balarāma. Kṛṣṇa's combination of softness and strength, intense delicateness and uncompromising hardness, is extremely attractive. Whenever we witness or receive benefit from the prowess or strength of any creature, human being, or nature itself, we can gain an awareness of the current of Kṛṣṇa's power, even when exhibited to an infinitesimal extent.

Intelligence

OF

INTELLIGENT

Brute force and power certainly are Kṛṣṇa's energy and can be witnessed everywhere in creation and destruction on a micro and macro level. Any strength at all is the energy of the Lord. Yet there is also a kind of strength and power in which we feel Kṛṣṇa's presence in a sweet way. Whenever force and strength protect, shelter, love, aid, provide, and nourish, there is Kṛṣṇa, the supreme father and mother of all living beings. It is said that Kṛṣṇa cares for us like a mother lion carrying her cubs gently in the same teeth that tear larger creatures apart. Using our own strength and power without personal desire to control others, but rather to help them, connects us with this opulence of Kṛṣṇa's prowess. All our strengths are gifts meant to serve others, not to harm them.

Meditation 14: Sex Life

I am sex life which is not contrary to religious principles (*Gītā* 7.11)

Sex should be related to pleasing Kṛṣṇa, who has designed the function of sex to be connected with creation. The main criterion in the *śāstra* for righteous sex is procreation. Children produced should be trained as devotees, which is much easier if they are born within marriage. Limiting procreative sex to marriage also benefits the parents, as it practically and mentally connects pleasure to responsibility and service. Further limiting sex to only the most favorable time for procreation and a deliberate preparation of the parents' mental state produces the most beneficial result. The closer sexual behavior is to the ideal of responsibility and service, both with regard to the sexual partner and the offspring, the more "pious" results one incurs. Also, as our sexual behavior gets closer to responsibility and service, we can experience Kṛṣṇa's presence there and be aided in our *bhakti*. As one gets further from this ideal, *bhakti* becomes more and more difficult, though ultimately *bhakti* is independent of material circumstances. There are also sexual behaviors that by their very nature cannot be offered in service and are therefore great obstacles to *bhakti*, just as there are foods which cannot be offered to Kṛṣṇa.

However, sex in line with dharma and creation can go beyond being pious. It can be an act in which Kṛṣṇa Himself manifests. The couple connects with each other, and with the child they hope to create a circle of love whose center is Kṛṣṇa's pleasure. Kṛṣṇa is the potency and vigor of the sexual act, the life of parents manifesting the life of the child, the bonds of affection, and the very taste of pleasure itself. He is the paradox of simultaneous individuality and union, which is at the heart of sexual relations. When sex is done not only according to scriptural rules but as an offering of devotion to the Lord, it is a cause of liberation from lust. It is transcendent and glorious.

Meditation 15: Kandarpa, God of Love

Of causes for procreation, I am Kandarpa, the god of love (Gītā 10.28)

There are many reasons we have children. We may want the experience of caring for another, watching them grow and change, and influencing their lives. We may enjoy teaching and guiding them, seeing bits of ourselves in them, and perhaps a way of starting a new chapter. Often, people have children to continue their name and dynasty to secure a sense of immortality through their descendants. Children may also be an insurance policy for old age care or a way to continue the family business. They may be a contribution to society by giving the world well-trained population. They may be the fruit of loving care between spouses. Children may be a symbol of status and accomplishment when they win honors and gain material success. For some, children are just a natural and perhaps an inconvenient result of lust for sexual pleasure. Of all these causes and more, Kṛṣṇa is the feeling of attraction, love, appreciation, and caring between a man and woman who demonstrate their commitment in a spiritual ceremony of lifetime loyalty. Sometimes immature spiritual practitioners reject such affection as selfish, but the more mature relish it as one of Kṛṣṇa's potencies for attracting a qualified soul to take birth on earth.

SEX LIFE

WHICH IS NOT CONTRARY

TO

religious

principles

Meditation 16: Ritual

I am the ritual (*Gītā* 9.16)

At various times in the day we have our rituals, our habitual systems for what we do regularly. We also have "rituals" for how we connect with, and please others. Vedic rituals are systems for pleasing and connecting with Kṛṣṇa. *Bhagavad-Gītā 9.16* uses the Sanskrit word *kratuḥ,* that He is such Vedic rituals. These rituals are processes for connecting our consciousness, actions, and desires with the Supreme. We may think of Kṛṣṇa as only the goal of such rituals, but He is also the process itself. The way we light the sacrificial fire, for example, and the rules for what is done in what way and in what order represent Kṛṣṇa's desire for how He likes things. In an ordinary family, the mother may want the dishes put in the kitchen cabinets in a particular way, and when the other family members honor those wishes, they practically act in friendship, respect, and possibly love for her desires. In Kṛṣṇa's case, however, His desires are nondifferent from Himself. Therefore, when we are attentive to the details of ritual, it is not a mechanical thing, but a deep connection with Him in every part of the procedure.

Meditation 17: Sacrifice

I am the *yajñaḥ-smṛti* (*Gītā* 9.16)

Here the Lord says that He is *yajñaḥ*: the ceremonies we perform to connect with Him, which includes our chanting of the holy name, our offering of grains into the sacrificial fire, our worship of the Deity, and our various processes of meditation. Generally, we think of these ceremonies as a means for obtaining the favor of Kṛṣṇa rather than their being Kṛṣṇa Himself. But here Kṛṣṇa says that he is also that very means. So, as we offer our lamp, for instance, we can feel the process of lighting the lamp, purifying our hands and the lamp, moving our hands in a circle to offer the lamp, and doing everything according to the scriptures as being Kṛṣṇa Himself. These activities are Him, because He gives the directions in the scriptures, which indicate what He loves, what gives Him pleasure, and what He knows is good for us. This pleasure is His own internal potency, and therefore identical with Him.

Meditation 18: Offering to the Ancestors

I am the offering to the ancestors (*Gītā* 9.16)

Losing someone close to us causes great pain and mental disturbance. Overwhelmed with grief, we may lose our footing for a while. We may want to do something for those who have passed, such as an offering of love and peace. To facilitate the natural desires to benefit departed family members, many cultures perform ritual offerings to long departed ancestors. Such offerings, according to *śāstra,* do help our family members wherever they are now, and are gifts of love and gratitude from the living. Any offering of genuine love means that Kṛṣṇa is present. He is pleased with gratitude, and he is pleased with love. He is pleased to see family traditions continue and our respect for those who came before. He cares about the continuity of piety and respect; therefore, He is personally present in such offerings.

Meditation 19: Healing Herb

I am the healing herb (*Gītā* 9.16)

Kṛṣṇa as the healing herb sooths our troubled minds and aching bodies. As lavender He brings calmness. As echinacea, goldenseal, or turmeric He cures our infections; as marigolds He cools our sunburn; as arnica He reduces our bruises; and as basil He speeds the healing of our cuts. In His form of mint, He heals our upset stomach and as ginger quietens nausea; as chamomile He soothes mosquito bites and as parsley, He overcomes our bad breath. He restores our memory and concentration as rosemary and mitigates depression as St John's wort.

But it is I
who am the
ritual,
I the
sacrifice,
the
offering
to the ancestors,
the
healing
herb.

hare kṛṣṇa hare kṛṣṇa

kṛṣṇa kṛṣṇa hare hare

hare rāma hare rāma

rāma rāma hare hare

Of sacrifices
I AM THE
chanting
OF THE
holy names

Each healing herb grows from the same earth, in the same sun, drinking the same water. Yet each plant has specific remedial power and specific ways of preparation and use. Such power is in the humble and simple plants of the earth because such power is Kṛṣṇa Himself. Even advanced and sophisticated pharmaceuticals are often made from the chemicals of healing herbs. Although disease is part of having a material body, Kṛṣṇa is not callous to the suffering of illness but manifests Himself in interplay between these plants and our bodies to restore health. People often mindlessly consume various remedies, seeing the plants' energy and their own body's processes as only chemical and mechanical systems. The greater truth is that the Supreme Life, Kṛṣṇa, is the healing power of medicine.

Meditation 20: Transcendental Chant

I am the transcendental chant [mantra] (*Gītā* 9.16)

Kṛṣṇa is the Absolute Truth, the Supreme Personality of Godhead. As the All-powerful, Kṛṣṇa can manifest Himself in whatever form He chooses, including sound. If we doubt the power of sound, we can consider how music, poetry, and words in general can have so much power over people. The advertising industry exemplifies the power of words and jingles to sell any product. Even in our personal lives we experience the effects of someone's words. We may become inspired after hearing a lecture, or we may struggle for weeks because of a hurtful comment thrown our way. Music has the power to change our mood and emotions, too. Some sports teams use music to psych themselves up before a big match. Some songs have the power to make us feel hopeful, sad, or angry, etc.

If there is so much power in ordinary sounds, certainly the supreme sound can be the Supreme Powerful personally and directly. The literal meaning of "mantra" is that which frees the mind, and Kṛṣṇa is there as sound to personally free our mind from the habits and attachments that bind us to illusion and misery. The accessibility of Kṛṣṇa in His sound form is a great mercy for us, both personally and in our helping others to attain to spiritual life.

Meditation 21: Chanting of the Holy Names

Of sacrifices I am the chanting of the holy names [japa] (*Gītā* 10.25)

When we are in love with someone, we often – or even constantly – think of that person and think of many different ways to spend time with him or her, no matter what else needs to happen in our day. When we deal with those we love, such loving dealings usually center around what we can do for them or how we can spend time with them. And often, time is one of the most precious gifts we can give someone. Another precious gift is the sound of their name. We all love to hear our name, to see it in print, and to know that others remember our name. We will hear our name clearly out of a great sea of dozens of conversations that blur together in a crowd. Of all the ways that someone can connect with us, saying our name is immediate and direct, grabbing our interest and attention.

So, of all the ceremonies and processes given in scripture and by sages to be in the presence of God, the supreme is the quiet personal repetition of His name. We have heard many times that Kṛṣṇa is His name. In addition, Kṛṣṇa is the act of our repeating that name in a very private way, just between Him and us, with deep appreciation and affection for Him.

This ceremony, this sacrifice of giving our time to the holy name, is not the sacrifice that makes us feel we're losing a limb or giving up something that we hold very dear, but it fills our hearts with even more love for the person that we are spending time with. In this way, our *japa*, our quiet chanting of the holy names, is the highest sacrifice of divine connection.

I AM THE
syllable
AUM

Meditation 22: The Syllable Om

I am the syllable *oṁ* (*Gītā* 9.17); I am the syllable *oṁ* in the Vedic mantras (*Gītā* 7.8)

The letter "o" in the syllable *oṁ* is a combination of the two vowels "a" as in "up" and "u" as in "put." The Sanskrit language makes use of *sandhi*, the merging of two vowels to make a new vowel based on what sound biologically occurs when the separate vowels are said together. In this case "a" and "u" make the combined sound "oh" as in "home." Kṛṣṇa says that He is the sound "a," not because it is the first letter of the alphabet, but because it is the base sound from which all other sounds come. It is the sound that we make using only the throat, with no manipulation of airflow using the tongue, teeth, or lips. Jīva Gosvāmī says that the "u" represents Rādhā (or Lakṣmī or Sītā) and the "m" represents the *jīva*, ourselves. *Oṁ* is therefore the complete reality in sound.

Several times in the *Bhagavad-Gītā*, Kṛṣṇa identifies Himself with *oṁ* or advises the chanting of *oṁ*. It is the sound that started creation and pervades all reality. It is part of many mantras and prayers in the scriptures and as given by the *ācāryas*. It is simple and short, yet deep and profound. Similarly, Kṛṣṇa also seems simple to some – a little cowherd boy calling His herds with a flute he keeps tucked in His belt. But the profundity of His personality, power, knowledge, and love spread unlimitedly in all time and space. Such is the glory and power of *oṁ*.

Meditation 23: Butter

I am the butter [melted butter] and the fire (*Gītā* 9.16)

When we look at melted butter, we can see its rich golden color, especially when it is in the form of ghee, just like Kṛṣṇa's golden *dhotī*. The golden ghee forms a foundational part in cooking as it is the basis of most chaunces. It helps to absorb the flavor of the spices and spread them through the preparation. Kṛṣṇa is the ghee that spreads flavor through our lives by infusing everything with His divine love. Ghee is also a component in *Āyurveda* as part of *pañca-karma* – a cleansing ritual that rids the body of all toxins and restarts stagnant systems within. Kṛṣṇa, in the form of His names or sacred literature, also cleanses us from all our *anarthas* and restarts our dormant love for Him whenever we take up the process of becoming Kṛṣṇa conscious.

Meditation 24: The Offering

I am the offering (*Gītā* 9.16)

We know that Kṛṣṇa expands Himself into every atom of the material universe. This doesn't mean that everything material is conscious of itself like the *jīvas*, but it does mean that Kṛṣṇa is aware of His energy, much as we are aware of our fingernail tips or hair. The nails and hair in and of themselves are not alive or conscious, but as they are connected to our bodies, we as the *jīvas* are aware of them.

In the same way, when Kṛṣṇa says that He is the offering He means that whatever we offer Him – fruit, flowers, vegetables, ghee, etc. – is already part of Him, because the material energy is also part of Kṛṣṇa. We may then ask, what is the point of offering anything to Him? And the answer is "love."

It is much like the relationship between a father and his small children. The father is the provider, and whatever the children have is because the father provides it. So logically, the children can't really give their father anything, because all they have belongs to him already, but when a little girl decides to make her father breakfast, his heart melts. This is not because she gave him something that he didn't already have, or that the breakfast deserves five stars, but because his daughter made him an offering filled with her love.

Additionally, we see that Kṛṣṇa is the offering because Kṛṣṇa is Himself love. We have the capacity to love because we are part and parcel of Kṛṣṇa. The point of the offering is the loving exchange between the *jīva* and Kṛṣṇa.

Meditation 25: Father

I am the father of this universe (*Gītā* 9.17)

Most religions describe God as the Supreme Father of the universe, so it's no surprise that Kṛṣṇa describes Himself in this way too. Usually, we interact with many fathers; perhaps we, ourselves, are fathers, or we may have dealings with our own father, or the father of our children, or those who are fathers to other children. In addition to human fathers, we see fathers in various species of mammals, fish, insects, and birds. Kṛṣṇa is the epitome of fatherhood. He is the provider, maintainer, teacher, guide, protector, confidant, and well-wisher of every being. As the perfect father He loves all equally and never envies His children; indeed, like most fathers, He aspires for each of His children to achieve greatness. He is happy to stand in the background and let His children take the credit.

Meditation 26: The Mother

I am the father of this universe, [and] the mother (*Gītā* 9.17)

Kṛṣṇa describes Himself, not just as the supreme father, but also as the mother. In our present day, if God is described as the Supreme Mother, the assumption is that the Supreme Being must be feminine. Yet Kṛṣṇa describes Himself to be both the original male and the ultimate mother. How can we understand His statement? Of course, Kṛṣṇa has His incarnation as a woman, Mohinī-mūrti, who is the object of worship for the supreme goddess of the material world, Prakṛti devī. Also, the great saints explain that God is both male and female as Lakṣmī-Nārāyaṇa, Sītā-Rāma, Rādhā-Kṛṣṇa, and so forth. Such divine couples are one in identity though They appear as two persons for pastimes of enjoyment.

Our bodies were formed and nourished from our mother's body. As a mother loves her children regardless of their defects or crimes, so Kṛṣṇa always loves us. As mothers in many species will sacrifice safety, health, and even life for their children, Kṛṣṇa ultimately and voluntarily gives everything to His beloved children. Śrīla Prabhupāda's commentary on Kṛṣṇa's assertion that He is the mother is fascinating.

Approaching the subject from a different angle, Śrīla Prabhupāda's writes:

> In the material existence we create different relationships with different living entities who are nothing but Kṛṣṇa's marginal energy; under the creation of *prakṛti* some of them appear as our father, mother, grandfather, creator, etc., but actually they are parts and parcels of Kṛṣṇa. As such, these living entities who appear to be our father, mother, etc., are nothing but Kṛṣṇa. In this verse the word *dhātā* means "creator." Not only are our father and mother parts and parcels of Kṛṣṇa, but the creator, grandmother and grandfather, etc., are also Kṛṣṇa. Actually, any living entity, being part and parcel of Kṛṣṇa, is Kṛṣṇa.
>
> (*Bhagavad-Gītā* 9.17 purport)

Thus, not only does Kṛṣṇa personify the qualities and role of a natural mother, but also in the love we receive from the mothers in our lives, we can feel a little of the love and caring of Kṛṣṇa.

Meditation 27: The Support

I am the support (*Gītā* 9.17)

Support can be seen at all levels of society as well as the natural world. In a gross sense, houses and buildings need support. Arches are built, sometimes without mortar, so that one stone rests on top of the other. Cement attaches bricks to form walls; buildings rest on a foundation; and beams hold the roof of a house. In a subtler sense, creatures in nature give each other support, from parent animals helping their young, to trees nourishing each other via their root system, even nourishing stumps left by loggers. Among humans, even strangers lend support to helpless people and change their lives. All kinds of support are Kṛṣṇa, and underlying the physical and emotional support of this world is Kṛṣṇa's unwavering support for us. His support is our strength, and not acknowledging and accepting His support

HIS
support
gross and subtle
IS OUR STRENGTH

leads to "crumbling of the bricks" – discord between family members and other disputes and challenges. Even when the external manifestations of support seem to vanish, Kṛṣṇa is always there holding us and ensuring that we are never vanquished.

Meditation 28: The Grandsire

I am the grandsire (*Gītā* 9.17)

Kṛṣṇa says that He is the grandsire. In the animal kingdom the word *sire* is used to refer to the father of a particular animal and the grandsire is the grandfather. So Kṛṣṇa is the forefather, the original person from whom all other persons have their origin. We are parts and parcels of Kṛṣṇa as His marginal potency just as a little child is genetically and bodily linked to his father and his grandfather.

The First Canto of *Śrīmad-Bhāgavatam* explains that when creating this material world, Kṛṣṇa expands into Mahā-Viṣṇu who, by His breathing, creates all the universes, which appear like bubbles coming out of His pores. Mahā-Viṣṇu then expands into all these millions of universes to create diversity – the 8,400,000 species of life. Then, Kṣīrodakaśāyī Viṣṇu expands to not only be within every living entity as the Supersoul, but also within every atom of every living entity and every material object. In this way, Kṛṣṇa is the grandsire, the master creator, behind everything and everyone.

Meditation 29: The Object of Knowledge

I am the object of knowledge (*Gītā* 9.17)

The ultimate result of knowing anything is to know Kṛṣṇa, the source of everything, the sum total of everything, the soul of the universe, the form of the universe, and the personality of the universe. Whatever is the object or goal of our curiosity, learning, or research is within Kṛṣṇa and part of Kṛṣṇa. Such is true even if we want to learn about death and destruction, for Kṛṣṇa is that, also. Ultimately, if we know Kṛṣṇa, even to a minute degree, we know "everything" in the sense of knowing the essence and the purpose of everything. Once we know Kṛṣṇa, therefore, we can use all else we know for the highest good, for the benefit of ourselves and others.

Meditation 30: The Purifier

I am the purifier (*Gītā* 9.17)

We conditioned souls, if we are honest, can understand our need for being purified. Our motives, desires, thoughts, emotions, and actions are often out of sync with what we believe is best for ourselves. Our espoused ideals remain above our actual lives. On the physical, emotional, mental, ethical, and social level we find ourselves choosing the impure out of habit, pressure from others, fear, expediency, or a host of other reasons and justifications.

If we are interested in real happiness, health, and peace, we try our best to purify ourselves. We may make healthy – or at least healthier – food choices, read and watch things that we hope will edify us, and have relationships with those who bring out our best. We may go further to enroll in self-improvement courses, go to therapy, or take up a self-help discipline. But if we are fully honest, we will find that none of these paths are completely purifying. Certainly, Kṛṣṇa is present in whatever extent our diets, therapists, and other efforts bring us to a higher level of consciousness. He is the only real purifier. It is His voice in our hearts that confirms the helpful and cleansing truth of whatever action we need to take against the things that drag us down. Thus, we give ultimate credit to Him. At the same time, to realize our eternally pure and glorious nature, we take to Kṛṣṇa's service directly, and so find that all we sought elsewhere is included.

Meditation 31: The Goal

I am the goal (*Gītā* 9.18)

The Oxford English Dictionary defines *goal* as "the object of a person's ambition or effort; an aim or desired result." It can also be defined as a destination of a journey. Having goals gives our lives meaning, purpose, and drive. Achieving our goals not only gives us a sense of permanent completion but also opens up unknown vistas to us, further goals and destinations that we could not have seen from our original starting point.

Furthermore, having a well-defined goal also immediately gives us a clearer understanding of the directions we need to follow to attain that goal. For instance, if we enter a destination on our GPS, it can immediately tell us several things: which turns are correct, which turns are wrong, and alternative routes that will get us to our destination even though some take a bit longer than others.

Whatever clarity we get from our various goals in life is increased a thousandfold when our goal is loving service to Śrī Kṛṣṇa. All our goals in this world, the effort we make to reach them, and the accomplishment we feel upon their attainment, are a tiny part of the satisfaction and understanding we get when we make Kṛṣṇa our goal. All other objectives we focus on can be part of the overall purpose of pleasing and connecting with Kṛṣṇa.

Meditation 32: The Sustainer

I am the sustainer (*Gītā* 9.18)

If we think about sustenance or a sustainer, we may ask ourselves, "What keeps me alive?" And the answer is not just air, food, water, or blood. Being alive has many facets. Although we may be breathing, we may be figuratively dead on an emotional, creative, or spiritual level.

For a mother and father, it may be the happiness of their children that sustains them; for a child it may be the love of the parents; for teenagers it may be friendships at school. For a homeless person it may be a tree or a tent; for artists it may be the facility to express themselves in the way that they feel most comfortable. For a musician it may be to make music; for a writer it may be to tell a story; for a policeman or fireman it may be to help others.

However, both on the physical and subtle levels it is really Kṛṣṇa who sustains everyone. He is air, water, and sunlight. He is the life of everyone and the total of all relationships. When we feel physically, emotionally, creatively, and socially sustained through another way, it is really Kṛṣṇa's energy working through those ways.

In *Bhagavad-Gītā 9.18* the Sanskrit word used for *sustainer* is *bhartā*, which can also be translated as *husband*. Like a husband who enjoys the beauty of his wife, Kṛṣṇa enjoys the beauty of His creation and the living beings. He takes care of us in the same way that a gardener takes care of plants. He nurtures and cultivates us to come closer to Him.

Meditation 33: The Master

I am the master (*Gītā* 9.18)

When we hear the word *master,* we may conjure images of our boss, or an English lord in his manor, or someone who is top in their field, like a master chef or master painter. In general, we associate qualities of power and control with a master, someone who has the last word.

To be master also means to have followers or servants. For some this idea of a master may ignite a fire of resistance within them; others may think of a master as an inspiring person in their field of interest, someone they admire or look up to or who has come out on top against the odds. Sometimes we may even feel envious of such masters rather than feeling inspired by them: They've already made it to the summit, and we are stuck in the mud way down in the valley.

It's fairly easy for masters in any field of activity to remind us of Kṛṣṇa, the Supreme Master. Of all the ways Kṛṣṇa manifests in the world, His being the master is perhaps one of the most obvious. He is the supreme boss, the supreme expert, the supreme powerful, and supreme controller. While we may admire His mastery and feel inspired by His control, we may also envy Him and wish to be a master ourselves.

Unfortunately, when we feel we are a master, such an idea can be like a weed invading the heart. We may think we possess the people in our lives: our spouse, children, parents, friends. We may think we own our house because we've paid for it with our own bone-grinding work. When the weed of being master of all grows tall enough in our hearts its fruit ripens into a feeling of dissatisfaction with people, situations, and life in general. In this mood we become unwilling to help others, thinking our own lives are more important.

On the other hand, when we are conscious that only Kṛṣṇa is the master and we are His servants, then even a position in the world of mastery, in terms of leadership and expertise, will not inflame our egos. We can lead as Kṛṣṇa's servant, knowing that in whatever field we have gained mastery, it is all His grace.

Meditation 34: The Witness

I am the witness (*Gītā* 9.18)

We may think of a witness in a legal sense, as someone who gives testimony regarding those who participate in a crime. A witness, however, isn't necessarily involved in something negative. The term could simply refer to someone observing our life, like a mother observing her child growing up from a baby to a toddler. It could refer to friendships spanning across decades, people with whom we've shared deep life experiences, people who have witnessed us grow into the people we are today.

Kṛṣṇa says that He is the witness, but this does not mean He is a meanspirited tattletale recording only our bad actions. As the Supersoul in the heart of every living entity, Kṛṣṇa is the Supreme Witness. He is the friend who has been with us since the beginning of time, spanning across all our lives, not just this one.

We may sometimes feel alone or that no one really knows or cares what we do. Others may look at the results of our actions, but few – if any – pay attention to all the details of our efforts and desires. Ah, but there is a witness. Kṛṣṇa sees our sorrows, our joys, our struggles, stumbles, and triumphs. He is witness to all our actions as the most loyal friend, choosing to stick with us no matter what. He is simply waiting patiently for us to recognize that He has always been there and always will be and to finally turn to Him. He is a witness because He deeply cares – about every detail of our inner and outer life. Knowing He is with us gives a sense of connection and security that can't be found anywhere else.

Meditation 35: The Abode

I am the abode (*Gītā* 9.18)

Sometimes we think *home* is synonymous with *house,* but it isn't. If we've relocated to another country or town, we feel we've left home for another place, a place that is not yet home. What makes us peg the word *home* to certain places and not others? Is it just four walls and a roof over our heads at the end of the day?

Home is the place we want to go to when we've had a rough day – to close the door, put up our feet and read something, have silence, or collect our friends around us. Home is the place where we feel we can be our most authentic selves, a place of safety where we can recalibrate when life is a bit stormy. Home is the place where we collect our memories. So, from this broader perspective, home is not just a house but a collection of people, experiences, and memories.

Sometimes, what is supposed to be our home, our place of safety, is the place where we feel the most unease and fear. Perhaps our home is taken away due to financial constraints, or the people we live with fill our hearts with fear and discord. In such cases, we feel lost and without a lifeline, but Kṛṣṇa always gives hope.

Kṛṣṇa says that He is the abode. On a cosmic scale He manifests the universes – our cosmic homes – after which we return to Him at the time of dissolution. Kṛṣṇa is our real home. When Nanda Mahārāja and Mother Yaśodā decided to leave Gokula and move to Vṛndāvana, the other cowherd men and women also packed up their homes and moved with Kṛṣṇa. They didn't really need to, but they just couldn't picture home without Kṛṣṇa.

Kṛṣṇa Himself has an eternal home, Goloka Vṛndāvana, and He is so attached to that home that He takes it with Him in some form wherever He goes, together with all His friends and family. It is difficult for us to fathom a sense of security without a home, but Kṛṣṇa is our home. Many *sannyāsīs* and *vānaprasthas* travel the globe without having a permanent home, nevertheless, they always feel at home because Kṛṣṇa is their home and shelter. For them their "home" is even in an airport waiting lounge! Kṛṣṇa is the abode in all circumstances. If we turn to Him in times of tragedy, joy, love, and whatever life gives us, we may see that Kṛṣṇa's shelter is always "home" no matter where we are. If we turn to Him, we carry home in our hearts.

Meditation 36: The Refuge

I am the refuge (*Gītā* 9.18)

A refuge is a shelter, a place of safety and protection. We consider much in our life a refuge. Physically, we take refuge in buildings, screens on our windows to ward against bugs, clothing, skin creams, and places with food and water. Socially, we take refuge in family, friends, groups, and governments. We may also feel that our own gross body is a refuge. For many of us, our subtle body can seem like a refuge. We may feel protected by our intellect, knowledge, skills, and so forth. However, with even a little introspection we can understand that all material refuges are like fallible soldiers. They are unstable and temporary. None of these fallible soldiers can offer us real protection without Kṛṣṇa's sanction. "If Kṛṣṇa wants to kill you, no one can save you; if Kṛṣṇa wants to save you, no one can kill you."

Although our material refuges are shaky and insubstantial, we can take the feeling of security that we get from them – like a baby in a mother's arms – and multiply that by millions of times to get a small sense of the real, supreme, eternal, and total refuge, Kṛṣṇa. Śrīla Prabhupāda writes, "[Devotees] boldly take to that shelter which is like an umbrella against the sun of repeated birth and death." (*Śrīmad-Bhāgavatam* 3.21.17 purport)

Meditation 37: The Dearmost Friend

I am the most dear friend (*Gītā* 9.18)

Most of us have or have had a close, special friend or friends in our life. Sometimes friendships even exist between humans and animals, or even between animals that are usually enemies, like a lion and the deer that became best friends, or a cat and mouse. The Internet is filled with stories of such unlikely animal friendships. There is something magical about friendship and how it can transcend boundaries. The sense of friendship we get in this world gives us a small taste of the friendly love of Kṛṣṇa, a friend who is not just dear but the "most dear". Our worldly friendships, however magical and long-lasting they are, will always end. Sometimes those endings are bitter and painful, full of betrayal and grief. But even the best friendships of this world end with death. Kṛṣṇa, in contrast, is not only the dearest friend but a friend with no expiration date, a friend who will help us no matter what, all hours of the night or day. He is our friend when we act rightly and our friend when we make the most grievous mistakes. Whatever He does for us is for our benefit. Our gratitude for our friendships in the world and the joy we experience through them can fill us with the desire to be a friend of the Supreme Friend, Kṛṣṇa, as well – to be faithful to Him through life's ups and downs and to act to fulfil His desires.

TOMPKINS
SQUARE
PARK
resting
PLACE

Meditation 38: The Basis of Everything

I am the basis of everything (*Gītā* 9.18)

Life's craziness can sometimes stretch our minds and abilities in a million directions so much that our minds feel like a spider's web: sticky because it attracts thought patterns, and stretched in all directions to keep a hold on reality, where the slightest breeze can disintegrate the fine tendrils of our remaining composure. Work, children, spouse, friends, service at the temple, home, cleaning, cooking, taxes, preaching, *sādhana* . . . on and on these threads of responsibility stretch.

Sometimes it's not just the little bits of life that collectively overwhelm us but rather real and actual pain and trauma that hook onto our consciousness and spread distress everywhere. It can be the void of a loved one's death, the shards of a broken marriage or relationship, a betrayal, a failed business venture, or the infection of criticism and deceit. And sometimes we are even stretched by the beauty of life, such as a job promotion, good feedback on a project, or our children's excelling at something. Sometimes we go through a rollercoaster of contradictory experiences – one evening we may be celebrating our child's achievement at school and on the way home there is an accident and then an emptiness; we may excel at work one year and lose our job in the next because of financial cutbacks. We may be battling with an addiction and after years overcome it and finally put our lives together again.

Sometimes the banyan tree of life spreads too many branches and roots that go in all different directions, which twist and turn, go upside down and inside out, and . . . it's chaos. In whatever way life stretches us, we often get to a point where we ask ourselves: How did we get here? How is one part of our lives connected to another vastly different part?

And the answer is in Kṛṣṇa, as always. Even the most fragile or chaotic spiderweb has its anchor points. Even the largest banyan tree has its trunk from which all branches and roots sprout. Similarly, as Kṛṣṇa says, He is the basis of everything. And He literally means everything. To the spiderweb, He is the anchor points; to the banyan tree He is the trunk; from Him comes everything and within Him everything has its basis.

It's sometimes difficult to swallow that Kṛṣṇa is the basis of our lives' tough lessons, but often we forget that He is the basis of our greatest successes, too. He gives us the intelligence by which we get that promotion, by which we solve that conflict. He is the guiding hand that helps us raise our children and guide our relationships. But often when things go well, we think ourselves the root of our glory.

Still, there is immense hope and grounding grace in the realization that Kṛṣṇa is the basis of everything. Our happiness, our tragedy, our anger, our experiences, our lessons – Kṛṣṇa has them all under control. From Him comes everything.

Meditation 39: The Resting Place

I am the resting place (*Gītā* 9.18); the ultimate resting place of all this universe (*Gītā* 11.18)

Oases are green jewels scattered in a desert shimmering with mirages. They are the treasure for all animals and travelers looking for a repose from the burning heat. They are bathed in cooling shade, providing much needed water for dry thirsty throats. They are calming resting places, giving the strength again to face the ocean of fire.

Deserts, however, don't always take shape in rolling sand dunes. Many of us are more familiar with the burning glare of sunlight from city skyscrapers or the melting asphalt of an overcrowded sidewalk as we rush to work. We may also know the deserts of loneliness in working environments filled with people that don't share our goals and ideals or intellectual abilities. We may know the oppressive humdrum of a hundred voices bombarding us in classrooms, in tightly packed office cubicles, or in airport check-in lines, a sea of voices making demands of us, making us yearn for the quiet oasis of our homes.

What are our modern-day oases? They may be a park bench in the shade of a giant tree, or a little rowboat on a pond with only the waterfowl sporting about. Maybe our resting place is the ability to fall back onto our beds just to take a twenty-minute nap. Perhaps it is the relief of joining friends for a meal or at a temple.

A resting place is therefore a sanctuary, a place where we go to take shelter from the difficulties of life. It may be a physical place or a mental space we enter for inner space and privacy.

In the *Kṛṣṇa Book* we read about how loving, trusting relationships can also be resting places. Lord Balarāma took rest by placing His head on the lap of a cowherd boy while Kṛṣṇa massaged His feet; Kṛṣṇa also took rest in the same way; Arjuna sometimes rested his head on Kṛṣṇa's lap; Kṛṣṇa provided a seat and resting place for His friend Sudāmā Brāhmaṇa when Sudāmā visited Him in Dvārakā. Lord Kūrma's back is the resting place for the Mandara mountain, which enables the demons and demigods to churn the Milk Ocean for the pot of nectar. Kṛṣṇa in His form of Mahā-Viṣṇu is also the resting place for the conditioned souls when the universe is destroyed. Kṛṣṇa often gave the Pāṇḍavas peace of mind when their lives were in extreme turmoil.

Whatever rest we find anywhere, from loving friendships to our homes and furniture, is really Kṛṣṇa, the supreme resting place. And, resting in him directly is the most peaceful and restorative.

Meditation 40: The Withholder of Rain

I withhold the rain (*Gītā* 9.19)

A young child often loves to play with water. In that play, the child may leave on the tap and make puddles throughout the house. Then the parent says, "Enough," and cuts off the water supply. We may assume rain and water to be something automatic and feel entitled to an unending supply. Indeed, when Kṛṣṇa "turns off" the rain, we suffer greatly in the form of drought, a desperate crisis to live through. As droughts worsen, they affect businesses and homes; gardens and livestock die. But, other times, when there is too much rain, we desire that Kṛṣṇa withholds the water. Floods bring destruction and death as much as droughts. On a minor level, we may ask Kṛṣṇa to withhold rain because we are planning an outdoor event! Whether apparently harming or benefiting us, the withholding of water is not impersonal – Kṛṣṇa has His hand on the planet's tap.

Meditation 41: Giver of Rain

I send forth the rain (*Gītā* 9.19)

Rain is the natural purifying system for water in the world. It is a system of genius, kindness, and beauty. The sun evaporates water from the earth, cleans it, and resends it as rain that nourishes the ground, the plants, and the air. It forms rivers that feed into lakes and seas. All this is done by the hand of the kind, amazing, intelligent Kṛṣṇa who organizes life and the world in cycles of taking and giving, ending and beginning. Seeing the evaporation of water, one might feel anxious and upset, thinking Kṛṣṇa is only taking. But whatever He takes He returns in a better form – cleansed and renewed strength and life.

Meditation 42: Death Personified

I am death personified (*Gītā* 9.19); I am all-devouring death (*Gītā* 10.34)

Death is a form of God to whom even the atheists must bow down and surrender all. In most cases, it is an involuntary giving up of all possessions, relationships, knowledge, skills, and most of all, our material identity. Although death is a great mercy to a conditioned soul who has more varied desires than can be accommodated in any one life and body, it is also a renunciation as well as an admission of subordination. Death reminds us that we own nothing; nothing was ever ours. The actual owner, Kṛṣṇa in the form of death, can and does come at any time, without even a so-called courtesy of warning or announcement. We must live ready to drop all and go elsewhere at His bidding regardless of our religious, political, or moral philosophy.

The renounced order of *sannyāsa* is the way to reclaim death and voluntarily submit to this inevitability of our own accord. *Sannyāsa* involves not the attempt to wrest Kṛṣṇa's power away by suicide, but, rather, a total willingness to abide by Kṛṣṇa's order and practically use everything according to His will. Even those who never formally take the *sannyāsa* order can live a life of death to illusion, alive in reality. When we voluntarily let go of what Kṛṣṇa is taking from us, we see not "death" but our loving friend.

Meditation 43: The Generating Principle

I am the generating principle of all that is yet to be (*Gītā* 10.34)

Only when we look back in life do we understand how we were being prepared for who we are now or what we are doing now. Before any idea exists, before there is a seed, before there appears to be anything, Kṛṣṇa is there, generating through His clever intertwining of everything the principles that are yet to be.

At any given time, we probably do not fully understand the meaning, purpose and direction of who we are and what we are doing. Such is true even when we seem to be following our own plan down to the smallest detail. However, Kṛṣṇa is using what is happening now to generate the future.

The path toward any destination – whether enlightenment, heaven, or hell – is often a gradual one, made of baby steps from where only an intermediate objective is seen, and even that is sometimes foggy. Even though we may not always like to think of how our small actions, thoughts, and attitudes inexorably unfold into a manifestation, Kṛṣṇa is Himself that principle. Working in sync with His desires means that we delight in wonder at the mystery of the unfolding process.

Meditation 44: The Generating Seed

I am the generating seed of all existences (*Gītā* 10.39); I am the eternal seed (*Gītā* 9.18); I am the original seed of all existences (*Gītā* 7.10)

When we were children, we may have done a school project of growing seeds. We kept the seeds layered between tufts of cotton, well-watered and checked every day. To our excitement we finally saw sprouts appearing. It is amazing to watch a seed transform into a flower, tree, or shrub.

Seeds of plants, zygotes, eggs – all types of seeds surround us. Most of the world has the seed of a grass – wheat, rice, barley, oats, rye – as the staple food. The leaves, fruits, or flowers we eat all depends on a seed. There are also seeds of ideas, journeys, relationships, love, and sin. Within any seed is the set of instructions, the blueprint, for a mature manifestation. Within a seed is also concentrated nourishment and a protective boundary. Ultimately there is a soul, a life, a *jīva*, who in the right circumstances will use the instructions and nourishment to transform, breaking the protective boundary and becoming something far greater and unrecognizable than the seed itself.

The science of devotion is also compared to a seed planted in the heart that, with the watering of hearing and chanting of God's names and glories, breaks the shell, totally abandons the false ego and designations, and finally blooms and fructifies into its eternal spiritual form in love of God. Kṛṣṇa, as seed, has within Him all that we discover in our loving relationship with Him. The beauty and fragrance that can manifest from the "Kṛṣṇa seed" is beyond even the wildest poetic conceptions of a materially conditioned soul. His seed contains unlimited desire trees that give anything upon request. Indeed, the Lord is the self-sufficient philosopher who has been fulfilling everyone's desires from time immemorial. Spiritually, the Lord assumes whatever form and relationship the loving, selfless devotee desires. Materially, the Lord supplies the fruits of one's desires and karma from false lordship of matter. In all cases, Kṛṣṇa is the divine and unlimited seed.

GENERATING
seed
OF ALL
existences

Meditation 45: The Creation

I am the creation (*Gītā* 9.18)

In general, people are attracted and amazed by creativity or the power to take some components and turn them into something uniquely useful, unexpected, or previously unthought of. We revel in our own creative energy – designing a new project, cooking something tasty, or finding a new way to arrange the furniture. That flow of creative energy, in us and others, is Kṛṣṇa as creation. That energy, that exuberance, that feeling of accomplishment – is Kṛṣṇa.

Meditation 46: Annihilation

I am the annihilation (*Gītā* 9.18)

There is something spellbinding about destruction or endings. News headlines usually feature people cheating on each other and ripping apart their marriage, murders, and devastation when homes are burned to the ground. We are awed by nature's power to destroy through gigantic waves, lava flow, intense wind, quaking earth, and forest fires. What mesmerizes us is the way in which things and people can apparently utterly cease to exist. We may tend to get anxious and morose when we focus on various kinds of annihilation, but these devastations are a form of Kṛṣṇa. In a positive way, Kṛṣṇa annihilates our illusion and the false identities that hamper our authenticity in all areas of life. When the universe ends, He is the personification of annihilation in His form as Mahā-Viṣṇu. He identifies Himself as "Time I am, the great destroyer of the worlds." (*Bhagavad-Gītā* 11.32)

Aside from dramatic and sudden annihilations, time gradually and completely destroys everything. Ah, but nothing is really destroyed. Energy is not destroyed. What is annihilated is only the current form. Through time, death, earthquakes, and so forth, Kṛṣṇa is the form-changer, keeping the essence of the energy but adjusting the external manifestation. These changes are meant for facilitating the various desires of the living beings, whether positive or negative, and thus the apparent annihilations are another form of His loving exchanges with conditioned souls.

Meditation 47: The Beginning

I am the beginning of all beings (*Gītā* 10.20); Of all creations I am the beginning (*Gītā* 10.32)

Starting something, anything, requires a burst of energy, determination and hope. It's a throwing off of sloth and excuses. It's a risk of never finishing, or of the task being harder than imagined, or even impossible. It's an excitement and a dare to the future. Sometimes a beginning is an acceptance of a difficult duty. In some beginnings we don't personally participate but only witness. We do not have the power to stop the first winter snows, and even if we wish to, we cannot unlock the first flowers of spring. And even when we want time to stand still, the sun always rises. Kṛṣṇa's wives in Dvārakā would curse the cock that crowed at the break of dawn because it would mean the start of a new day, prompting Kṛṣṇa to get up from bed.

Beginnings can be daunting. How do we begin life again after a failed marriage or the death of a loved one? Where do we begin with raising children? Lord Brahmā has the mammoth task of re-creating much of the universe at the beginning of each of his very long "days." Talk about a daunting undertaking! But what does he do? He takes shelter of Kṛṣṇa and so receives the inspiration to proceed. Think of all Devakī's pregnancies. With the birth of each baby, she had to face not the ecstasy of a new soul placed in her care but the terror of losing them to Kamsa's hatred. She managed to get through it each time by always maintaining her connection with Kṛṣṇa, who Himself came to herald the beginning of Kamsa's end.

Kṛṣṇa is not only the spark of excitement or hope that we experience with new beginnings, but also the foundation of our strength when the beginnings bring with them despair and misery. Fortunately, Kṛṣṇa never has just a beginning in mind but also a middle and an end.

Beginning
OF ALL
CREATIONS...
Middle
End
OF ALL BEINGS

Meditation 48: The Middle

I am the middle of all beings (*Gītā* 10.20)

The middle is an interesting position. The roof of our house is held up by a middle beam. The key stone in an arch is the middle stone that keeps the arch together. The middle of a sandwich is where the juiciness is. Some children eat the middle of a slice of bread and leave the crusts, to the chagrin of their parents. A novel has its climax somewhere in the middle of the story. Going on a journey might mean many hours of travelling getting to our destination and then returning home, but in the middle we experience the reason for traveling.

Kṛṣṇa says that He is the middle. He is the pillars and beams that keep our spiritual lives upright and intact. Kṛṣṇa is the juicy part of life, like our sandwich. When we are on the mountaintop between climbing up and going down, Kṛṣṇa is the joy we feel at the view. He's at the climax of the story, and the purpose of our round-trip journeys. As the maintainer of the universe, He is the middle between creation and destruction.

Meditation 49: The End

I am the end (*Gītā* 10.32)

Endings may remind us of a used item that breaks, unused fruit that rots, or a crying baby that ends our sleep. Endings, however, aren't always bad. We may experience the end of pain if we take the right medication, diet, or herbs. A loved one fighting pain and illness is released from bodily suffering at death. The blistering heat of summer comes to an end with the cool breezes of autumn. A family may be holding their breath for the birth of their first child, and after nine months the waiting is finally over with the little one's first cry. We may nervously await our final exam results at school, and when the results are released, we finally breathe a sigh of relief. Whether the end is something we most fear, or most yearn for, or find most relief in, Kṛṣṇa is there.

Even in Kṛṣṇa's spiritual pastimes there is something akin to "endings" even though there is no time in Kṛṣṇa's world as we understand it. The *gopīs* yearn for Kṛṣṇa's association, a yearning that ends when He meets them in secret at the *rasa* dance. The cowherd boys' anxiety is ended many times when Kṛṣṇa saves them, for instance, from the forest fire or Aghāsura's belly. The older residents of Vṛndāvana wait all day for the end of Kṛṣṇa's time in the forest so they can see Him again. The entire *Śrīmad-Bhāgavatam* was spoken only at the end of Mahārāja Parīkṣit's life.

Kṛṣṇa Himself is the very end of all things. We may not always find it a lovely experience right away, but eventually we see how one thing's end is another thing's beginning. Kṛṣṇa is there in all endings and beginnings. The Supreme Author is fully aware of how each part of our story will end; all we have to do is agree to be part of His divine tale.

Meditation 50: Spirit and Matter

Both spirit and matter are in Me (*Gītā* 9.19)

Most of us understand reality as being made of matter and spirit, and we associate the spirit with Kṛṣṇa, and matter with illusion. When we chant Hare Kṛṣṇa or visit a holy place, we understand that we are doing something spiritual, and when we admire the beauty of the sunset or worry about a sick friend, we might think that we are absorbed in something material. This is not entirely the case.

We are spiritual beings within a material body, and we are aware of our body as if it were the soul itself. Indeed, our consciousness permeates our body and makes our body appear alive. In one sense, millions or billions of individual living cells comprise our body, and our body is, therefore, alive. Some parts of our body are not alive in any sense, however. The outer surface of our skin is dead cells, the ends of our nails have no blood or nerves within them, and our hair that is far from the root is not alive. Yet we are aware of our outer skin, the tips of our nails, and the hair that is tied in a bun or hanging on our neck. Both the living parts of our body and the non-living parts are "our body" and we have awareness of them.

For Kṛṣṇa, spirit is His internal energy, and matter is His external energy. But both are His energies and are part of Him as our hair and nails are part of our body. While matter has no awareness of itself as souls have, Kṛṣṇa is aware of matter, and thus in a greater sense, all is spirit.

Śrīla Prabhupāda explains:

> So those who have understood Kṛṣṇa along with His energies, he sees the energy, because energy is not different from the energetic. He sees immediately Kṛṣṇa. Therefore, he does not see anything except Kṛṣṇa. So therefore, for him there is no material world. There is no material world. To a perfect devotee, there is no material world. Everything is spiritual. *Sarvaṁ khalv idaṁ brahma*. He sees everything Brahman.
>
> (Lecture on *The Nectar of Devotion*, Vṛndāvana. November 11, 1972)

Often when we do try to find Kṛṣṇa in matter, we find ourselves swallowed by that matter without a thought of Kṛṣṇa. One reason may be that even though matter is in Kṛṣṇa and He is in matter, people conduct "material affairs" to forget Kṛṣṇa. Indeed, certain activities – such as meat-eating, intoxication, illicit sex, and gambling – tend to make us experience Kṛṣṇa as absent and the world as only material, with no realization of spirit. at all. Interacting with matter as if our interactions matter to Kṛṣṇa and He is aware of them and feels them puts us in a state in which we find He is, indeed, everything.

Meditation 51: The Pilot of the Planets

I enter into each planet, and by My energy they stay in orbit (*Gītā* 15.13)

Whenever we look up at the night sky, be it through a telescope or with the naked eye, we are in wonder of Kṛṣṇa's power. Even those without any religious faith often find enchantment in heavenly bodies, and scientists devote their lives to the study of astronomy. The planets and stars stay in orbit, moving with such precision that can be accurately calculated over thousands of years. Yet, when humans create airplanes, their flights are far from perfect; they are often delayed, early, or even cancelled. Human-created satellites can drop from their orbit and re-enter earth's atmosphere due to various malfunctions.

The supreme pilot is Kṛṣṇa, who enters into each heavenly body like the captain of an airship. Kṛṣṇa has that perfect potency. His energy keeps the planets afloat, in their orbit, and in perfect timing. The pilot of the planets is also the pilot of our bodies and lives, keeping them exactly at the right place and the right time, with never an error.

Meditation 52: Digestion

I join with the air of life, outgoing and incoming, to digest the four kinds of foodstuff (*Gītā* 15.14)

Eating and digestion are unceasing, everyday human activities, generally done more than once a day. Some eating is thoughtless, and we simply assume digestion will work as it should. Eating is especially thoughtless when people eat meat, fish, and eggs – all of which are results of horrible suffering and violence and not designed for a human body to assimilate. Eating is also thoughtless when people eat what was produced in a laboratory rather than in the sun and rain. When people eat, they may be thinking only of enjoying their meal or satiating a great hunger, but they rarely pause to think of where their meals or their digestive power come from. Only when our digestive system doesn't move or assimilate the food optimally do we notice it. However, if we become still and pay attention to our inner workings, we can feel the various movements of air within our body that transport the food, combust it, and help it to travel through the various channels. It is Kṛṣṇa who joins with this air and does the miracle of moving our food from our mouth to stomach, to the secretion of chemicals from the gallbladder, pancreas, and so forth, to our small intestine, and to all the bodily organs' individual cells for their maintenance.

Meditation 53: Remembrance

I am seated in everyone's heart, and from Me come[s] remembrance (*Gītā* 15.15)

Kṛṣṇa giving us remembrance does not solely refer to remembering where we put our keys the previous day or what we need to do today. Rather, it also means remembering Kṛṣṇa Himself. While cleaning, for example, we can think of Kṛṣṇa cleaning our hearts. When we admire the sunset, we can think of what a wonderful artist Kṛṣṇa is. When we suddenly get an inspiration about how to solve a problem, we can thank Kṛṣṇa for giving us the memory of similar situations to solve the current problem. We can remember Kṛṣṇa in devotee *saṅga* and think of how Kṛṣṇa loves the association of His friends in Vṛndāvana.

Meditation 54: Knowledge

From Me come[s] knowledge (*Gītā* 15.15)

Research, study, reading, and listening with focus are all dependent on that little inner moment when we "get it" and understand. Many students cram their heads full of facts to pass an exam but cannot put those facts into practical use or remember even the raw information after a few days. The "ah-ha" moment, when it seems like a light has turned on in our awareness, comes from Kṛṣṇa. He is the one who, satisfied with us through our devotion or piety, decides what we will truly know. And sometimes He simply supplies knowledge directly without our making any specific effort to understand. We may think that we are the cause of our learning and knowing, or we may just take the process for granted, but Kṛṣṇa's personal touch is always there. Our awareness of that touch takes what is otherwise a common event throughout the day and turns it into an exchange of love.

Meditation 55: Forgetfulness

From Me come[s] forgetfulness (*Gītā* 15.15)

The sweet smell of vanilla and roasted almonds fills the air. The kitchen is warm from the heat of the oven. Inside the oven awaits a golden batch of cookies. The cookies are ready, and we offer them to Kṛṣṇa, excited about the opportunity about to offer them to Him and to share them with the devotees. After the offering, we bite into one cookie to test it before serving it at lunch. It tastes of cardboard. We forgot the sugar! How did *that* happen?

We may have other similar stories. We may forget our keys inside the car on the morning when time is running against us and the seconds are stacked like dominos. One moment of forgetfulness and it's an avalanche of missed appointments, late lunches, and whatnot else. Sometimes our spouse may tell us, "If I don't introduce you to someone, it's not because I'm rude; it's because I can't remember their names." Sometimes, just before plopping into bed at 10 p.m. we remember that we still have something that urgently needs to be completed before the morning.

Just as forgetting can embarrass us, it can also save us. Humans are programmed to forget physical pain. We can remember that we were in pain, but we can't actually remember the pain. In the same vein we generally cannot remember our past lives. It's often difficult to swallow what we go through in this life, so imagine if we were to remember our countless previous lives? To forget is Kṛṣṇa's mercy so we may have a fresh start; otherwise, it would be impossible for us to try to enjoy in this material world. Similarly, Kṛṣṇa does not want to force us to remember and love Him, because forced love is not love at all. To realize that our forgetting Him means He is close by granting that favor is a deep sweetness.

On the highest level of transcendence, Kṛṣṇa sometimes wants to forget that He is the Supreme Person and thus has His *yoga-māyā* potency cover the residents in Vṛndāvana and Dvārakā to facilitate His desire to have loving relationships with them. When Kṛṣṇa runs away from Mother Yaśodā, He is actually afraid of her – not just pretending, because He has "forgotten" that He is the Supreme Personality. Thus, the relationship of mother and son can fully exist. Without this element of forgetfulness, we are unable to relate to Kṛṣṇa in a truly intimate way.

Meditation 56: The Supersoul

I am the Supersoul seated in the hearts of all living entities (*Gītā* 10.20)

Plants turn toward the sun, spiders spin webs, butterflies migrate long distances. In this way Kṛṣṇa as the Supersoul guides and inspires all living beings. Awareness of the Supersoul in the heart of all living beings helps us to see them as something other than just their bodies or even individual souls. God is there. Each body of each living being is a temple wherein the Deity gives guidance according to that soul's receptivity. When we visit a temple made of bricks, wood, or stone, we remove our shoes, we bow our heads to the floor in reverence, and offer prayers. Yet everyone we meet is a temple – not only other humans, but animals, insects, and plants. Treating others with reverence and care is not just a matter of our relationship with that living being but also with the best friend and witness who stands beside them, observing and advising with love. If we could see each being standing next to God, universal love and respect would swiftly follow.

Meditation 57: Indra, the King of Heaven

Of the demigods I am Indra, the king of heaven (*Gītā* 10.22)

Rain, thunder, and lightning! Throughout history, the god of thunder is known as the chief of the gods whether named Thor, Zeus, and, of course, in the Vedic tradition, Indra. The word Indra literally means "chief" or the leader of the celestial beings who manage the universe. Rain is essential for life, a key part of the purification cycle that brings us clean water. And lightning is a major natural means – and certainly a dramatic and beautiful means – to take the nitrogen in the air and make it available to plants for fertilizer. How apt that the lord of the gods has such an intimate involvement with water and food.

From the thunderstorm and rain also come the necessary nutrients that help the plants to grow, and from the plants come our own nutrients. In this way Indra takes care of us on a material level, by providing us with water and food. Such is the mercy of Kṛṣṇa, whom Indra represents, that He amply provides for the physiological needs of rebellious souls. Rain and lightning are the work of a person, not simply of mechanical processes. And, though modern science can analyze thunder and lightning, the cause of this phenomenon continues to elude scientists, perhaps simply because they do not think to look for a powerful and loving person behind it!

Meditation 58: The Mind

Of the senses I am the mind (*Gītā* 10.22)

On the material platform we are dependent on our senses to understand and react to the world. Reading this very passage requires the sense of sight. Listening to our japa requires the sense of hearing. Honoring *prasādam* requires the sense of taste, and feeling the heat of the *ārati* flame or the drops of water sprinkled on our heads require the sense of touch. There are five other working senses also, but above all is the mind. The mind is our control room, the place where all information is collected, interpreted and distributed accordingly. That mind is a manifestation of Kṛṣṇa, who is the controller of our senses and whose interpretation of what our senses perceive is true and accurate. The Sanskrit word *go* means both cows and senses, thus Govinda is the ruler of the senses, and Gopāla the herder of the senses.

Prabhupāda writes in the *Kṛṣṇa Book*:

> Our minds can never be vacant. The mind is constantly occupied with some kind of thought, and the subject matter of such thought cannot be outside the eight elements of Kṛṣṇa's energy. One who knows this philosophical aspect of all thoughts is actually a wise man, and he surrenders unto Kṛṣṇa. The gopīs are the epitome of this perfectional stage of knowledge. They are not simple mental speculators. Their minds are always in Kṛṣṇa. The mind is nothing but the energy of Kṛṣṇa. Actually, any person who can think, feel and will, cannot be separated from Kṛṣṇa. But the stage in which he can understand his eternal relationship with Kṛṣṇa is called Kṛṣṇa consciousness.
>
> (Chapter 47: Delivery of the Message of Kṛṣṇa to the Gopīs)

OF
Mountains
MERU

When we think, feel, and desire in harmony with Kṛṣṇa, we know He is our very mind. When our thoughts, feelings, and desires are engaged in enjoying separately from Kṛṣṇa, we feel the mind is our own identity. When our minds manage and interpret our sense perception in such a way that all those senses are illumined with knowledge, then we are aware that Kṛṣṇa is our mind. When the mind is wild and unpleasant, we forget that our minds are actually Kṛṣṇa, but illuminating our mind with knowledge and becoming conscious that it is Kṛṣṇa allows our connection with Him to be re-established.

Meditation 59: The Meru Mountain

Of mountains I am Meru (*Gītā* 10.23)

There are great mountains on this planet – Everest, Matterhorn, Rainier, Kilimanjaro – but none like Meru as described in the sacred literature, *Śrīmad-Bhāgavatam 16.7*. Meru is a universal pivot with dimensions far beyond our imagination and perhaps beyond the credibility of those who base everything on their earthly experience. Kṛṣṇa is also far greater than anything or anyone or any idea of our experience. Many people find it difficult to understand that such a great, amazing, and powerful being can truly exist as the Supreme Person. Meru is the center of this universe as Kṛṣṇa is the center of all existence. Cosmology center d around Meru gives us a universal picture full of personality, beauty, and grace – what we would expect from the charming Kṛṣṇa.

Meditation 60: The Ocean

Of bodies of water I am the ocean (*Gītā* 10.24)

Vast, deep, almost immeasurable, the world's oceans captivate us. We go there for refreshment, peace, and meditation on the endless waves, the roar, and the moist, rich air. We play in the waves and run on the shore, sometimes forgetting the immense power and force into which we dip our toes. We see only the surface of changing colors, but beneath hides a world of glorious secrets, many of which we have not yet discovered. For the fish and sea life within the waters, the ocean is not just a manifestation of awe and reverence, but is home, safety, and beauty.

Kṛṣṇa is also large and vast beyond our comprehension. The shades of His love for us vastly outnumber the shades of the ocean water. Kṛṣṇa plays with us as a master, a friend, or a beloved, yet His strength and power are beyond measure. We cannot count His incarnations just as we cannot count the ocean waves. Like the ocean's depth, we can never know all the secrets of beauty and grace that are within Kṛṣṇa; there is always more to know and understand, more loving and wondrous surprises for all eternity.

Meditation 61: The Immovable Himalayas

Of immovable things I am the Himalayas (*Gītā* 10.25)

Immovable. Why would Kṛṣṇa used this quality to describe the Himalayas and not any of the myriad adjectives we commonly think of, such as majestic, massive, or frigid. Kṛṣṇa could have also described these mountains as the dwelling place of sages, mystics and *yogīs*, and maybe the occasional yeti. But the fact that the Himalayas are immovable is particularly what can provoke our awareness of Kṛṣṇa.

Immovability denotes some kind of security. We may think of a parent's love as immovable. No matter how many times we mess up, our parents still love us. And even more immovable is the promise of our spiritual master at the time of initiation. Our parents may love and guide us, but some day they have to move on when they pass away, or we move on to the next birth, or hopefully to Kṛṣṇa. But our spiritual master is our eternal guide. If we don't make it back home, he comes back into this miserable pool of material existence and finds us again.

OF BODIES OF
water
I AM THE
Ocean

In the same way Kṛṣṇa is truly immovable. He is always present everywhere at all times. His love for us is similarly immovable. We have been coming back to maya's abode for millions and millions of lifetimes, and still He loves us. He is immovable in His effort to bring us back to Him, to Goloka Vṛndāvana. This is the absolute certainty in a world of duality and uncertainty. Kṛṣṇa is ever-present, immovable, like the great Himalayan Mountains.

Meditation 62: The Banyan Tree

Of all trees I am the banyan tree (*Gītā* 10.26)

Complex, with no discernible beginning, middle, or end, the banyan tree represents the inscrutable Lord. In the *Bhagavad-Gītā* the whole material creation is compared to this tree, in that material life cannot be untangled but only cut down with the weapon of detachment. The banyan is a kind of king of trees, as the Lord is the king of all. Although not the tallest or the oldest, a banyan can still live an average of two to three hundred years and can spread over a vast area, claiming more and more territory. It's a tree of beauty like the most attractive Kṛṣṇa. Like Kṛṣṇa, the banyan provides shelter for many creatures, and it's a joy to sit with friends for a picnic under its branches with roots twisting, spreading, and forming cave-like structures – a living work of art. The banyan appears to be a great-grandfather of a being, reminding us of the original father, protector, and artist, Kṛṣṇa.

Meditation 63: The Monarch

Among men I am the monarch (*Gītā* 10.27)

Even in our modern world where kings and queens are either absent or just figureheads, people are still interested in even the ordinary doings of royal families. Children are fascinated with stories of royalty, dreaming of being a prince or a princess. Many books, television shows, and movies – whether fiction or historical – feature royal families.

The Lord's two main incarnations on this planet – Kṛṣṇa and Rāmacandra – both appear in royal families, and Rāmacandra reigned for thousands of years. An ideal king, like Lord Rāma, is like the ideal father to the citizens – caring, protective, and ensuring that citizens have happy and productive lives. Of all social roles humans can take in society, that of the ruler most closely resembles Kṛṣṇa's role with regard to His creation.

The interest and reverence given to government leaders are really meant for Kṛṣṇa, the supreme head of the supreme universal government. All our patriotism and national fervor should really be directed toward becoming universal citizens intent on pleasing God. And the leaders of society function best when they welcome Kṛṣṇa's empowering guidance.

Meditation 64: The Thunderbolt

Of weapons I am the thunderbolt (*Gītā* 10.28)

There is something mystical about a thunderbolt. It has immense power and emits instant and intense, although fleeting, light. We can think of it as nature's flash of inspiration, much like the "light bulb" moments we sometimes have for solving our problems but only a million times greater. We may wonder why these brilliant flashes of inspiration, which light up our consciousness for a few moments, don't stay longer. These flashes give us the greatest sense of relief, and then the darkness of life's worries come rolling in again like the unstoppable dark clouds that cover our consciousness.

Kṛṣṇa says that He is this thunderbolt that lights up our consciousness in a moment of realization. Kṛṣṇa is the flash of lightning, the lamp light that illuminates our consciousness with knowledge. However, Kṛṣṇa also says that He is the thunderbolt *weapon* – not just a blazing show of luminescence, but a weapon. In other words, Kṛṣṇa is not only our light but also the weapon to use against our material consciousness. When we do something with that flash of inspiration, it can become like a weapon.

OF
weapons
I AM THE
THUNDERBOLT

How else is Kṛṣṇa a thunderbolt? If maya enters our lives and builds high trees of *anarthas*, Kṛṣṇa will use the thunderbolt to destroy those trees rooted in our consciousness. This thunderbolt can take many forms like the purifying effects of *prasādam*, the cleansing association and truthful advice of devotees, uplifting melodies of kirtan, or the illuminating words of śāstra.

We can hear and see Kṛṣṇa's majesty in the rolling thunder and the flashes of lighting. As He is all sound in space (*Bhagavad-Gītā* 7.8) thunder is certainly included, and beyond that the power of that sound is reminiscent of a lion reminding all other creatures of their insignificance. The brilliant light reminds us that Kṛṣṇa is the source of all illumination (*Bhagavad-Gītā* 13.18) and can instantly light the dome of the darkest night. Such meditations may be scary in their awesomeness, but we can also think of the lightning like a twinkle in Kṛṣṇa's eye, desire to give us the joy of enlightenment beyond our scope of understanding.

In the thunderstorms of life, we can see Kṛṣṇa's immeasurable protection in the same way that He protected the residents of Vṛndāvana from the devastating flood, if only we reach out to Him. Kṛṣṇa is our ultimate weapon, providing us with flashes of insight on how to deal with trying situations in daily life as well as in preaching and other services. Unlike material lightning that only provides fleeting light and energy, Kṛṣṇa provides eternal light and energy, but it is up to us to use His light and energy in our "light bulb moments" to push forward and grow in our spiritual lives.

Meditation 65: The Surabhi Cow

Among cows I am the *surabhi* (*Gītā* 10.28)

For many of us the cow isn't exactly the animal that comes to mind when we think of cute and cuddly, but in recent years people have become more aware of the cow's good qualities. Cows love to skip and play, especially when they are let out of the barn after winter. They can be friends with other animals such as dogs, and cuddle up to their humans for a rub under the chin. They have best friends among the herd, and become anxious when separated from one another. But most of all, they are also magnanimous. Think about what mother cow gives us through her milk. Milk in and of itself is rich in nutrients, and Śrīla Prabhupāda often emphasized that it repairs and supports the growth of finer brain tissue, which makes us smarter. From milk we get butter and ghee, and let's face it, not even a sandwich works well without at least a little butter. Not only is ghee good for cooking, but it is also useful in Ayurvedic treatments. Yogurt is not only a delicious part of our meal but is also a cure for dysentery. From the milk we get cream, or we can simply boil it down to make burfi and we could never eat paneer *subji* without milk.

The cow's attitude of abundance is clear in how many by-products are derived from milk, but at some stage cows get old and produce less milk or stop all together. This is what makes the *surabhi* cow special. She, unlike the cows we know, gives limitless amounts of milk, as much as her owner needs and at any time of day. She embodies the quality of generosity.

Like the *surabhi* cow, Kṛṣṇa is limitless in His affection and love to all living entities. Like an unlimitedly giving cow, He supplies all the ingredients for intelligence and joy in life, material and spiritual.

Meditation 66: Yama, the Lord of Death

I am Yama, the lord of death (*Gītā* 10.29)

Stories of hate, rape and murder, fraud and money laundering, and myriad other crimes, are like a tidal wave of misery. We just have to glance at the news headlines to be aware of the daily horror. Some places in the world have it worse than others, and we may sometimes wonder, "Where is the justice? When will these perpetrators pay for their crimes?" It seems that their evil never ends. However, we can take solace in the fact that no matter how clever the criminals are, they all have to die in the end. Kṛṣṇa says that He is the lord of death, the ultimate dispenser of law. Some of us may have been deeply scarred by someone and may think that death cheats us of an opportunity to take revenge, but if we have firm faith in Kṛṣṇa and His law, we know He will exact exactly the right punishment for the deeds of the wrongdoer. A more uplifting thought, however, in the case of Kṛṣṇa's devotees, is that Kṛṣṇa promises to take personal charge of their lives, and therefore devotees generally do not meet Yamarāja. They are directly in the hands of Kṛṣṇa.

Meditation 67: Time

Among subduers I am time (*Gītā* 10.30)

So many means can be used to try to subdue an unruly person: sweet words, force, distraction, and promises. Water can subdue fire, and food can subdue hunger. In the natural world, plants, animals and humans try to overcome, subjugate, and in some way bring other living beings, and matter itself, under control.

Some of these methods work well, some work poorly, but none is always effective. No matter how expert we are at winning over obstacles, competitors, and enemies, we sometimes lose, and sometimes there is no clear winner at all. Yet one subduing force always wins, and that is time. Time eventually breaks everything down and back to its original parts. Time destroys all civilizations with their structures and histories. No one can ever defeat time, yet time defeats everyone. Time even changes the shape and nature of continents, rivers, and oceans. All must bow before inexorable time.

On a daily basis, time forces us to sleep, eat, and engage in other bodily functions. In the scriptures, time is often associated with the Lord and we can appreciate Him as the ultimate victor, the supreme. Regardless of our plans, His plans reign supreme. We can try to use time, to beat time, to save time, and to look forward in time, but a better alternative is to accept and surrender to time as a manifestation of our master. We can strive to remember Him in this moment, and dedicate each moment to His glory, always in the role of a servant and always submitting happily to His ultimate victory. In that mood, time takes nothing from us but rather fills us with His own unlimited sense of victory. Then we realize we are eternal. As eternal beings, time has no frightening meaning for us at all. Rather, time is only of concern to those who foolishly try to wrest the position of master from the Lord.

Meditation 68: The Lion

Among beasts I am the lion (*Gītā* 10.30)

To hear a lion roar unleashes involuntary fear. Lions are not the king of the jungle in children's fairy tales just because of their fluffy crown-like mane but for their power and majesty. Kṛṣṇa says that among the beasts we can see Him in the lion. Kṛṣṇa's absolute power and majesty are visible in how He instils fear in the lawless and demonic. For example, Kamsa sent demons to Vṛndāvana every day, and each of them could immediately sense Kṛṣṇa's power. Kamsa himself was shaken to his core by just a voice telling him of Kṛṣṇa's ultimate power.

On the other hand, the lioness is caring and protective of her cubs, and so is Kṛṣṇa with His devotees. If we look at how a lion carries her cubs, we see that she is in full control. The cub has only to relax and be carried. Unlike the baboon baby who has to hold on for dear life, the lion cub is carried by the power of his mother, and so it is with us, too. Kṛṣṇa is in full control – He carries us, and we are fully protected.

Meditation 69: The Purifying Wind

Of purifiers I am the wind (*Gītā* 10.31)

When there is a shift looming in our lives, we may say the winds of change are blowing, denoting the way being cleared for something new. A cool breeze can bring renewal to the senses after a long day of being cooped up at the office. Clothes hung to dry in the wind smell of freshness. A wind can dissipate smog that otherwise hangs over a city and claws its wispy fingers into our lungs. The rustling breeze shakes the dust from leaves so they can photosynthesize.

AMONG
SUBDUERS
time

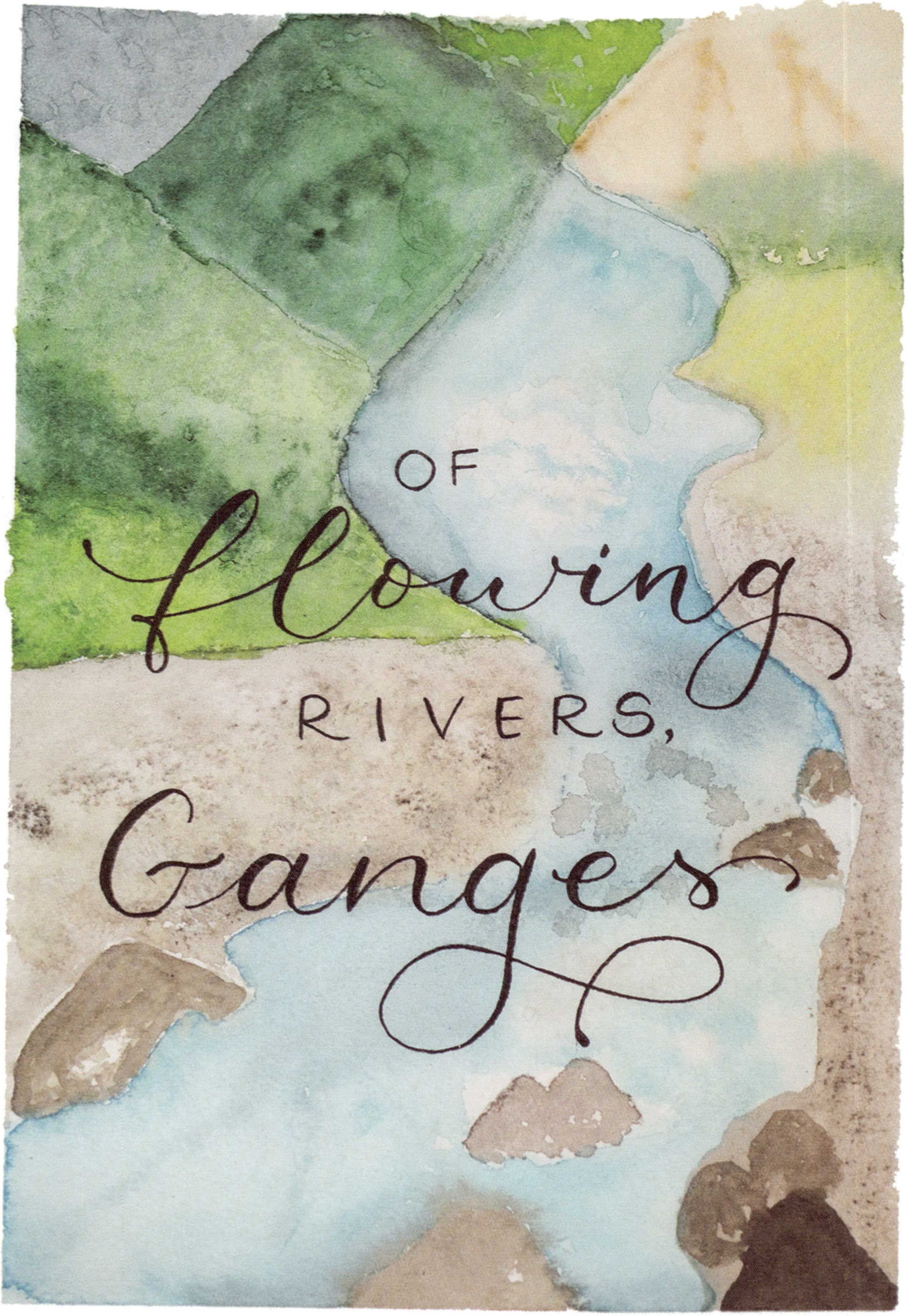
OF
flowing
RIVERS,
Ganges

In *Caitanya-caritāmṛta Madhya 21.113*, the vibration of Kṛṣṇa's flute is compared to a whirlwind. Its sound vibrates through the ether and picks up the hearts and minds of the *gopīs* like dried twigs and leaves. They drift and swirl in the ecstasy of Kṛṣṇa's love and settle forever at His lotus feet.

Whether through the air moving through His flute, or a breeze clearing out the musty smell from a storage room, Kṛṣṇa as the wind cleans and renews.

Meditation 70: The Shark

Of fishes I am the shark (*Gītā* 10.31)

The Sanskrit word for the fish that represents Kṛṣṇa is makara, an important aquatic creature in the scriptures. *Makara* also means the zodiac sign Capricorn. A traditional makara is usually depicted as a land animal in the front (like an elephant) and an aquatic in the back. Kṛṣṇa wears earrings shaped like makaras, and the makara is the vehicle for the goddess Gaṅgā, the demigod Varuṇa, and Kāmadeva (Cupid). In various places Śrīla Prabhupāda translates *makara* as crocodile, shark, or dolphin. It's doubtful that we'll encounter a makara in our lives, but we do read about, see photos of, or sometimes see a live shark, crocodile, or dolphin. These aquatic animals display power and cleverness and fascinate humans. Kṛṣṇa, like the sharks and crocodiles, is supremely expert in all that He does, patient for us to come to Him, and hungry. Of course, Kṛṣṇa's hunger is for love! Kṛṣṇa, like dolphins, is full of playfulness, helpfulness, and supreme intelligence.

There are also many analogies regarding fish in the scriptures which can remind us, upon contacting fish, of the Lord. For example, the conditioned soul is compared to a fish out of water, and Kṛṣṇa's eyes are compared to the beauty of a pair of swimming fish. (*Śrīmad-Bhāgavatam* 3.28.30)

Meditation 71: The Ganges

Of flowing rivers I am the Ganges (*Gītā* 10.31)

Devprayag is a small village near Rishikesh high in the foothills of the Himalayas. The village looks like it is carved from the sheer rock face on which it balances. To get there requires a strong stomach or an absence of fear of heights, as the two-lane road teeters dangerously on the edge of river gorges hundreds of meters below. It is well known to pilgrims as the place where the rivers Alakanandā and Bhāgīrathī converge and roar mightily. From here onward the river is called Gaṅgā, or Ganges. At the site of the convergence there is a stone staircase carved into the rocks and attached to it are heavy chains to which people cling when taking a bath in the glassy green-blue water.

At Devprayag we can experience a glimmer of Kṛṣṇa's power. And Kṛṣṇa, as the Ganges and sustainer of all, flows down to the sea and provides billions of people with sustenance and care. But the Ganges does far more than other rivers. Having come from beyond the universal coverings, and washed the Lord's feet, she at once gives both the touch of the Lord and her own blessings. In the same way, when we surrender to Kṛṣṇa, He immediately takes direct charge of our destiny, our karma, and washes it away, just like He washes it away in His waters as the Gaṅgā. He is magical, mystical, compassionate, awe-inspiring, and forgiving, manifesting these qualities in the Gaṅgā.

Meditation 72: The Spiritual Science of the Self

Of all sciences I am the spiritual science of the self (*Gītā* 10.32)

Of everything anyone can know and study, Kṛṣṇa is the science of knowing ourselves. Knowing ourselves means awareness of truth beyond space and time, and authenticity without anything false or pretentious. It is a science of personal discovery and joy. As we go through the process of transcendent scientific experimentation in spiritual life, it's not just that we find Kṛṣṇa and ourselves in a relationship. Kṛṣṇa Himself is our way of introspection, the meditations we do and the philosophy of self-realization that we study and reflect upon, guiding us in our very personal realization.

Meditation 73: The Conclusive Truth

Among logicians I am the conclusive truth (*Gītā* 10.32)

Looking at the Sanskrit words of this verse, Kṛṣṇa says He is *vāda*, which means a discussion following scriptural rules of logic (*nyāya*), done in a civil manner and aimed at finding truth. *Vāda* is in contrast to *jalpa*, arguments to establish one's own superiority, and *vitanda*, an argument aiming only to defeat others. It is a great pleasure to have the *vāda* type of discussion, as Kṛṣṇa is present in such reasoned agreement to find real understanding.

When we find something true, say something true, or hear something true, that is Kṛṣṇa. Of course, Kṛṣṇa is the Absolute Truth beyond past, present, and future. He is the truth beyond time, place, and circumstance. And He is also more "ordinary" truth, arrived at through logic. We can easily find Kṛṣṇa in logical truth as we use some logic during our day, trying to establish what is correct. Scientists devote their lives to looking for the truth about the material world, and their truths fill the daily news. Lawyers work to prove their case as true beyond a reasonable doubt. Teachers are looking for the right answers in their students' work. Even a small child asks a million questions, trying to figure out how life works and doesn't work. When we understand something to be true or when our logical discussion with others brings us to truth, Kṛṣṇa is that sense of satisfaction and conclusion.

Meditation 74: The Letter A

Of letters I am the letter A (*Gītā* 10.33)

Kṛṣṇa here is referring to the Sanskrit letter represented as an "a" in Roman characters. In Sanskrit, a letter's sound and name are the same, and the sound/name of this letter is made with open mouth, without the use of teeth, lips, or tongue. It is similar to the sound of "u" in the English word "bus." It is the basic sound upon which all other sounds build. Kṛṣṇa is, therefore, the essential substrate of the sounds we make to communicate, the essence of language. Of whatever language sounds any human makes or hears, Kṛṣṇa is the root sound.

Meditation 75: Inexhaustible Time

I am inexhaustible time (*Gītā* 10.33)

Kṛṣṇa is inexhaustible time, time that cannot be destroyed or diminished. Kṛṣṇa, the infinite without a beginning and an end, manifests as infinite time. *Jīvas* in the material world live and die by time. We are never more aware of the passage of time than when we are waiting for it to pass, or conversely, don't want it to pass. Little children usually can't wait for their birthdays to come, thinking that time will never pass, but it always does. When we lose a dear one, no matter how much we want time to stand still before they left us, we cannot. Time passes and before we know it, life has moved on whether we have moved with it or not. Time is the one unstoppable force of the material universe. As scary as it is, this principle is also filled with hope. Bad times will always pass, perhaps not quickly, but they do end at some stage. On the flip side, good times always come again but also end at some stage. This ever-presence of time throughout all changes is the constant of Kṛṣṇa.

Meditation 76: Fame in Women

Among women I am fame (*Gītā* 10.34)

Kīrtiḥ relates to fame in the sense of a glorious reputation, particularly regarding speaking about someone. When we speak well of others, thus spreading their fame, Kṛṣṇa wishes that we do so in a way that uplifts those who hear us, as well as the person we glorify. Our speech should be truthful, pleasing, and beneficial. When we speak in such a way, Kṛṣṇa is pleased, and present.

I
AM
CONCLUSIVE
truth

I AM
fame
fortune
fine speech
memory
steadfastness
AND
patience
IN
WOMEN

Although this opulence is "considered feminine" (purport 10.34), when we find anyone – male or female – glorified or famous in a way that uplifts others, our awareness of Kṛṣṇa can deepen. At the same time, we might ask why Kṛṣṇa particularly identifies Himself as fame in women (*nārīṇām*). Kṛṣṇa's statement serves to make us thoughtful about how the Lord views souls who are in female form. In general, selfish people tend to exploit those who hold less power than they. For example, humans exploit animals and less powerful people, and stronger animals exploit weaker ones. Thus, there is a tendency for males to exploit females, seeing females not as souls with their own glorious qualities and actions but as objects for their own pleasure. In fact, the śāstra is full of stern warnings to men not to see women as objects of sense enjoyment, as such a mentality is a gateway to degradation.

Kṛṣṇa is personally present whenever women are glorified with respect and genuine admiration. Those who thus praise women are dealing directly with Kṛṣṇa. The women being praised can offer respects to Kṛṣṇa, who wishes that we appreciate each other rather than becoming proud of the fame that superficially is due to our own credit.

In the scriptures there are many famous women whom the sages glorify. Gāndhārī is famous as a great performer of austerity for her voluntary blindness. Kunti is famous for her devotion to Kṛṣṇa, her tolerance in the face of adversity, and her deeply beautiful prayers. Sarasvatī is famous as the goddess of both arts such as music as well as wisdom. Bali Mahārāja's wife is famous for her frank speech in front of Lord Brahmā. Kṛṣṇa as the fame of such women, past and present, is like the sari he supplied to Draupadī, clothing these women in honor and reminding us that women have their individual excellence.

Meditation 77: Fortune in Women

Among women I am fortune (*Gītā* 10.34)

Kṛṣṇa is *śrī* in women. *Śrī* is a name for Lakṣmīdevī or for Rādhārāṇī and thus means the ultimate feminine. Lakṣmīdevī is called the goddess of fortune and is the energy of prosperity. *Śrī* means all aspects of a rich and satisfying life – all six ways of being opulent or prosperous. At the same time, *śrī* indicates one of those six opulences, which can be translated as "splendid beauty, gracefulness, and charismatic leadership."

Women are sometimes called the "fairer sex." Therefore, when we think of human beauty, we may more often think of women than men. Certainly, men may also exhibit great beauty, yet Kṛṣṇa identifies this opulence as "feminine." Kṛṣṇa is present whenever women have physical beauty combined with charisma, grace, and high character. Women who possess such beauty are dealing with Kṛṣṇa and therefore are happiest when they use that beauty in service to Him. When we appreciate feminine beauty, we do well to understand that such beauty is Kṛṣṇa and therefore worthy of our respect rather than exploitation. The same principle applies when people may not manifest *śrī* in their own form but create or manifest splendid beauty in the environment.

Kṛṣṇa is *śrī* in women as His female incarnation of Mohinī-mūrti who was able to bewilder even Lord Śiva. This incarnation reminds us that *śrī* in women is a most powerful manifestation of Kṛṣṇa, to be dealt with using extreme caution.

Meditation 78: Fine Speech in Women

Among women I am fine speech (*Gītā* 10.34)

Fine speech in this verse is *vāk,* the name of a divine goddess. The voice of a parent soothing a child is as much fine speech as the ability to deliver a well-planned seminar to hundreds. Because fine speech is one of Kṛṣṇa's feminine opulences, we can meditate on how women throughout history have greatly influenced human affairs through their charming or inspired speech. When a woman possesses cultured speech, she can express anything in a pleasing manner to benefit and uplift anyone she speaks to. Kunti's prayers to Kṛṣṇa in the Bhagavatam, or the songs of the *gopīs* in separation from the Lord, are examples of such fine speech in women. Kṛṣṇa is present in such speech among women.

Kṛṣṇa Himself generally uses gentle and persuasive speech. His speaking to Arjuna and to Uddhava are important examples of how He influences the world through His speaking. But the Lord's fine speech can also be cutting. In this prayer to His disc weapon, the Sudarśana chakra, we can mediate on the power of speech to illuminate like a powerful weapon: "O master of speech, by your effulgence, full of religious principles, the darkness of the world is dissipated, and the knowledge of learned persons or great souls is manifested." (*Śrīmad-Bhāgavatam* 9.5.7) For an example of such fine yet sharp speech in a woman, we can turn to Bali Mahārāja's wife, Vindhyāvali, who used cutting speech (*Śrīmad-Bhāgavatam* 8.22.20) to establish that her husband should surrender to Vāmanadeva.

Meditation 79: Memory in Women

Among women I am memory (*Gītā* 10.34)

Kṛṣṇa remembers the needs and desires of each living entity as a woman remembers what each of her children enjoys eating and playing with. When women remember all their countless chores and duties in life, that represents Kṛṣṇa, who remembers all our karma and desires.

The quality of memory or *smṛti* means to have the ability to remember that which has been experienced. This does not refer to having a photographic memory of experiences but rather to ultimately remember one's spiritual existence. To forget spiritual existence is called *aśruta-smṛtiḥ* (*Śrīmad-Bhāgavatam* 4.28.59) and to remember the Supreme Lord is *hari-smṛtiḥ* (*Śrīmad-Bhāgavatam* 8.10.55). As a mother always remembers her children, even when they are far away or rebellious, so Kṛṣṇa in his feminine opulence of memory always remembers us and desires us to have the ultimate memory of our relationship with Him.

Meditation 80: Steadfastness in Women

Among women I am steadfastness (*Gītā* 10.34)

Here Kṛṣṇa uses the word *dhṛtiḥ*, meaning firmness. Such firmness or steadfastness in women is particularly seen in motherhood. Children have many demands and can be petulant and ungrateful, yet the mother is firm in her dedication and care. The mother's relationship of concern and love is lifelong regardless of the child's mistakes or even rejection of the mother. Thus, the mother's love for her child is an example in this world of Kṛṣṇa's steadfast love for us. Indeed, Lord Brahmā compares the Lord's steadfastness and tolerance with the living entities to that of a pregnant woman whose child is kicking in the womb. (*Śrīmad-Bhāgavatam* 10.14.12) Mother Yaśodā constantly meditates on how to take care of Kṛṣṇa; she dresses and ornaments Him; she even wants Him to wear shoes to the forest so that His feet are unharmed by thorns and pebbles. When Kṛṣṇa throws a tantrum and breaks a butter-filled churning pot because His mother doesn't want to breastfeed Him, Mother Yaśodā steadily goes after Him and firmly decides to teach Him a lesson by trying to tie Him to a grinding mortar. Thus, Mother Yaśodā's love is not just about feeding and cuddling Kṛṣṇa but also addressing His mischief. When we thus look at women remaining firm in their duty and love, we can think of Kṛṣṇa and how He vows to bring us back to Him, even when we make it difficult.

Meditation 81: Patience in Women

Among women I am patience (*Gītā* 10.34)

There are women who are patient with their husbands in times of difficulty, giving sage advice along with loving service, and such patience is Kṛṣṇa. A good example in the scriptures is Gāndhārī, who patiently cared for her misguided husband, Dhṛtarāṣṭra, while lovingly advising him to seek peace and reconciliation with his nephews. Similarly, Kṛṣṇa is patient with the wayward souls, serving them as the voice of conscience and the words of scripture, along with giving them sun, water, food, and opportunities to come to the right path.

The patience of women is also widely seen in motherhood, even among women who are not patient with their husbands or other men. Young children especially require mothers to exercise tremendous patience. It takes thousands of repetitions for children to learn the simplest things; young children want to hear, say, or watch the same thing literally thousands of times, and children cause much mischief and chaos in their playful and curious behavior. Yet mothers are extraordinarily patient, and this patience of women is also Kṛṣṇa. Kṛṣṇa is also patient with the aspiring transcendentalist, whose surrender and faith matures in what is generally a very gradual way.

Meditation 82: Intelligence in Women

Among women I am intelligence (*Gītā* 10.34)

While Kṛṣṇa is the analytical intelligence, *buddhi*, of any intelligent person, among women he is especially applied intelligence or *medhā*, which Prabhupāda defines as "the ability not only to read many books on different subject matters but to understand them and apply them when necessary." (*Bhagavad-Gītā* 10.34, purport) Women often excel in verbal abilities, which is a manifestation of Kṛṣṇa Himself.

Furthermore, there is an important reference to the *medhā* type of intelligence, a feminine opulence, along with Lord Caitanya and the *saṅkīrtana-yajña*, in the *Śrīmad-Bhāgavatam* (11.5.32) as follows:

kṛṣṇa-varṇaṁ tviṣākṛṣṇaṁ
sāṅgopāṅgāstra-pārṣadam
yajñaiḥ saṅkīrtana-prāyair
yajanti hi su-medhasaḥ

Translation: "In this Age of Kali, people who are endowed with sufficient intelligence [*su-medhasaḥ*] will worship the Lord, who is accompanied by His associates, by performance of *saṅkīrtana-yajña*."

There is sociological evidence that women are particularly blessed with this type of intelligence, as Śrīla Prabhupāda writes:

> Women generally assemble in great number in any sort of religious function. In every country and in every sect of religion it appears that the women are more interested than the men. This simplicity of acceptance of the Lord's authority is more effective than showy insincere religious fervor.
>
> (*Teachings of Queen Kunti* 3: The Most Intelligent Woman)

Kṛṣṇa identifies Himself with the intelligence of women who show this glory of sincere surrender to the Lord, and thus take part in the *saṅkīrtana-yajña*.

Meditation 83: The Gāyatrī

Of poetry I am the Gāyatrī (*Gītā* 10.35)

Kṛṣṇa says *Bhagavad-Gītā* that the *gāyatrī mantra* is He Himself in poetic form. So *gāyatrī* is God as poetry. Śrīla Prabhupāda mentions in the purport to *Bhagavad-Gītā* 10.35 that *gāyatrī* is the sound incarnation of Brahman (all-pervading spirit) and therefore allows us to realize *ahaṁ brahmāsmi*: I am a spiritual being separate from the body and mind. Interestingly, although the *Bhagavad-Gītā* says *gāyatrī* is the sound incarnation of Kṛṣṇa, the *Śrīmad-Bhāgavatam* (3.13.35) says that Kṛṣṇa is the incarnation of the *gāyatrī*. That's because they are nondifferent and can be looked at from either perspective.

The Brahma-*gāyatrī* is complete knowledge. Caitanya Mahāprabhu, speaking to His disciple Sanātana Gosvāmī, says that *gāyatrī* contains *sambandha* and *abhideya*, or identity and the process to realize it. (*Caitanya-caritāmṛta, Mad-*

hya 25.147) Our identity is that we are a part of the Supreme Truth, and our process is to meditate on that Truth. The Brahma-*gāyatrī* also contains *prayojana*, or the result of such meditation, a condition of joyfulness and enthusiasm.

In the *Bhāgavatam 's* description of Kṛṣṇa's incarnation as Varāha, the sages say that the *gāyatrī mantra* is the touch of the Lord's skin. (*Śrīmad-Bhāgavatam* 3.12.45) Kṛṣṇa's skin is very soft. The *Bhakti-rasāmṛta-sindhu* describes the Lord's skin as so delicate that if He just brushes against a plant, His skin will change color. There are many descriptions in sacred writings, especially in *Ānanda-vṛndavana-campū*, about how the Lord's skin is soft like butter. One can feel the touch of the Lord simply by chanting the *gāyatrī mantra*.

Kṛṣṇa's touch is described as follows:

> By the touch of Lord Kṛṣṇa's hand [in His form of Nṛsiṁhadeva] on Prahlāda Mahārāja's head, Prahlāda was completely freed of all material contaminations and desires, as if he had been thoroughly cleansed. Therefore, he at once became transcendentally situated, and all the symptoms of ecstasy became manifest in his body. His heart filled with love, and his eyes with tears, and thus he was able to completely capture the lotus feet of the Lord within the core of his heart.
>
> (*Śrīmad-Bhāgavatam* 7.9.6)

Meditation 84: The Months November and December

Of months I am Mārgaśīrṣa [November– December] (*Gītā* 10.35)

The months of November and December are the harvest season in India and in much of the world. Regardless of the exact month, most cultures have a festival of joy and gratitude after the main harvest, and the time for such celebration represents Kṛṣṇa. Families gather, feasts are cooked, songs are sung, and prayers are offered to the Lord. Harvest time acknowledges Kṛṣṇa as the greatest philanthropist, the greatest voluntary giver, the supplier of all, and the giver of nourishment. Although Kṛṣṇa identifies Himself with these particular months, anytime we have reason to be thankful, anytime we "harvest" a good result, and anytime we eat a satisfying and healthy meal, we can feel ourselves in touch with the grace and kindness of the Supreme.

Meditation 85: The Season Spring

Of seasons I am flower-bearing spring. (*Gītā* 10:35)

Spring brings hope of warmth after winter and new life after everything has been dormant for most of the cold season. The spring sun begins to thaw the icy grip of winter by its gentle warmth. The increase of temperature and light signals the plants to awaken and produce leaves and flowers. Similarly, Kṛṣṇa thaws the coldest of materialistic hearts by steadily and warmly shining the sun of His knowledge on them. Just like spring brings forth new blossoms, so, in touch with Kṛṣṇa, a cold self-absorbed heart sprouts blossoms of appreciation that grow into love. Kṛṣṇa is an entire season of joyful, warm unfolding into endless varieties of flowers – colors, shapes, fragrances, and sizes. In the youthful dawning of the springtime of Kṛṣṇa, we each awaken to our individual flavor of loving service to the Lord for His appreciation and happiness.

Meditation 86: The Gambling of Cheats

I am the gambling of cheats (*Gītā* 10.36)

Kṛṣṇa's opulences are found in the best of everything, even the best kind of cheating. Generally, in cheating, those who are cheated are bewildered and do not realize their true position. They do not explicitly agree to be cheated. Yet gambling is such an amazing form of cheating that all parties agree to the process, each hoping to move treasures from the others' pockets to their own without any honest exchange of goods or services. While there is the excitement of risk in many honest ventures, in gambling the risk is of losing one's own allotted wealth with nothing of value received in exchange. In these ways gambling reminds us of Kṛṣṇa's wonderful illusory energy that covers our natural connec-

November
OF MONTHS
I AM
December

I AM ALSO THE
gambling
OF
cheats

tion with Kṛṣṇa, a connection that benefits us without any cost, but instead we believe we are competing for limited resources. This illusory energy muddles our minds so that we swerve from the path of honesty, hoping for the thrill of quick and easy gains in the world, when in truth we already are fully heirs to the glory of God, as are all His creatures.

Meditation 87: The Splendor

Of the splendid I am the splendor (*Gītā* 10.36)

What makes something excellent, spectacular, glorious, and dazzling rather than ordinary and plain, or perhaps wretched? What is splendid in this world has attributes that fill us with wonder and admiration. There is the pageantry of royal weddings or Oscar awards, architectural wonders such as the Parthenon, the Colosseum, and Taj Mahal, and natural wonders such as the Grand Canyon and Victoria Falls. Sunsets and rising golden moons, artistically decorated cakes, and expertly executed dance performances can also invoke the specific sense of happiness we call "wonder." Kṛṣṇa is that elusive quality that infuses an activity, a place, a thing, or a phenomenon with the ability to inspire us with amazement.

Meditation 88: Victory

I am victory (*Gītā* 10.36)

Being number one. There is something so magnetic and powerful about being first, about having won a top position. We see this hunger for victory in all facets of life. On the sport field opposing teams battle it out until the last whistle. In the classroom, students compete for first place. In the business world people compete to win a major deal or get a promotion. People often try to have the last word in an argument. Achieving victory is a strong driving force in the world. At its most mundane and basic level, being victorious is about declaring supremacy, being above something or someone else, but that is not always bad. To be victorious means to have the ability to be faced with a challenge and not be defeated. Someone who has suffered from an addiction, be it alcohol, pornography, gambling, or abusive behavior, knows how sweet it tastes to be able to say no to that drink, that risky website, pulling that lever, or striking out in anger. Kṛṣṇa is that victory. He is in the elated feeling when we take a risk and come out successful.

In the *Śrīmad-Bhāgavatam* we see how Kṛṣṇa is victorious in every fight with the demons. But we also see how He lets His devotees conquer Him. When the cowherd boys wrestle with Kṛṣṇa and Balarāma on the pasturing grounds, the cowherd boys win. Kṛṣṇa and Balarāma have to carry their victorious friends on their backs as the winners' prize.

Kṛṣṇa is the sweetness and rush of victory. He is the victory we are all searching for. He is the ability to defeat our bad habits and attain the supreme victory, love of God.

Meditation 89: Adventure

I am adventure (*Gītā* 10.36)

To yearn for adventure is a quality of the soul, and Kṛṣṇa Himself is adventure. Kṛṣṇa and the cowherd boys had adventures every single day. One day the boys almost got burned by a forest fire; one day they were swallowed by Aghāsura; another day Kṛṣṇa and Balarāma fought with Dhenukāsura and his cronies; the residents of Vṛndāvana lived through a terrible storm and took shelter under Govardhana Hill. While experiencing these situations, they were filled with the ecstatic *rasa* of fear, and afterwards, they relished retelling these events to each other.

In every encounter with the demons in Vṛndāvana the cowherd boys and other residents feel that Kṛṣṇa Himself is the adventure that they are experiencing. Kṛṣṇa is the mystery of how things will unfold, the anticipation of discovering how Kṛṣṇa will reveal the story, the wondering of how Kṛṣṇa will save the day. So, it is with us. Our adventures are directly Kṛṣṇa, and with each one we can go deeper into our relationship with Him and introspection about ourselves.

I AM
adventure

OF
SECRET THINGS
silence

We sometimes find that it is the difficult situations that make the best stories later, like missing a train in a foreign country, taking a wrong turn on the way to an interview, coming out of the supermarket to find that the car had been smashed or stolen, or dealing with some last-minute mishap just before a big event. While we are living through these situations, our conviction that Kṛṣṇa is directly the adventure itself brings us to a state of curiosity and anticipation about how He is working in our life, rather than frustration, anger, or fear. And in hindsight, when we have lived through them, we can choose to see that Kṛṣṇa has taught us valuable lessons to bring us closer to Him.

Meditation 90: Punishment

Among all means of suppressing lawlessness I am punishment (*Gītā* 10.38)

Criminals who flout the law create fear and chaos in society. News headlines always detail one crime or another. In societies where there is due process and convicted criminals are punished, honest citizens can focus on their lives rather than protection. Kṛṣṇa is the protective parent or older brother who protects us from a bully. Kṛṣṇa is the system of law and punishment that enables a sense of security. In places where such a system functions well and justly, the freedom we feel going to work, or to shop, or to walk through a park in the evening is Kṛṣṇa, who in His form of punishment has suppressed lawlessness in our lives.

Meditation 91: Morality

Of those who seek victory I am morality (*Gītā* 10.38)

Kṛṣṇa is victory, but Kṛṣṇa also says that of those who seek victory, He is morality. That tells us something about what kind of fight Kṛṣṇa wants us to fight. Kṛṣṇa did not ask Arjuna to annihilate the Kauravas just for the sake of having a great battle story. He wanted Arjuna to slay them for the sake of restoring morality and religious principles to the world. We see sometimes how righteous people come into positions of power but are later swayed by their power to act in an immoral way. We see presidents, who are supposed to be beacons for morality, come under the sway of power and lust and either embezzle millions or have affairs that are splashed on the front pages of the newspapers. Lawyers may sometimes tweak the law to win a case. These people may win in the short run, but ultimately, they lose because they gave up morality. Sometimes we see how someone loses on a material level even though they remained virtuous. The Pāṇḍavas lost their kingdom to Śakuni's cheating. Mahārāja Parīkṣit was condemned to death by a brāhmaṇa boy who had lost his sense of morality and virtue. However, we see that these people, who have lost on a material level, won far more because they stayed virtuous throughout difficult situations. The Pāṇḍavas won their kingdom back and gained power of the world. Mahārāja Parīkṣit died in seven days, but he gained the ultimate spiritual knowledge by hearing the *Śrīmad-Bhāgavatam*. Therefore, morality is the real victory, even when it seems like we have lost something. And that sense of feeling victorious because of having done what is right, what is fair, and what is just – is Kṛṣṇa.

Meditation 92: Silence

Of secret things I am silence (*Gītā* 10.38)

Keeping things confidential often challenges people. We may think we can break silence to share with just one very trusted person, but soon the secret becomes public knowledge. Instead, when we are truly and deeply silent about confidences, we find Kṛṣṇa. The greatest confidential information is about our personal relationship with the Lord. Private and sacred, it is safe in our inner silence that we share only with Kṛṣṇa.

Gaining inner wisdom – that which is a "secret" to most of the world – is best done with a receptivity that gives us a silent break in our own mental chatter. In seeking understanding or advice, we have to apply silence in order to listen and learn. Śrīla Prabhupāda explains in the purport to *Bhagavad-Gītā 10.38*: "Among the confidential activities of hearing, thinking and meditating, silence is most important because by silence one can make progress very quickly." Silence is the deepest act of listening by which we open ourselves internally to the most confidential knowledge. That act of silence not only invites Kṛṣṇa, but represents Him as a total giving of peaceful attention.

OF
WISE
wisdom

Meditation 93: Wisdom

Of the wise I am the wisdom (*Gītā* 10.38)

Our lives are oversaturated with sources of knowledge, some legitimate, some not. Some of us learn by going through school all the way to a PhD, and some of us learn on the job. But knowledge does not equate to wisdom. Wise people draw from experience and learning, both formal and informal. Therefore, wisdom, insight, discernment, and acumen are the most valuable features of the wise.

Wisdom cuts through our confusion, clarifies the cloudy, and lights a path brightly when we can only dimly see. Wisdom is the spark of epiphany, of realization and understanding, the so-called "common sense" that is ironically rare and precious. Sometimes wisdom is communicated in a look, a gesture, or a short phrase. And sometimes it's transmitted in a book of hundreds of pages. But it is the insight of the wise – their wisdom – that is the manifestation of Kṛṣṇa Himself. The greatest wisdom of the wise cannot affect us without Kṛṣṇa confirming the insight and manifesting as the wisdom Himself. Therefore, a truly wise person's wisdom is a manifestation of Kṛṣṇa as wisdom. When we feel that grasp of truth from the wise, we know that Kṛṣṇa has appeared as our understanding.

Universal Form Descriptions from the Śrīmad-Bhāgavatam

His skin
AND
SIX OTHER LAYERS
ARE THE
generating
CENTERS
of
VEDIC
hymns

Universal Form Descriptions from the *Śrīmad-Bhāgavatam*

We often hear the phrase "Mother Earth." The earth is our mother in the sense that she gives birth to our sustenance and wealth in the form of minerals and vegetables. The earth as a personal entity is not just a metaphor or a poetic device but a fact. Just as there is a goddess with the form of a planet, Kṛṣṇa Himself has a universal form, a body that has the moon and sun for His eyes and the mountains as His bones. Mahārāja Parīkṣit asks Sūta Gosvāmī about this form and this is part of his answer:

> *bhagavato guṇamaye sthūla-rūpa āveśitaṁ mano hy aguṇe 'pi sūkṣmatama ātma-jyotiṣi pare brahmaṇi bhagavati vāsudevākhye kṣamam āveśituṁ tad u haitad guro 'rhasy anuvarṇayitum iti.*
>
> When the mind is fixed upon the Supreme Personality of Godhead in His external feature made of the material modes of nature – the gross universal form – it is brought to the platform of pure goodness. In that transcendental position, one can understand the Supreme Personality of Godhead, Vāsudeva, who in His subtler form is self-effulgent and beyond the modes of nature. O my lord, please describe vividly how that form, which covers the entire universe, is perceived.
>
> (*Śrīmad-Bhāgavatam* 5.16. 3)

In this section we look at many descriptions from the Second and Eighth Cantos of *Śrīmad-Bhāgavatam* of how we can appreciate Kṛṣṇa as the universe. The universal form is a person, a loving person who is vast and expansive in His acceptance of all living entities. Every creature, quality, and community have a place in this form of Kṛṣṇa and serves a purpose. We hope that these meditations help you to not only learn about Kṛṣṇa but also learn about your relationship with Him through the universe.

Meditation 1: The Lord's Mouth and Voice

The mouth of the virāṭ-puruṣa [the universal form of the Lord] is the generating center of the voice, and the controlling deity is fire (*Bhāgavatam* 2.6.1)

A voice is something that can burn us worse than fire or heal us faster than any doctor. Whether it is the voice in our mind or the voice that comes from our mouth, it has a creating power like nothing else. Much of our reality is shaped by the voice of our thoughts. Our mental "voice" takes objective facts and ascribes meaning to them, such as "She said that because she loves me," or "He did that because he is dishonest," or "I'm a resilient person who can do that," or "I'm useless and will never accomplish anything."

In terms of the audible voice, we get deeply hurt when a loved one says something thoughtless and mean to us. A fearful situation seems all right when we hear a loved one's voice, as when a frightened child in a dark room calls for Mother, and she comes and says, "I am here."

A voice – whether mental or audible – is like a fire that can be used to warm, positively transform, and purify, or conversely destroy and turn things to ashes and smoke. The voice from Kṛṣṇa's mouth is the fire of knowledge that enlightens us and burns our ignorance.

Meditation 2: Vedic Hymns: The Lord's Skin and Touch

His skin and six other layers are the generating centers of the Vedic hymns (*Bhāgavatam* 2.6.1)

When we attend a traditional fire sacrifice for a wedding, spiritual initiation, or other religious ceremony, we hear chanting of Vedic hymns. The sound of the Sanskrit syllables and the traditional varieties of tone and pitch not only soothes and uplifts from a musical perspective, but also lightens and clarifies our awareness. These hymns are soft and gentle yet substantial and protective. Kṛṣṇa's skin is also very soft – a leaf brushing against His skin will alter the color. And, as the skin protects the body, the sounds of the Vedas protect us all (who are in the universal body of the Lord) from harm. The skin also keeps pathogens out and the internal organs moist and in place. Similarly, our chanting of the Vedic hymns keeps us from becoming infected with the lower modes of nature. These hymns raise us to goodness and ultimately to transcendence by putting us in touch with the Supreme through sound. The hymns also give us direction for our proper place in society and ultimately in the universal body, and, like bodily skin, give structure and direction to the flow of relationships and resources.

As when we want to touch someone, we contact their skin, when we want to contact the Supreme, we hear or recite the Vedic hymns, including the *mahā-mantra*: Hare Kṛṣṇa, Hare Kṛṣṇa, Kṛṣṇa Kṛṣṇa, Hare Hare/ Hare Rāma, Hare Rāma, Rāma Rāma, Hare Hare.

Meditation 3: Vedic Hymns: The Lord's Brain, His Cerebral Passage

The Vedic hymns are the cerebral passage of the Lord (*Bhāgavatam* 2.1.31)

Prosthetics are possible for our limbs, and transplants for most of our organs, but no one has done a brain or head transplant. In rare cases when doctors remove half the brain because of severe brain damage, patients regain their faculties after a while, but to get a whole new brain is, as yet, unheard of. The brain is irreplaceable in modern medical science. We see that sometimes a severely injured patient is put on a ventilator, but if the brain is dead, the ventilator does not help restore the patient's life The Vedas are therefore the cerebral passage of the Lord, because like the brain it is indispensable. Because the Vedas and Kṛṣṇa's words are nondifferent from Him, this means that Kṛṣṇa is indispensable.

The brain is the place where knowledge is stored and the platform from where we retrieve information by which we act. Without the *Bhagavad-Gītā, Śrīmad-Bhāgavatam,* and *Śrī Caitanya-caritāmṛta* we would be lost. The Vedas are the brain of a religious community, the spiritual knowledge of that tradition. Without it our spiritual community would not have the flow of awareness through the cerebral passage and thus and cease to function.

On an individual level, when Kṛṣṇa cut off Śiśupāla's head with His Sudarśana *cakra,* he died immediately. But Śiśupāla was dead long before because he had cut himself off from Kṛṣṇa by being offensive. The same happens to us. If we cut ourselves off from spiritual knowledge, we are dead. The Vedic hymns are therefore our source of life, the cerebral passage of the universal body.

Meditation 4: The Lord's Words

From His words came all the Vedic mantras (*Bhāgavatam* 8.20.25–29)

Scriptures which contain the mantras to connect with the Lord come from His own words. We often say we want to see God, and we may also want to hear God, touch God, smell God, and interact with Him with all our senses. We can certainly hear Him through the Vedic mantras because He directly spoke them. He is telling us how to approach Him, how to find Him, how to access Him. Whether these mantras are chanted with our voice or another's, the sound is truly the voice of the Lord.

Meditation 5: Brāhmaṇas: The Lord's Face

The virā*ṭ*-puru*ṣ*a's face is the brāhma*ṇ*as (*Bhāgavatam* 2.1.37)

It's the vision of sages, intellectuals, scientists, and in general those who work in the field of ideas that guides society in the right direction. The voice of such persons communicates their vision to the rest of us. The ears of such *brāhmaṇas* take in information from the scriptures and also hear the needs of human society. Thus, such persons act as the overall face of the Lord to guide all of society.

FROM HIS
words
CAME ALL THE
VEDIC
mantras

ON HIS LIPS
WAS
greed
hare kṛṣṇa
hare kṛṣṇa
kṛṣṇa kṛṣṇa
hare hare
hare rama
hare rama
rama rama
hare hare

Meditation 6: The Lord's Tongue

His tongue is the productive center of different foodstuffs and delicacies for offering to the demigods, the forefathers and the general mass of people (*Bhāgavatam* 2.6.1)

We put food on our tongue, but the tongue of the universal form produces food! And what wonderful food! The food from His tongue is not meant directly for us; it's for us to offer to our forefathers whose culture and values nourish us; to the demigods who, as agents of the Lord, provide for us; and as general charity. We thus act as servants or agents of the Lord's own taste of His tongue to provide for others' taste when we give them food in in ritual offerings or as charity. The connection between Kṛṣṇa's pleasure in eating and in sharing that pleasure with others becomes our source of happiness.

Meditation 7: The Lord's Tastes

The juice or essence of everything is His tongue (*Bhāgavatam* 2.1.30)

Imagine the taste of a juicy watermelon or mango, or the sound of mantras being chanted melodiously, or the touch of a loved one's hand. All have one thing in common we might not think of: moisture. The enjoyment, taste, or *rasa*, of anything we eat, hear, and feel requires some moisture to function properly. When our eyes are dry, we can't see. When our mouth is dry, everything tastes like cardboard. When the wax in our ears dries and clogs them, we can't hear. We need *rasa* or "juice," literally and figuratively, to have our senses interact with their objects and experience pleasure.

The source of that juice is Kṛṣṇa's tongue. Kṛṣṇa loves eating. His tongue loves the taste of food prepared with love for Him, like our mothers cook with love for us. Mother Yaśodā enjoys making milk sweets for Kṛṣṇa with her own hands rather than asking one of her servants. The cowherd boys' mothers all cook with love for their boys, and the cowherd boys love sharing their food with Kṛṣṇa. And Kṛṣṇa relishes their offerings because they are made with such love. From the Lord's enjoyment of this *rasa* on His tongue comes all the *rasa* in our own lives.

Meditation 8: The Lord's Lips and Greed

On His lips was greed (*Bhāgavatam* 8.20.25–29)

We are all familiar with the feeling when "our eyes are bigger than our stomach." Our eyes, or rather our mouth, tells us that we can absolutely have another savory, or that we for sure have space for dessert. Our mouth drives our greed. It wants to be satisfied right now. But later, we regret it.

Our lips are not only greedy to eat but also to speak. We may know the feeling of disappointment when talking to someone about a problem only to find that person using our problem as a segue to talk about themselves, on and on. Maybe we've also been that person. Greed to speak may also appear when someone says something we are sure is wrong, and we feel an uncontrollable urge to correct the person or defend ourselves.

Our stories of greedy mouths and lips are more often linked with embarrassment and regret, but Kṛṣṇa succeeds in being greedy in a transcendental way, making it glorious. When He assumed the form of Govardhana Hill, He cried, "Āniyora! Āniyora! Give me more!" And Nanda Mahārāja and the cowherd men had to give Govardhana everything they had to satisfy His desire. Lord Caitanya was so greedy to chant the holy names of Kṛṣṇa that He explained grammar to His students by connecting everything to Kṛṣṇa's holy name.

The Lord's pastimes of greed are infinitely more palatable than our own; when our greed pulls at our lips, it may be discouraging. At such times we can remember that greed for transcendental pleasure is not a bad thing. To be greedy for *kīrtana* or discussing Kṛṣṇa is glorious as greed rests on the Lord's own lips. If we become greedy for loving service, our lips lift us out of our embarrassment and regret and fill us with joy.

Meditation 9: Medicinal Herbs: The Lord's Nostrils

His smelling powers generate the Aśvinī-kumāra demigods and all kinds of medicinal herbs (*Bhāgavatam* 2.6.2)

The world around us is filled with mystical and medicinal herbs. We use these fragrant or strong-smelling plants to keep us healthy and alleviate disease. Kṛṣṇa's sense of smell creates these herbs and the Aśvinī-kumāra demigods who are the chief celestial physicians. They are the experts in Āyurveda. So expert were they, that they could give old Cyavana Muni a rejuvenated young body.

Healing herbs help us not only physically but also mentally. In many cases the smell of herbs is an integral part of healing, or in some cases is the medicine itself.

Our sense of smell acts only as a receiver. The Lord's smell acts as a creator. When the scent of healing enters our body, that smell is the Lord's breath as a heavenly doctor. He breathes upon us His loving care to soothe or invigorate, to relax or to strengthen, to build up or to cut out as needed in the moment. This smelling power of the Lord, taking the form of divine doctors, medicine, and then healing through scent perception, is a loving link between Kṛṣṇa and us. Our senses are linked with His through His care for us, and all we receive benefit from is His mercy. Kṛṣṇa's form is the ultimate medicine. He is thus our one true physician.

Meditation 10: The Wind: The Lord's Nostrils

In the [Lord's] nostrils, he [Bali Mahārāja] saw the wind (*Bhāgavatam* 8.20.25–29)

The wind blows away smog and pollution. It can also spread pollution or wildfires. In any case, wind brings a change to circumstances. Wind is Kṛṣṇa taking a breath through His cosmic nostrils. We open doors or windows on a hot day and are grateful for the relief. Other times that very wind brings difficulty, as when moving air sends winter cold seemingly into our very bones and we wrap ourselves every tightly in wool to little avail. Yet both the welcome wind and the bitter wind are the air that comes through the Lord's nostrils. Our apparent fortune and misfortune dance on that wind like a pearl dangling from the center of Kṛṣṇa's nose, moving back and forth with His every breath. While we may not understand in the moment why the same wind at different times brings seemingly welcome or unwelcome sensations, we can know that the feeling of wind means a close connection to our beloved Lord.

Meditation 11: The Generating Centers of Our Breathing: The Lord's Nostrils

His two nostrils are the generating centers of our breathing and of all other airs (*Bhāgavatam* 2.6.2)

We don't really think about breath and breathing unless we're running a mile and get winded, wondering why we haven't practiced more. We become aware of our nostrils when we are sick, and our nose becomes red from blowing or blocked from inflammation. When we have a cold, bronchitis, asthma, or hay fever, we learn the value of moving air, of breathing, and what it feels like to have no air.

When we've been stuck inside all day and finally get the chance to go for a walk, we feel the release of tension when we breathe the outside air. It refreshens the mind, and we feel as if any cobwebs that we may have had are blown away.

With every inward breath, our breath supplies essential gases to each of our bodily cells, and with every outward breath, it removes the waste gases. When the universal form of the Lord breathes, we each – little cells within His form – get our breath. In turn our waste gases nourish the plants whose waste gases then nourish us. And all are nourished by the breathing of the Lord in His magnificent universal form.

HIS TWO NOSTRILS
ARE THE
generating
centers
OF OUR
breathing
AND OF ALL OTHER
airs

Meditation 12: Sense of Smell

Material fragrance is His sense of smell (*Bhāgavatam* 2.1.29)

It is early evening and silent clouds sail through the sky. The evening breeze carries with it the promise of rain as a subtle smell. All around, the air acts as a messenger, carrying smells of flower gardens or evening meals being cooked. These smells can fill us with tranquility and even curiosity . . . Is that fresh bread I'm smelling? On the other hand, maybe the early evening is disturbed by the stinging smell of smoke, signaling a fire and setting off our alarm bells. Where is the fire? What's caused it? We know action is needed.

Kṛṣṇa says that all material fragrance is His sense of smell. It's easy to think of Kṛṣṇa's enjoying the smell of richness when we smell roses or a home-cooked meal. But how is it that we can find Kṛṣṇa's sense of smell evident in a rotten corpse or in of any of our bodily excretions? These smells serve as warning signals. Kṛṣṇa's sense of smell manifests as these odors to steer us to safety. Kṛṣṇa's smelling creates all the fragrance of the world, communications meant for our good, out of His love. What caring love letters He sends us!

Meditation 13: Producing Various Fragrances

His breathing energies produce different kinds of fragrance (*Bhāgavatam* 2.6.2)

Our breath and breathing certainly produce odors but generally of an unpleasant kind! A dentist is likely to say that the human breath is nothing to write poetry about. Toothpaste, mouthwash, or mints are our handy tools before an important meeting or when we have the potential of a romantic encounter.

We also breathe through our pores to some extent, and again, that smell is one we try to prevent or mask with various creams, sprays, and potions. Our sense of breathing through the mouth and pores may give us joy or give others distress depending on the quality of our hygiene and the smells around us.

Kṛṣṇa's original form, on the other hand, has a unique fragrance of a mixture of sandalwood, musk, aguru (oud), and camphor. The *gopīs* use their breathing and smelling to find Kṛṣṇa when He hides by detecting His bodily aroma. The breath from His mouth is so enticing that bees sometimes hover around thinking there are fresh flowers. Kṛṣṇa doesn't have to wear garlands or scented oils, but their fragrance gives Him pleasure when they are offered with love.

Yet the fragrance coming from the breath of the universal form includes all types of smells and therefore seems quite different from what the *gopīs* search for in Vṛndāvana's groves. But aren't even the fragrances we label as distasteful also beautiful in another sense? The smell of excrement tells us to avoid it and thus stay healthy, and that smell also indicates the process of life – what is eaten can again return to earth and provide nutrients for the next crop of food. Thus, all fragrances of this world bring pleasure either directly or indirectly and thus can be understood as the Lord's breath.

Meditation 14: Air: The Lord's Breath

The omnipotent air is His breath (*Bhāgavatam* 2.1.33)

Without notice, without thought, in the background, air flows into our nose, our diaphragm muscle moves, and our lungs fill. Extracting oxygen, the tubes and vessels in our lungs let go of carbon dioxide. The oxygen is essential for digestion, a kind of chemical fire, just as oxygen is needed for any fire. As the air around us becomes the breath of life within us, it further divides into five kinds of *prāṇa*, or flows of energy. If we focus our attention on this *prāṇa* and regulate its flow attentively, we can still the mind and focus as part of dedication to our spiritual practices, or even just for brief relief and peace.

From our perspective, the air outside is lifeless matter, which becomes the very breath of life as soon as it enters our nostrils. Yet we exist in the universal body, and the air surrounding us is the Lord's breath of life. It is His means of supplying oxygen to some life forms, nitrogen to others, and carbon dioxide to others. The movements and eddies of air are

Material
fragrance
is His sense of
smell

HIS EYES ARE THE
generating
centers
OF
ALL
KINDS OF FORMS
AND THEY
glitter
and
illuminate

His own breathing as He both gives and removes the gases for each life form, which focus on their various objectives, leaving the influx and outgo of air as an unnoticed and automatic process, heedless of the Supreme Life giving them life. But that air is Kṛṣṇa's *prāṇa*, full of His potency, and when we do turn our attention to it, when we are mindful of it, when we notice and slow its flow, filling our lungs deeply, it's easier to feel His presence around us and through us.

Meditation 15: Generator of Forms: The Lord's Eyes

His eyes are the generating centers of all kinds of forms, and they glitter and illuminate (*Bhāgavatam* 2.6.3)

We take photos because we want to capture something in memory, something we can return to later to remember a larger experience. In fact, photos can play a big role in augmenting our mind's ability to remember events. Without photos we have only our imagination and our fading memories of the people and places we have known and experienced.

The human eye, like a photo camera, is our body's tool to capture the world and is a wonderfully complex mechanism of sight. It has many precisely planned parts: the cornea and retina that work together to reflect and transmit light from objects, and the optical nerve that transmits what we see to our visual cortex. Despite the eye's wonder and complexity, it cannot see things out of proximity and can only see what is already there to a limited degree. Our eyes are only via-mediums between our brain and the outside world. They cannot create the things we look at, only perceive them.

Kṣīrodakaśāyī Viṣṇu, however, creates the material world by glancing over it. Just imagine, His sight creates everything that we see: the clouds, the flowers, the mountains, the materials that make up our houses, cars, and other amenities. Our eyes can only perceive what already is there, but the whole creation is created merely by Kṛṣṇa looking at it.

Thus, the world is one gigantic photobook, reminding us of what Kṛṣṇa has created. We can look at the world and see pictures of Kṛṣṇa everywhere, because He is nondifferent from His energies.

Meditation 16: Sun and Planets: The Lord's Eyeballs

His eyeballs are like the sun and the heavenly planets (*Bhāgavatam* 2.6.3)

Eye contact invokes emotions. Imagine having an in-person conversation without the other person ever looking at us. Their lack of visual engagement may fill us with a range of emotions, such as frustration, indignation, confusion, or even loneliness. Eye contact may fill us with disgust if we judge that the other person as someone of questionable morals. If the other person is a friend or partner, eye contact may fill us with happiness.

Eye contact carries with it great power because it establishes a connection between two people. We *jīvas* have such a connection with Kṛṣṇa, not only as our companion in the form of the Supersoul. He is also observing us as His universal form through the sun, moon, and heavenly planets. The sun and moon are Kṛṣṇa's eyes. Through them, Kṛṣṇa witnesses our lives, our pitfalls, our triumphs, our questions, doubts, and all our activities. This thought may fill us with peace or horror, depending on what kind of activities we perform. A person walking home at night may feel safe as the bright moon lights the path home, but a thief by no means wants to be observed while going about his nocturnal pursuits. The sun, moon, and stars shining means there is Someone who knows us, is looking at us, and is waiting for us to look at Him too.

Meditation 17: Outer Space: The Lord's Eyepits

The sphere of outer space constitutes His eyepits (*Bhāgavatam* 2.1.30)

When we think of the human eye pit, we may think of darkness, of eye muscles, of blood vessels, or of a place in our body that hurts when we have serious sinus problems. We might imagine a horrific sight of an empty eyepit with eyeballs popping out.

Kṛṣṇa's eye socket, His eyepit, is vast and beautiful and mystical. The dark outer space of our universe, or our solar system, is Kṛṣṇa's eyepit, and the sun and moon are His eyes. When we peer up at the heavens on a dark night and see the stars, we also see Kṛṣṇa's eyepit. And it is not a place of horror, as in a mortal body, but of mystic wonder.

Meditation 18: Sun: The Power of Seeing

The eyeball is the sun as the power of seeing (*Bhāgavatam* 2.1.30)

The power of seeing is something that many of us take for granted until we have to get glasses or contact lenses. Darkness, or the lack of seeing, often fills us with fear. In the dark the slightest sound may sound like a thief breaking in, but when we switch on the light, we see it is our cat playing at the door with a ball of string. We also depend on our eyes to navigate traffic or to see our loved ones.

Regardless of how healthy our eyes are, we depend on the sun to see. We use electricity, batteries, or flames, true, but the illuminating power of any light source comes directly or indirectly from the sun. We are, therefore, totally dependent on the sun for light and therefore for sight. We see because Kṛṣṇa sees. It is His eye that allows our seeing.

Kṛṣṇa's eyeball is the sun and source of all sight. He not only gives us material sight but also spiritual sight. The sun not only shines on the outside, but can, by Kṛṣṇa's mercy, also shine in our consciousness, if we'll only let it.

Meditation 19: Day and Night: The Lord's Eyelids

His eyelids are both the day and night (*Bhāgavatam* 2.1.30), When His eyes were open it was daytime, and when they were closed it was night (*Bhāgavatam* 8.20.25–29)

The night creeps in, the sun is setting, and the stars are lighting up one by one. After a long day we are finally winding down. When we do get to bed and close our eyes, a feeling of relief washes over us. On the contrary, if a nightmare torments us in the dark of night, we may feel relief at being able to open our eyes and switch on the light. The day and night hold promise and opportunities for different reasons. Even during the day, we blink our eyes thousands of times. If it weren't for that blinking, our eyes would dry out and we wouldn't be able to see properly. In the same way, Kṛṣṇa blinks His eyes. The days and nights are His eyes blinking. During our day His eyes are open and during our night His eyes are closed. It's mind-boggling to think that Kṛṣṇa also blinks His eyes. The demigods don't blink their eyes, so why does Kṛṣṇa? It is for our benefit. It is in His blinking we find our rest and recreation, or activity and endeavor.

Meditation 20: Dawn and Dusk: The Lord's Dress

The terminations of days or nights are His dress (*Bhāgavatam* 2.1.34)

There is something magical about dawn and dusk. The mystical deep-blue light of the pre-dawn heralds the end or beginning of night. Sometimes, in wide open spaces the juncture of day and night can be seen at the same time. On one side is the dark blue of the night and on the other the blazing copper and gold of day. In the middle is the magical sphere where the two meet.

And so is Kṛṣṇa's dress described in many places in the *Śrīmad-Bhāgavatam*. The Lord often wears a golden helmet and a lightning-yellow *dhotī*. We can almost imagine Kṛṣṇa moving through the sky, His yellow cloth fluttering and His golden helmet glittering as the dawn light shifts from yellow to copper to gold. His golden saffron colored clothes fold over His dark bluish form like the sky and sunlit clouds as day and night join. Sometimes, where the day and night meet, we can almost see a flash of His shimmering blue, brown, and green peacock feather.

THE
eyeball
IS THE
sun
AS THE
POWER
OF
seeing

Meditation 21: Vedas and Sound: The Lord's Neck

On the neck [Bali Mahārāja saw] all the Vedas and all sound vibrations (*Bhāgavatam* 8.20.25–29)

When peacocks call, their necks visibly vibrate, reflecting the luminescence of their feathers. While sound is formed with the mouth, it originates in the neck with the vocal cords. The coordinated vibration allows us to whisper, speak, and sing. From our vocalizations we coordinate with others to act, and we express ideas.

We have this capacity with the sounds from our neck because this capacity also exists in the Lord's form. The Vedas start with the primeval sound, the *praṇava, oṁ*. As these sound vibrations move up the neck and out of the mouth of both the universal form and Lord Brahmā, they create all the wisdom and forms of the universe.

Meditation 22: The Lord's Ears are the Receptacles of all the Vedas

His ears hear from all sides and are receptacles for all the Vedas (*Bhāgavatam* 2.6.3)

In forests and mountains, we may hear echoes coming from all directions and struggle to find the source. It's like nature has an organic, natural surround sound system. Even in a theatre the sound sometimes seems to be coming from left, right, below and above – in all directions – as an immersive experience. We hear sounds around us every day, but even if we are fortunate to have two working ears, we can't always discern where sound is coming from.

Imagine misplacing our cell phone just before going to bed. The next morning, out of the shower and on the way to our room, we hear the phone alarm ringing. We walk around following the sound, not sure where it is, tilting our ears this way and that, trying to hear where it is coming from, and finally we find it. Kṛṣṇa doesn't have to tilt His head to hear the source of a sound. His ears can hear from all directions at once, always knowing the source, no matter how soft the sound is.

Kṛṣṇa's ears hear everything from all sides and all distances, yet it is the Vedas for which they are especially the receptacles. Just as when we hear many things but especially note the sound of our name or someone speaking favorably about us, in the same way, the Vedic sounds particularly attract Kṛṣṇa's ears. He also hears His devotees' calls. He hears the cowherd boys call His name when they are in trouble, whether eaten by Aghāsura or in danger of being burned by a forest fire. Kṛṣṇa hears Draupadī calling out to Him when she is being disrobed in the assembly hall of the Kurus. Even when she calls out for help in the forest, unable to feed Durvāsā Muni and his thousands of disciples, Kṛṣṇa hears her all the way in Dvārakā.

When we speak verses or knowledge from the Vedas, Kṛṣṇa's ears catch that sound no matter where we are. His ears hold that sound carefully, just as a container or receptacle keeps its contents safe from spilling or getting dirty.

Meditation 23: Sky and Sound: His Sense of Hearing

His sense of hearing is the generating center of the sky and of all kinds of sound (*Bhāgavatam* 2.6.3)

Throughout the scriptures we learn that sound creates space. The sound of *oṁ* churns the unmanifested material energy, from which space emerges, and is the foundation of everything material.

What is the "sense of hearing"? It's our ability to receive waves and vibrations through space and translate them into something meaningful. We often have a reasonably good idea of where the sound is coming from in space, in terms of direction, distance, and possibly movement of the source. Kṛṣṇa also has a similar sense of hearing although He can hear with any part of His body and can hear the whispers of thoughts in our minds and hearts. While we hear through space, His hearing generates space and sound itself.

The sounds that surround us at this moment – sounds of nature like wind and water, of humans, animals, and birds, and of machines such as motors and alarms – are from the Lord's own hearing and travel through the space that His hearing creates. We are hearing what He has heard first as if our hearing is within His hearing.

ON THE
neck
ALL THE
VEDAS
AND
ALL
sound
VIBRATIONS

HIS SENSE
of
hearing
IS THE
GENERATING
CENTER OF THE
sky
AND OF ALL KINDS OF
sound

and in His
WONDERFUL ACTIVITIES
AND STEPS WAS THE
fire
OF
sacrifice

Meditation 24: *Yajña*: The Lord's Steps

In His wonderful activities or steps was *yajña*, fire of sacrifice (*Bhāgavatam* 8.20.25–29)

Viṣṇu is the controlling deity of the legs and feet (*Bhāgavatam* 2.10.25) that enable humans to do their duties, all of which should be done as *yajña*. The term *yajña* as used in śāstra almost always means a performance or ceremony of connection with the Lord. In ordinary language we can say these are religious rituals, but such a phrase perhaps gives an erroneous impression of a mechanical action. The reality is that such ceremonies are a means of a loving connection. Having some time to connect deliberately with the Lord is essential for everyone in human society. Such ceremonies and rituals are found in all religious systems and all societies.

Many times, such religious observances are connected with fire. Of course, there is a literal *yajñic* fire, which is part of religious rituals, but there is also the fire of the ghee lamp, which is part of the *ārati* ceremony. And in every religion, there's some kind of fire that's used in rituals, such as lighting of candles or lamps. Fire and light are often associated with spirituality in terms of both vision and the burning away of anything unwanted. The Lord's steps are associated with this fire of *yajña*, because we often talk about moving forward or taking a step toward purification.

The Lord's stepping also enables us to walk so we can perform all our duties within this world. These steps of the Lord are called *havyaṁ karmabhiḥ*, or the *yajña* offering (made into a fire) of our worldly responsibilities. This implies that every step we take and every action we do can be a kind of religious ritual. For people in general, religious ritual is a small part of their day, if any, and the rest of the time is spent working to make a living. But our form of livelihood should also be a kind of religious ceremony. We can meditate on our attempts to integrate *yajña* and work as the Lord's steps, and we can remember His walking when we move about in our day.

Meditation 25: Lusty Desires: The Lord's Touch

In His touch were lusty desires (*Bhāgavatam* 8.20.25–29)

In the *Bhagavad-Gītā* (10.28) Kṛṣṇa says that of all causes for procreation He is Kāmadeva, the god of desire. And in the universal form that Lord Vāmana exhibits, *kāma* is in His touch. The Fifth Canto of *Śrīmad-Bhāgavatam* explains that when the princess daughters of the mystic snakes touch the body of Balarāma, both they and the Lord feel desires for love. The association of touch with desire is true among all species of life in this world. Touch certainly communicates romantic desires – generally associated with the Sanskrit word *kāma,* and that Śrīla Prabhupāda here translates as "lusty desires." Of course, as any of Kṛṣṇa's senses can work as any other sense, He can communicate His desires in ways other than touch, and our desires to serve Him can also be communicated with our other senses.

In addition to lusty desires, touch communicates desires for friendship, for partnership in business, and for parental love. But of all types of desires in all types of relationships and of all the ways to communicate those desires, romantic or lusty desires are quite strong and through touch are communicated in full intensity. Indeed, it is because of this power of touch that many traditional societies have rules to physically keep men and women from any situation in which they might touch each other, even accidentally or slightly.

Throughout our day we can notice when we intentionally avoid touch so as not to inadvertently indicate a desire. We can also notice when we touch others for the purpose of communicating or indicating a desired relationship, whether romantic or another type. The Lord also has touch, and the desires kindled and increased through His touch are of pure love and total satisfaction eternally.

THE HAIRS ON HIS BODY
ARE THE CAUSE OF ALL
vegetation
PARTICULARLY THE trees AND THE
blue sky

Meditation 26: The Cause of all vegetation: The Lord's Bodily Hairs

The hairs on His body are the cause of all vegetation, particularly of those trees which are required as ingredients for sacrifice (*Bhāgavatam* 2.6.5)

Human hair is a strange thing. We also know the feeling of not shaving in a long while, be it face or legs or armpits. At some stage the overgrowth looks like a forest, but, unlike the hair on our heads, a profusion of bodily hair is not necessarily attractive.

However, Kṛṣṇa's bodily hair, even overgrown, is beyond any beautiful conception in this world, yet vegetation can give us some idea. The forests enchant us by their beauty. As the trees gently sway in the wind, their leaves fluttering in shades of green in the sunlight, we get some sense of the beauty of Kṛṣṇa's hair. Flowers and fruits in vegetation are like ribbons and jewels in that hair. Like the hair on our bodies that protect our skin, vegetation protects the soil. And the vegetation, as the Lord's hair, used in religious *yajña* and rituals have particular beauty and use. The wood of the sandalwood tree is used to worship and cool the Lord, which we then use as *prasādam* in hot summers. Kuśa grass adds grace to fields and forms the priests' sitting mats and sacrificial ingredients. Wood is fed into the sacrificial fire, which then dances like flowing shining hair. Kṛṣṇa's hair is thus an integral part of a *yajña* as the twigs and sticks igniting the fire.

Meditation 27: Trees: The Hairs on His Body

The trees are the hairs of His body (*Bhāgavatam* 2.1.33)

Walking through or next to a forest or on a tree-bordered street surrounds us with the "tree-hairs" of Kṛṣṇa's body. We thus get an immediate sense of walking on the form of the Lord. We know that putting our feet on the Lord's form is forbidden and most disrespectful, but in His form as the universe, it is unavoidable. If the trees are His bodily hairs, then we walk among those hairs on His body. How intimately connected we are with Him! We are so small, like a tiny creature walking among the hairs on an arm, yet our relationship with the Lord is as His cherished friend, His part and parcel. As we live and walk among His bodily hairs, we can feel how close we are to Him, how loved, and how naturally connected we are. We then gain respect for the trees, the ground or path upon which we walk or ride, and our relationship with the Lord's form.

Meditation 28: The Clouds are the Hair on His Head

The clouds which carry water are the hairs on His head (*Bhāgavatam* 2.1.34);

On the hair [of the Lord, Bali Mahārāja saw] the clouds (*Bhāgavatam* 8.20.25–29)

Perhaps we sometimes lie on our backs on the grass and gaze at how the clouds seem to form recognizable shapes, or we briefly check the sky to try and gauge the weather. With His hair of clouds, Kṛṣṇa gives us beauty, rain, and shade. Like clouds, Kṛṣṇa's thick curly hair can form a fluffy frame around His face. His curls have soft moving edges like puffs of cottonwool balls or the kind of clouds that little children draw in their pictures. There are also wispy clouds, which are like Kṛṣṇa's bits of hair that fly out of His otherwise neat bun, and various hair arrangements, to scatter across His face and neck. Kṛṣṇa's hair is a glossy dark color, like rain-filled storm clouds. Sometimes, when Kṛṣṇa is moving large herds of cows from one place to another, or when He is running toward Bhīṣma on the battlefield, the dust in the air covers His hair, which then appears ash-colored, like white-gray clouds in a royal blue sky.

We don't often think of hair in general unless we have to wash it or if someone pulls at it. In the same way, the clouds of Kṛṣṇa's hair drift silently by without us taking much notice unless we need rain or shade or sunshine. They are also very far away, but just by gazing upward at them, intimately connects us with Kṛṣṇa.

THE
hairs on His head
and face
ARE THE
reservoirs
FOR THE
clouds

ON HIS
nails
WERE ALL THE
stones

Meditation 29: His Hair are All the Drugs and Herbs

On the hairs of His body were all the drugs and herbs (*Bhāgavatam* 8.20.25–29)

On our arm is a soft short carpet of bodily hair. This hair helps to keep us healthy by regulating body temperature and increasing the touch sensations of our skin, helping us feel pesky insects. As our hairs assist the health of our body, Kṛṣṇa's hairs give health to the whole creation. His hairs are medicinal; they help cure disease and realign the body and mind of the inhabitants of the universe.

When we drink herbal teas, plant herbs, harvest herbs or use herbal medicine and pharmaceuticals derived from herbs, we can turn our awareness to the fact that these fragrant, balancing, healing, relieving plants are the Lord's bodily hairs. Viśvanātha Cakravartī Ṭhākura describes in *Mādhurya Kaḍambinī* how a devotee on the platform of *prema* feels ecstasy at the fragrance and taste of the Lord. We smell and taste something of Kṛṣṇa whenever we cook with herbs, eat food prepared with herbs, or walk through an area where they are planted. When our sensory sensations are filled with loving appreciation for Kṛṣṇa – "Oh, you smell so nice!" – we grow in our love for Him.

Meditation 30: His Nails are the Breeding Ground of Electricity

His nails are the breeding ground of electricity, stones, and iron ores (*Bhāgavatam* 2.6.5)

Electricity is directly related to magnets, which are in turn related to iron. If we think of the nails in this verse as being on Kṛṣṇa's toes, we can think of how, when the Lord walks, His toenails spark electricity like matches striking a matchbox. Similarly, the touch of the Lord's fingernails spark ecstasy and spiritual realization in His devotees. That the Lord's nails are electric and magnetic is indicative of how attractive He is. His devotee Prahlāda described himself as iron and the Lord as a magnet attracting him. Indeed, the very name "Kṛṣṇa" means "all attractive." When we use magnets or turn on electrical appliances and objects, we are in touch with the Kṛṣṇa's beautiful nails. Those nails are so brilliant that they shine with a beckoning luster, drawing even those who are already impersonally realized to personal devotional service. Those nails are illuminating, energizing, and attracting. They are electric and magnetic.

Meditation 31: The Animals of his Nails

The horse, mule, camel and elephant are His nails (*Bhāgavatam* 2.1.35)

The animals mentioned here are the typical "beasts of burden" in various parts of the world. These creatures that serve humans by carrying them and their goods are Kṛṣṇa's nails, perhaps on both His fingers and toes. Our nails protect the delicate ends of our appendages and also act as tools and aids in our work, as these animals do. They assist us and make our lives easier. Therefore, when we care for the animals who render service, we are caring for the Lord's nails. Our own nails that we cut and clean (and perhaps decorate) are so insignificant by comparison! Of course, at the time of this writing, few humans use such animals for work, relying instead on hand-carried wheeled carts or motorized wheeled vehicles. Yet, at least in some places in the world, the Lord's nails act as assistants not only to Him but also to us in the form of sentient beings who move us around and carry our stuff.

Meditation 32: On His Nails are All Stones

On His nails were all the stones (*Bhāgavatam* 8.20.25–29)

Deep red ruby, reflecting diamond, multi-colored shimmering opal, lavender amethyst, streaked marble, and dotted granite – the soft earth contains hard stones of beauty. More mundane stones are in soil as well – the ordinary gray or brown rocks we sit on and build our walls and homes with. Just as our soft fingers have hard nails, these various stones are on the nails of the Lord's lotus-like hands. When we use stones for beauty or function, we can meditate on how the Lord's nails are so beautiful on His hands. We can recall how Kṛṣṇa in Vṛndāvana uses His nails to write messages to His friends on flower petals and leaves. In the Lord's Nṛsiṁha form of half-man, half lion, He uses His stone-like fingernails to tear apart the cruel demon Hiraṇyakaśipu who had severely tortured his own son, Prahlāda. And, in His incarnation of Vāmana, He uses His stone-like toenails to pierce the universal covering and bring to us the Ganges River from the spiritual realm.

Throughout our day, we may have many occasions to look at our hands and nails. Perhaps they are pinkish with a white half-moon at the root. Perhaps they are especially attractive. Certainly, they are useful. And they can remind us that the Lord's nails are as beautiful as rubies and diamonds and as useful as the stones that form the foundations of our structures in this world.

Meditation 33: Animals: The Lord's Belt

Wild animals and all quadrupeds are situated in the belt zone of the Lord (*Bhāgavatam* 2.1.35)

Who would think that the universal form of the Lord needs a belt or a belt zone at all, but He does, and all the wild animals and quadrupeds live there. In our world these animals' skins are the source of most belts. While devotees of Kṛṣṇa avoid leather from the slaughterhouse, traditional cultures use leather after animals meet their natural death. There are belts of dark leather, colored leather, and leather with golden or silver studded holes. Police officers sometimes carry their weapons in leather holsters worn on their hips. We can find a whole range of leather belts with little pockets for our cell phones and wallets, to keep everything safe and together. Some of us may have embarrassing stories to tell of when we depended on a belt to keep our pants up but it didn't.

The belt zone is also the area of our core muscles, the area that keeps the upper torso upright and the lower back from hurting. If those muscles are damaged or malfunctioning, we experience all sorts of hip pains, back pains, and bad posture.

Whether we think of a belt as a fashion accessory that keeps our pants from falling or our core muscles as something that need exercise, our belt zone is an integral part of our functioning.

In the same way all wild animals and quadrupeds are integral to the functioning of the biosphere. The horses, camels, mules, and bulls all used to play a vital role in transport, farming, and travel. Wars have been fought on the backs of horses and elephants. Wild animals like wolves play an important part in the balance of nature as was discovered recently in Yellowstone National Park in the United States. When wolves were reintroduced, the entire ecosystem was gradually restored, affecting even the way the rivers flowed.

Today the function of many quadrupeds has been reduced to leisure rides and, unfortunately, as an item on the mealtime menu. Or they end up in zoos or as our pets. However, in their natural place the wild animals and quadrupeds bring balance to our society and natural world, because they are Kṛṣṇa's belt zone.

Meditation 34: Protection: The Lord's Lotus Feet

His lotus feet serve as protection from all kinds of fear (*Bhāgavatam* 2.6.7)

The mountain goat is a mind-boggling creature. It looks like the gangster from the animal world, idle and looking for trouble, but when it comes to climbing, it is the boss. Mountain goats can ascend near-vertical cliffs, looking like they walk on nothing but air. They are the poster child for sure-footedness.

Not only mountain goats but also humans depend on their feet for safety. Ladies who wear high heels for the first time know how it feels to wobble along on those heels – something as simple as walking suddenly becomes a full-brain task. And when children climb up a tree or the roof and are not able to come back down, they need to be caught, and the person doing the catching must have a firm stance. We often see small children clinging to a parent's leg when they are shy or scared. If we somehow lose mobility in our feet, like being on crutches, learning to walk again after an accident, or even just from cutting our toe – we lose some of our security, or safety.

His lotus feet
SERVE
AS
protection
FROM ALL
KINDS
OF
fear

On a much grander scale Kṛṣṇa's feet serve as protection from all fear. In many paintings of Kṛṣṇa holding up Govardhana Hill during Indra's attack, the residents of Vṛndāvana are standing safely at Kṛṣṇa's feet, without fear. Just as our feet give us stability and balance, Kṛṣṇa's feet are the source of dissipating fear. He is the ultimate stability and balance, and His feet never falter.

Meditation 35: Water and Rain: The Lord's Genitals

From the Lord's genitals originate water, semen, generatives, rains, and the procreators (*Bhāgavatam* 2.6.8)

Our experience on earth is that semen can produce offspring of the same species in a female of that species. But the Lord's semen can produce abundance and species of all kinds. It is the water of the rains, it can produce those who procreate the various forms of life, and it can produce all kinds of fertility in all species and all varieties within all species.

Kṛṣṇa says that He is the father of all living beings. So even though externally there are many fathers, the only ultimate father is the Lord. Therefore, the semen in all fathers of all species is the semen of Kṛṣṇa. Whenever we see pregnant creatures or creatures sitting on eggs, we can understand that the living being in the egg and womb is coming from the potency and virility of Kṛṣṇa. When the rains fall, it is the semen of the Lord coming to bring life, fertility, and abundance to us all.

Meditation 36: The Cause of Pleasure: The Lord's Genitals

His genitals are the cause of a pleasure that counteracts the distress of begetting (*Bhāgavatam* 2.6.8)

There is something intensely powerful about the pleasure generated by our genitals, so powerful that it makes us forget the consequences of our acts. This pleasure is Kṛṣṇa. In this material world, sex is the highest form of pleasure, the closest thing people will come to experiencing bliss, and by Kṛṣṇa's mercy He gives us the possibility to experience such bliss. He is that bliss Himself. The pleasure of the genitals is a momentary, tiny reflection of the full pleasure of spiritual life. That full pleasure is compared to an unlimited ocean, and sexual happiness to a drop of water in a desert.

Yet the world is captivated by genital pleasure and filled with images intended to excite us with sexual lust. The advertising industry functions on exactly this principle. Kṛṣṇa intends this pleasure to be a compensation for the difficulty of raising children. The Lord wants good population in the universe, and He wants parents to lovingly and responsibly care for those children. Of course, children do bring much joy, satisfaction, and love into one's life. The great moralist Cāṇakya said that a home without children is a void or desert. But no one will deny that being a parent is a difficult job requiring much self-sacrificing of resources, time, and energy. The intense pleasure of conceiving children counteracts the difficulty of bearing and raising them.

Sadly, in today's world people often try to take the pleasure without the responsibility. Such behavior is a kind of theft – like taking a salary without doing any work. In modern society many people indulge in irresponsible sex, even intentional one-nighters. And these affairs all have deep running psychological effects and financial implications. The girl and boy who just want to have some fun at a party end up with having to take care of a baby. The husband and wife who have severe financial constraints want to alleviate their stress for one night and end up with another child to feed in nine months. Expecting parents and new parents know the stress on the body and mind that comes with having a new-born baby, something that they did not think about while making that baby.

But those who actively seek Kṛṣṇa and cultivate a relationship with Him experience pleasure and bliss in all areas of life. Such certainly includes using the genitals in married life, and also in raising the resulting children in love for Him.

Meditation 37: Waters: The Lord's Semen

In His semen were all the waters (*Bhāgavatam* 8.20.25–29)

A swift stream flows through a forest and under a bridge. A lake has lilies and lotuses at its edges and boats crossing it. A mighty river flows in the middle of a great city. Waterfalls roar and tumble and surge off cliffs, churning the river below. And the great oceans and seas house a multitude of life. Water pours from our taps and comes up from our wells. All these waters are the semen of the Lord. According to Ayurveda, semen is the most concentrated part of the body's energy, designed to create new life. Therefore, waters of the earth are the essence of life in our bodies, our food, our air – everything. We are alive, nourished, cleansed, and functional – because of water. This water is Kṛṣṇa's potency and full of vitality.

Meditation 38: Death and Envy: The Lord's Rectum

The evacuating outlet of the universal form of the Lord is the abode of the controlling deity of death, Mitra, and the evacuating hole and the rectum of the Lord is the place of envy, misfortune, death, hell, etc. (*Bhāgavatam* 2.6.9)

Our regular releasing of solid waste, that foul-smelling embarrassing routine of earthly embodied beings, is yet a measure of our health and vitality. It is at once the rejecting of indigestible matter from our food and the means by which we keep ourselves free of toxins. While we may think of the holy and pure Lord as being far away from our toilet business, when we squat or sit and release our waste, we can remember that the Lord's universal form also has a means of dealing with what is unneeded and is an obstruction to happiness.

Death sits within the universal anus, releasing living beings from bodies that are no longer useful in the fulfilment of their desires and their karmic destinies. It may appear that some die "untimely" or before the general full span of time. But the universal anus is always healthy and therefore arranges for each being's bodily death at exactly the right time and place for that individual. And, as the excrement of all beings provides nutrients for the soil that facilitate new life, those who die take with them what they have learned as fertile ground for progress in the next life. Such can be our meditation as we witness our body letting go of its waste.

Furthermore, we learn that the demigod Mitra, meaning "friend," lives in the universal anus and rectum. Certainly good digestion and elimination is our friend, yet in the universal process of evacuation there is also envy, misfortune, and suffering. The feeling of wishing others ill due to our envy of them, or the sinking dread we feel when others envy us, resides in this part of the universal body. Envy is the opposite of love, and though it also exists within the ultimate reality, it is in the form of something putrid to be discarded. Just as one feels relief after evacuating, letting go of our own envy, or letting go of caring about others' envious actions, brings us lightness and freedom. Blocked up envy we hold on to is a kind of mental and spiritual constipation for which we need the laxative of appreciation and forgiveness.

Meditation 39: The Lord's Jaws and Teeth

His jaws of teeth are Yama, god of death, who punishes the sinners (*Bhāgavatam* 2.1.31)

When we are angry, we often clench our teeth. Our jaw tightens. And so does the Lord's. The Lord does not like to give punishment to those who are sinful, because He is naturally merciful and understands the ignorance and foolishness of sinful actions. Yet He also has to protect those who are being harmed by the sinful. So with great determination He clenches His jaw and teeth and awards those evil doers the natural reactions of their sins. When Arjuna sees the universal form, all the soldiers are rushing into the Lord's mouth and being crushed by His teeth.

Whenever we see or hear of some criminal getting punished, such punishment is the crunching of the jaws of the Lord. While we may clench our jaw in anger and frustration at some sin, the Lord's jaws destroy the sinful activities of rebellious living beings. Just as chewing transforms the bodies of plants into our own body through the digestive process, the Lord's jaws destroy sinful living entities and create a peaceful prosperous universal body for all the pious living beings.

Meditation 40: Affection: The Lord's Teeth

The art of affection is His set of teeth (*Bhāgavatam* 2.1.31)

There are three major divisions of smiling that Rūpa Gosvāmī discusses: *smita*, *hasita*, and *vihasita*. Smita is when the teeth are not visible, but there is a distinct change in the eyes and cheeks. Smiling in which the teeth are slightly visible is called *hasita*. When the teeth are distinctly visible in a smile, that is called *vihasita*. Throughout our day, we smile at others and they smile at us. Our smiles indicate some level of affection, truth, and connection, but Kṛṣṇa's visible teeth in smile is the pinnacle of love and joy.

In *Śrīmad-Bhāgavatam* 3.28.33, Kapila describes the Lord's teeth in this way:

> With devotion steeped in love and affection, the *yogī* should meditate within the core of his heart upon the laughter of Lord Viṣṇu. The laughter of Viṣṇu is so captivating that it can be easily meditated upon. When the Supreme Lord is laughing, one can see His small teeth, which resemble jasmine buds rendered rosy by the splendor of His lips. Once devoting his mind to this, the *yogī* should no longer desire to see anything else.

Meditation 41: Ignorance: The Lord's Back

The back of the Lord is the place for all kinds of frustration and ignorance,
as well as for immorality (*Bhāgavatam* 2.6.10)

Darkness and night bring with them an ominous mystery – a time when criminals prowl and plunder. Darkness brings with it fear and frustration – fear of the unseen possibility of danger and the inability to see what we are doing. Someone turning their back on us, or we turning our back on someone, also brings a kind of darkness – of absent communication and personal disconnection. When the disconnect is strong enough it may even turn evil. It seems contradictory that this disconnect of immorality, frustration, and ignorance would also be part of Kṛṣṇa, but it has to be because otherwise Kṛṣṇa wouldn't be the complete whole. We can see that ignorance, frustration, and immorality sprout from a place of neglect and disconnect to what we know we should do but aren't doing. And although we feel hopeless when such feelings of ignorance and frustration overwhelm us, we may find solace in the fact that Kṛṣṇa's universal body has a space for us even when we forget Him. So even in our darkness Kṛṣṇa is there.

Meditation 42: Rivers: The Lord's Veins

From His veins flow the great rivers and rivulets (*Bhāgavatam* 2.6.10)

The stream flows fast over rocks, tumbling and swirling. Sunlight filters through trees on the stream's banks to light up parts of the churning water, switching back and forth between light and shadow. The rapidly flowing water picks up soil to carry to the sea yet runs so fast that the water is darkly clear. Fish, insects, and frogs gain sustenance from the stream. As it slows closer to the sea, it begins to drop the soil it carried from the mountains, fertilizing the land. In the great universal body of the Lord, these streams are the veins – the channels of life-giving liquid that deliver nutrition and remove waste. The huge rivers of the world define countries' borders, encourage centers of human habitation, dictate the movements of animal herds, and transport goods from surplus to need. They are the main blood vessels of the Lord, messengers of His heartbeat of life itself.

Meditation 43: Mountains: The Lord's Bones

On His bones are stacked the great mountains (*Bhāgavatam* 2.6.10)

The human skeleton is the stuff of horror stories. Imagine any scary story without some kind of skeleton or corpse! On the other hand, without our skeleton we will just be blobs of flesh and fluid. The skeleton is the structure of our body. Without it we would have no stability, little form, and not be able to physically function in the world. On Kṛṣṇa's bones are stacked the mountains of the earth and ocean. The mountains are stable and majestic, their structure and form giv-

THE BACK
OF THE
LORD
IS THE PLACE
FOR ALL KINDS OF
FRUSTRATION
AND
IGNORANCE
ASWELL
AS
FOR
IMMORALITY

FROM His
veins
FLOW THE GREAT
rivers
AND
rivulets

AND ON HIS
bones
ARE STACKED THE
GREAT
mountains

ing shape to the earth. Their peaks influence rainfall and serve as storage for water in the form of snow. The mountains under the ocean give structure to the foundation on which the land rests and gives habitation for the creatures of the water. These mountains give form to Kṛṣṇa's universal body.

Meditation 44: The Lord's Arms

The Lord's arms are the productive fields for the great demigods and other leaders of the living entities who protect the general mass (*Bhāgavatam* 2.6.6)

The arms are one of the most active parts of our bodies in terms of regular use. We use them so often that if they get hurt, we become handicapped, unable to do most of our normal activities. If our brains are the executive center of our body, our arms are the executors. In the same way, Kṛṣṇa is the Supreme Chief Executive Officer, and the demigods are the executors. They are the ones who manage affairs in this material world according to Kṛṣṇa's order. They manage the seasons, rainfall, plant growth, and so forth.

The Pāṇḍavas, leaders of living entities, also used their arms to protect their citizens. Kṛṣṇa sometimes addressed Arjuna as "mighty-armed one". When the Pāṇḍavas were in exile and travelling through the forest, Bhīma picked them up and carried them on his body and arms so that they wouldn't have to walk all the way.

Kṛṣṇa vowed not to take up weapons, or "arms," during the Battle of Kurukṣetra; rather, He acted as Arjuna's charioteer. However, when Bhīṣma launched a fierce attack on Arjuna, Kṛṣṇa violated that promise by jumping off the chariot, picking up a broken chariot wheel, and rushing toward Bhīṣma, intent on killing him. Thus, He also used His arms to protect His devotee.

The demigods providing our necessities, leaders protecting us, or anyone using their arms for our benefit are resting on the Lord's arms. They embody Kṛṣṇa's attention and care.

Meditation 45: His Arms are the Demigods

His arms are the demigods headed by Indra (*Bhāgavatam* 8.20.25–29)

A broken arm or sprained finger is a painful reminder of how much we use our limbs. We lift, carry, and move things. We use our arms for balance, to cook, clean, play instruments, and much more. All our limbs are important, but our arms are like the executive leaders of the firm that is called our body. They are the doers.

In the same way the demigods are the arms of Kṛṣṇa's universal body. Lord Indra is the chief who controls the rain and clouds, without which we are in deep trouble. Agnideva controls fire. Varuṇa controls bodies of water. In this way, a particular demigod controls each sphere of this material world in some way. Kṛṣṇa is the owner of this material world, but His executors, the demigods, make sure it runs properly, as Kṛṣṇa wants.

However, sometimes it looks as if the universe is going haywire. There's a flood when it's supposed to be dry, and there are no rains when it's supposed to rain. One day it's blazing hot and the next day everybody is wearing warm jackets. We may ask, "What's happening? Does Kṛṣṇa also sporadically sprain His finger, or break His arm?" The answer is "No!"

Seeming irregularities in the demigods' management doesn't mean Kṛṣṇa's arms are damaged. We can be sure that Kṛṣṇa never breaks an arm, not in His two-handed form, His four-handed form, or His universal form. Yet it is a fact that, according to stories in the *Bhāgavatam*, demons sometimes take over the demigods' posts and cause havoc. In such instances, out of affection for the Lord the devotees serve Him by restoring order as if they were tending to His injured arms.

Each of us contributes to universal harmony when we live according to Kṛṣṇa's laws and engage in acts of sacrifice, such as the *saṅkīrtana-yajña*. At the same time, even when things look a bit out of order from our perspective, we can be sure that Kṛṣṇa is in control, and His arms, and all other limbs, are fully functional in terms of fulfilling perfect situations for the desires and karma of all living beings. We may not see how it all fits together because we are so small. At such times, when we are confused, we can take shelter in the arms of our beloved Lord and trust that He will guide us.

Meditation 46: His Arms are the Kṣatriyas

His arms are the kṣatriyas (*Bhāgavatam* 2.1.37)

We always associate the government and weapons with arms. In fact, we refer to weapons as *arms*. Therefore, it is not surprising that the "arm of the law" is associated with government. Arms, of course, also protect. They protect by using weapons, and they protect by hugging and sheltering. Ideally, the government is like a parent with a large family. In the same way as parents provide the necessities for their children and family, the government provides necessities for the citizens. Whenever the government is protecting its citizens either with weapons or with necessities, it acts as the arms of the Lord.

Meditation 47: Fire: The Lord's Mouth

His mouth is the blazing fire (*Bhāgavatam* 2.1.29)

During the battle of Kurukṣetra, Arjuna asks to see Kṛṣṇa's universal form and Kṛṣṇa obliges. Kṛṣṇa then changes His form into that of all-devouring time. Arjuna sees all the soldiers on the battlefield rushing into Kṛṣṇa's mouth, like moths rushing into a flame. They are mesmerized by the light, thinking they will find warmth, only to find death. At the same time, those soldiers found real light, as all those who died in Kṛṣṇa's presence attained their original forms after death.

Fire is one of nature's most destructive forces. An out-of-control forest fire fills onlookers with fear and wonder. It consumes everything in its path and leaves only ashes and ruins in its wake. People in general, and sometimes even firefighters, are powerless and can only look on, waiting for the fire to burn itself out. At the same time, fire is also one of the most useful elements, for warmth, cooking, and light.

Our mouths are in one sense also like this blazing fire. Sometimes our words can be like a blazing fire that brings death to people in various ways. A judge orders the death penalty and parents ground their errant children, killing all hopes of a free weekend. We can also speak fire through hurtful words, burning with them the trust in good relationships. Of course, words can be like fire in a beneficial way, burning ignorance and shining with understanding. Our words can burn away falsity and illusion, not through hurt but through truth spoken from the deepest compassion.

The words from Kṛṣṇa's mouth may sometimes seem harsh and destructive to materialistically minded people. But to His devotees, the Lord's speech warms their hearts and lights their path through the darkness of ignorance.

Meditation 48: Creation: The Lord's Glance

This great ocean of material creation is but the casting of His glance over us. (*Bhāgavatam* 2.1.31)

Perhaps we have looked at an empty cookie jar and wished that we could look some more cookies into existence. Or perhaps when we are driving long distance and the gas light flickers on, we look at it and try to will it to turn off. Whatever lack we have, be it cookies, milk, gas, or something else, just looking at the empty space won't make that item reappear. We are doomed to go into the kitchen and bake more cookies or quickly find the next gas station.

Kṛṣṇa, on the other hand, can look at an empty space and bring to life whatever He wants. This great ocean of material life of which we are tiny fragments is the creation of but one glance from Kṛṣṇa. Our bodies exist because Kṛṣṇa's glance has brought into being the material realm from which our bodies get their components. But Kṛṣṇa's glance is mostly for us, hoping that we may look across the material ocean and see Him, as He sees us.

Meditation 49: Modesty: The Lord's Upper Lips

Modesty is the upper portion of His lips (*Bhāgavatam* 2.1.32)

Often when we are shy, we press our lips together so that they look thinner, or we use our lower teeth to softly bite our upper lip. Kṛṣṇa is also modest. Although He's the creator and maintainer, He hides Himself so that we can imagine glorious nature to have arisen of her own accord. He doesn't sign His artwork in the dawn and dusk. We imagine that the intelligence, memory, and forgetfulness He gives us to be of our own doing. And, in His pastimes He often pushes His devotee forward to get the credit. While Kṛṣṇa sometimes modestly looks down and moves the upper portion of His lips, He is grateful when we acknowledge His craftsmanship, power, grace, and intelligence – both in this world and in His eternal pastimes.

Meditation 50: Hankering: The Lord's Chin

Hankering is His chin (*Bhāgavatam* 2.1.32)

The English idiom "sticking one's chin out" means to show determination in getting what we want, to stand fast in our opinion, or to do what is right. Those who want something intently – who hanker for it – often lead with their chin and have a "chin out" posture. Kṛṣṇa does not hanker for, or desire, in the sense to which we are accustomed as conditioned souls. Conditioned souls are in a constant underlying state of fear and lack. We hanker for relationships, things, and situations that we hope will fill the gaps in our lives and give us security, love, and peace. But Kṛṣṇa has the original hankering of which ours is but a reflection. His hankering is for playful exchanges with those who love Him and care for Him. His hankering is to please those who are dear to Him. And this hankering rests upon His chin.

Meditation 51: Dharma: The Lord's Heart

On the heart of Lord Murāri he saw religion (*Bhāgavatam* 8.20.25–29)

Dharma (or religion) means a code of what is good and right, what is aligned with the desire and will of the Lord, and what is in harmony with creation. The ultimate dharma is loving service to the Lord Himself. There are also many subordinate dharmas, including temporary dharmas relating to our material situation of body and mind. Dharma, in all its forms, is the Lord's heart. The heart is about the essence of a person's life and what is most precious. To live in alignment with the way the cosmos runs, and the purpose of creation, means to be in the heart of the Lord and to be dear to Him. When we choose the path of *śāstric* codes, when we choose to follow Kṛṣṇa's desires, we can feel that we are in His heart. The beating of our heart reminds us of how dharma is the essence, the identity, the defining characteristic of reality like the heart is to the Lord's universal body.

Meditation 52: On the Lord's Chest are Pleasing Words and Truthfulness

On the chest [he saw] pleasing words [*ṛtam*] and truthfulness [*satyam*] (*Bhāgavatam* 8.20.25–29)

Śrīmad-Bhāgavatam (3.28.25) states: "The *yogī* should concentrate his mind on the Lord's nipples, which resemble a pair of most exquisite emeralds." On this beautiful chest of the Lord's universal body are *ṛtam* and *satyam,* pleasing words and truthfulness. Just as we embrace our dearest ones to the upper part of our chest, the Lord cherishes these two parts of speech. One is speech that is true in the sense of seeing the spiritual reality everywhere and in everything, and the other is speech that is pleasing. This pleasure comes from a connection with *Brahman*, with the spiritual. Whenever we are aware of the spiritual equality of all beings and speak with that awareness of connection and equality, we are thus resting on the Lord's bosom. Similarly, when we present such spiritual realization and truth in poetic and pleasing ways that bring pleasure to our listeners, the Lord is holding us to the shining emerald jewels on His upper chest. Therefore, when we speak in these ways, we are respectfully and tenderly held in Kṛṣṇa's embrace.[5]

5 Information from the Eleventh Canto verse and commentary, courtesy of Hari Parshad Dāsa

ON HIS
chest
THE
Goddess
OF
fortune
WITH A
lotus flower
IN HER HAND

Meditation 53: On His Bosom Rests the Goddess of Fortune

On the bosom [he saw] the goddess of fortune, with a lotus flower in her hand (*Bhāgavatam* 8.20.25–29)

One's beloved wife should be embraced to one's chest. In other words, one should always protect one's wife with great love and affection. Such is done by the Lord Himself with His own wife, the goddess of fortune. In whatever incarnation or form of the Lord, His dear wife is always present in the *śrīvatsa* curl of hair on His chest. She is called the holder of the lotus, or sometimes by the name Kamala, meaning "lotus" itself. The holder of the original spiritual lotus – of which the lotuses we see are dim replicas – rests on the Lord's bosom. For some of us, lotus flowers may be part of our daily lives as part of our natural environment and thus spark our remembrance of the Lord's wife on His chest. For those of us who rarely, or never, encounter natural lotuses, our remembrance can be sparked when we see men's chests, whether bare at the beach or clothed in business suits. We then remember that on the Lord's bosom – unlimitedly more comforting and protecting than any man's – is the most beautiful, most auspicious, most loving, and kindest supreme goddess whose favor everyone is seeking. Additionally, whenever we see opulences of any kind, these opulences or forms of prosperity are in the jurisdiction of the goddess of fortune and are therefore resting on the bosom of the Lord.

Meditation 54: On the Lord's Chest are all the Clusters of Stars

On the Lord's bosom he saw all the clusters of stars (*Bhāgavatam* 8.20.24)

Śrīmatī Rādhārāṇī is the Ganges in which the elephant of My mind enjoys pastimes. She is the shining of the full autumn moon for the *cakora* birds of My eyes. She is the dazzling ornament, the bright and beautiful arrangement of stars, on the border of the sky of My chest. Now today I have gained Śrīmatī Rādhārāṇī because of the highly elevated state of My mind. (*Caitanya-caritāmṛta, Antya* 1.191)

Just as the goddess of fortune is on the chest of the Lord in the *śrīvatsa* curl of hair, her supreme form also resides there as an arrangement of stars. Sometimes it is also said that the Lord puts a pearl necklace on the chest of His beloved, and that necklace looks like a cluster of stars. Our night sky with its glittering jewel-like stars is the Lord's chest decorated with His beloved.

Meditation 55: Oceans: The Lord's Waist

The ocean is His waist (*Bhāgavatam* 2.1.32); on the Lord's waist he saw the seven oceans (*Bhāgavatam* 8.20.24)

The seven oceans are the link between large continents like a waist is between the chest and hips of a human body. Like a waist holds the upper and lower body together, the oceans unite the continents and keep the planet together as a whole. As an attractive waist is a key feature in a body's beauty, so the oceans mesmerize onlookers who find delight simply in gazing at the expansive, unfathomable depths.

One's waist is flexible, able to move in many ways. Similarly, the oceans' waters shift and bend in contrast to the land on its borders. Walking near the ocean, we see the swaying of the waves, crashing sometimes to our right and sometimes to our left, which seems like Kṛṣṇa's waist turning and twisting in a dance. The sometimes fast, sometimes slow wave movements are like a dance changing in beat and speed and rhythm according to the changes in music. Like a belly dancer ripples the abdomen, so the ripples and eddies in the ocean are the dance moves of the Lord.

Meditation 56: Passing Ages: The Lord's Movements

The passing ages are His movements (*Bhāgavatam* 2.1.33)

The lanes of our memory are as varied as the seasons wandering across our time on earth. Some lanes are filled with warm sunlit memories, some with cold and dreary empty spaces – places we do not often visit. But sometimes when we walk these lanes, they show us the passage of time. Looking back, we see the faint traces of our steps getting from there

ON THE LORD'S
BOSOM HE SAW
ALL THE
Clusters
of
stars

THE
Ocean
IS HIS
waist

to where we are now. Sometimes this awareness fills us with relief, sometimes with regret, sometimes with gratitude, and sometimes with bitterness. But the road continues, and we must go forward, as we have no choice.

Stacking enough time, minutes on minutes, leads us to decades, centuries, millennia. In the material world, this passage of time is an unbreakable law, so fixed that even death can't fight it. Yet we try to fight it with everything we have. Our consumer culture is based on remaining forever young, retaining youth while we still have it, regaining it when lost. Our science is geared toward making us infallible. We fight cancer, getting treatments to buy us "time." We get pacemakers to safeguard us from heart attacks. We have come to fear time because it brings death and separates us from what we are attached to, but however attached we are, time marches on its slow pace across the ages.

This "marching" of time and the passing of ages are Kṛṣṇa's movements. As the universal form, Kṛṣṇa says, "Time I am," and we measure time in the movements of the planets and stars in relation to one another. Such movements are Kṛṣṇa's movements – the movements of His universal body. Thus, we can feel that Kṛṣṇa is moving through our life as the passing of time. This movement of the Lord as the universe reminds us of the movements of little baby Dāmodara waddling like a baby elephant, Vrajarāja Kṛṣṇa dancing with the *gopīs*, and Gopāla racing with the cowherd boys. Such movements of the Lord can fill us with wonder and delight as time changes and adjusts everything. With His movements come great happiness and loss but also great experience and deep realization.

Meditation 57: The Cause of Material Creation

The supreme cause of material creation is His intelligence (*Bhāgavatam* 2.1.34)

Our intelligence is the birthing place of all that we materially produce. We have a vision, a goal, an inspiration, a plan. We look in our memory for similar things done in the past that may guide us. Using our intelligence, we then design, consult, navigate, and consider options. Compared to how we create, the Lord creates effortlessly. He sleeps and breathes out the universes. However, His intelligence is the supreme cause, evident throughout the created world.

We use intelligence to consider aesthetics and beauty in design, and when doing so we can recall the intelligently created beauty of the natural world in all its varieties. We can use our intelligence to design interrelated systems, remembering how the planets' movements and the karma and desires of all living beings in this universe are coordinated. His interweaving and creation are beyond our comprehension but not beyond our appreciation. With our intelligence we do our best to relate to a variety of people; Kṛṣṇa can relate to everyone perfectly in ways that totally satisfy both the person and Himself.

While there are many causes for our creations, the supreme cause is our intelligence. Similarly, although there are many intermediate causes for the overall creation, the supreme cause is the magnificent intelligence of Kṛṣṇa. Appreciating Kṛṣṇa's intelligence in this creation is perhaps one of the easiest ways to be conscious of him throughout our day, and further remembering Him when we use our intelligence in creation makes that meditation so much easier and sweeter.

Meditation 58: His Intelligence Contains Lord Brahmā, the Demigods and the Great Saintly Persons

In His intelligence were Lord Brahmā, the demigods and the great saintly persons (*Bhāgavatam* 8.20.25–29)

In human society there are intellectuals, advisors, and professors. There are religious persons and saintly persons. And the Vedas tell us that above this planet are even more qualified beings who guide the universe with a broad vision of the meaning and purpose of life. We read in the *Bhāgavatam* that Parīkṣit Mahārāja took shelter of Śukadeva Gosvāmī during the last seven days of his life. He inquired from Śukadeva Gosvāmī what a man is to do at the end of his life even though he himself was a highly intelligent person. We also read that Kṛṣṇa and Balarāma went to the school of Sāndīpani Muni although They Themselves possess supreme intelligence. We also often need guidance in our lives when we are unable to see what road to take in our lives. In those moments we take advice of people who have more experience than we and who are better able to see the whole picture. While Kṛṣṇa provides everyone's intelligence and is personally the intelligence of intelligent people, these people are also His intelligence. When we interact with saintly people on earth or when we get the protection and blessings of celestial beings, we are thus guided by the Lord's personal intelligence. By putting our trust in saints and celestials, we connect not just with their own wisdom and understanding but with the intelligence of the all-knowing and all-compassionate Lord.

Meditation 59: The Moon: The Lord's Mind

His mind is the moon, the reservoir of all changes (*Bhāgavatam* 2.1.34)

The moon has always been associated with the mind, including the idea that a full moon creates mental instability. Here the moon is identified as Kṛṣṇa's mind, exemplifying changes. We all know too well the changeability of our own mind and its tendency to wax enthusiastic over something today, and then wane over the same idea tomorrow, having considered other factors hitherto overlooked in our initial optimism. We also know very well the mind's tendency to "wander" or move in various ways to various subjects, both when we relax and when we are trying to focus our attention.

When our mind changes from the skeptical to the willing and back again, we can remember the moon's cycles and how, despite its appearance of growing and shrinking, it truly remains constant.

The Lord's mind is also always constant and fixed though He appears superficially to sometimes favor some persons and not others or to give and then withdraw His favor on the same person. Sometimes a bright moon lights our way in the darkness, and sometimes we are left on a moonless night to stumble and feel our way inadequately. Yet despite these appearances from our perspective, the moon is always there. The clarity or lack of it in our lives, the apparent blessings and difficulties, are all an appearance only. Similarly, Kṛṣṇa is always there, and we can always have His guidance if we but go beyond such appearances.

One aim of all types of yoga is a fixed and peaceful mind, and Kṛṣṇa's lotus feet are the ultimate resting place for the mind. One whose mind is fixed at the Lord's lotus feet automatically and easily gets detached from the modes of material nature and feels peace and relief. When we see the beauty and peacefulness of the moon, we can recall the ideal state of the mind. And when our mind rests in this ideal state through our yoga practice, we can remember the beauty of Kṛṣṇa's moon-like mind.

Meditation 60: Rudra: The Lord's Ego

Rudradeva is His ego (*Bhāgavatam* 2.1.35)

The Lord begins the manifestation of the material world with a glance. That glance is time itself, and is also the personality Śiva, or Rudra. Rudra, meaning anger, is another name for Śiva because Śiva destroys the universe, and such destruction is associated with anger. Also, Śiva is the lord of materialistic ego that is, as we know all too well, associated with anger. Our false materialistic ego is the mood of a controller, a lord, of this world. It is the sense of identity separate from Kṛṣṇa, separate from other living entities, and separate from the natural world. That ego gives us a conception of ourselves as perfect, powerful, and a worldly enjoyer. However, in this mood of separation from Kṛṣṇa, our false ego feels incomplete and therefore threatened. Full of fear and hankering, false ego naturally leads to anger.

In spiritual life, our false materialistic ego should gradually dissolve so that the real ego of being a loving servant of Kṛṣṇa emerges. While we are in that process, the false ego will still raise its ugly head in anger from time to time. And we may find ourselves in the presence of others' egotistical anger or destructive force, as well. At such times we can remember that the Lord's form of ego is Rudra himself. Yet Rudra, through anger, has a benevolent function in the universe. His role of destruction leads to another creation – death is the basis of life. Crumbled ruins of buildings become the soil of new civilizations, new life, and new opportunities for souls to fulfil their desires. Therefore, the essence of the false ego's existence comes from Kṛṣṇa's loving kindness in giving us the freedom to be a fool and discover the truth the hard way, if we so desire it.

HIS
mind
IS THE
moon
THE
reservoir
OF ALL
changes

Meditation 61: Birds: The Lord's Artistic Sense

Varieties of birds are indications of His masterful artistic sense (*Bhāgavatam* 2.1.36)

Peacocks, hummingbirds, cockatoos, flamingos, cardinals . . . so many of the birds on this planet exemplify artistry. Their feathers, often iridescent and shimmering, dress them in countless colors, hues, and tints. Their forms are often graceful, and their movements in flight can equal or surpass the greatest dancers. Only a master of artistic sense could design the way colors and patterns form on birds both at rest and in flight, creating a functional form for flying that is also decorative. Human mastery of aesthetics in functional design, such as landscaping, furniture, and clothing, pale before the birds made by the eye and hand of God. The colors and dancing of the birds themselves spark our sense of wonder at the talent that created them.

Birds can be indicative of artistry not only in their form and movement, of course, but also in their song. Some birds mimic human speech. Some can mimic any sound, some sound like that of laughter or crying, and some like the sweetest singer. Birds are, thus, a festival of color, movement, grace, form, and music. When we hear them, how can we not remember the master artist? Kṛṣṇa Himself is a musician, a dancer, and dresses expertly in many colors of cloth, glittering and shining. He sometimes dances like a peacock, and rides on an eagle through space. How easy it is for any bird to spark affectionate remembrance of Him!

Meditation 62: Humanity: The Lord's Residence

Humanity is His residence (*Bhāgavatam* 2.1.36)

In a very real sense, God is everywhere and lives everywhere. Yet where there are human beings, God is especially found. At least on this planet, only humans have systems of religion and spiritual practice. Those in lower species have little or no awareness of higher concepts and considerations. In the *Bhagavad-Gītā* (3.15), Kṛṣṇa says that the all-pervading transcendence always resides in acts of *yajña*, meaning ceremonies given in śāstra to connect with Him. If we want to find God's home, we will find it when we humans behave at the height of our humanity and regularly observe times of ceremony and celebration for communing with the Lord. To behave humanely, to really show our humanity, is to "build a subtle structure" where the Lord feels comfortable and at repose. There, in our spiritual ceremonies and in our acting according to our higher nature, Kṛṣṇa is present not only in a general way but also in a personal way, as He feels at home.

Meditation 63: The Lord's Musical Rhythm

The celestial species of human beings, like the Gandharvas, Vidyādharas, Cāraṇas
and angels, all represent His musical rhythm (*Bhāgavatam* 2.1.36)

In almost all cultures of the world, angels are depicted as singing and often playing instruments, such as harps and trumpets. The Vedic scripture describes all varieties of celestial beings who engage in singing, playing musical instruments, and dancing. Most of us probably are not aware of interacting with these beings in our daily lives, so it may seem difficult to use their existence as an impetus to remember Kṛṣṇa. However, we certainly have such interactions with these beings in art, poetry, and scripture. Additionally, sometimes human beings on this planet are so expert in playing instruments, singing, and dancing that they may appear to be from the celestial realms. Certainly, all such beings give us a little indication of Kṛṣṇa's musical rhythm and capability. It is said that when Kṛṣṇa, the master of all fine arts such as dancing, was dancing on the thousand hoods of the serpent in the Yamunā River, the celestial musicians were not able to keep up with the rhythm of His dancing and, in fact, found His rhythms bewildering.

VARIETIES OF BIRDS
ARE INDICATIONS
OF
His
masterful
artistic
sense

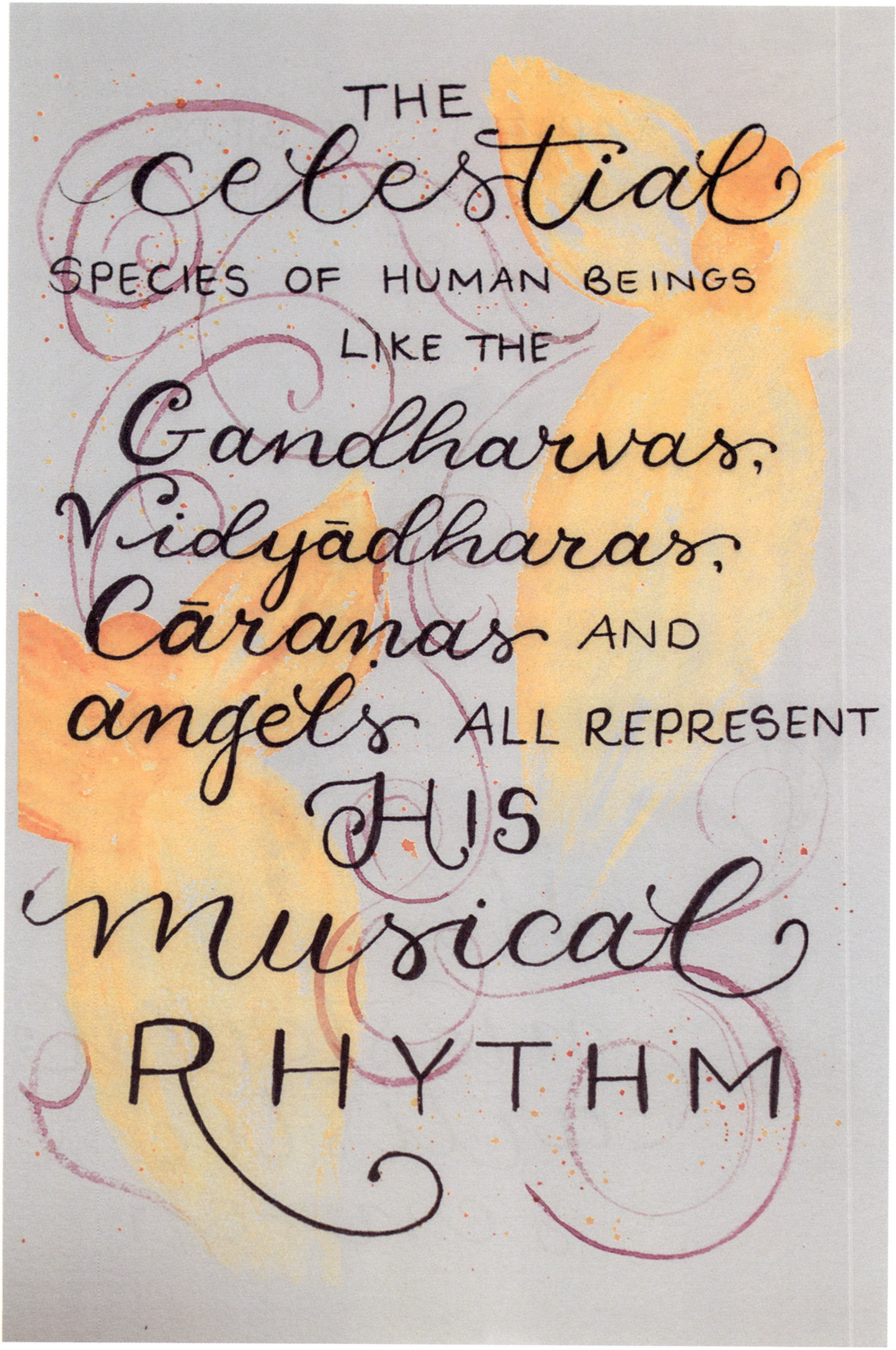
THE
celestial
SPECIES OF HUMAN BEINGS
LIKE THE
Gandharvas,
Vidyādharas,
Cāranas AND
angels ALL REPRESENT
HIS
musical
RHYTHM

Meditation 64: Demoniac Soldiers: The Lord's Prowess

The demoniac soldiers are representations of His wonderful prowess (*Bhāgavatam* 2.1.36)

Stories of soldiers and police are popular throughout the world. People love to read of fights between good and evil in which amazing strength and ability conquer threats to peace and kindness. We might expect that these righteous rulers and fighters are part of the Lord's body, and indeed they are the Lord's arms, but the soldiers on the side of evil are also part of Kṛṣṇa's universal body.

Although the motives and objectives of demoniac soldiers – and sometimes their methods of fighting – are selfish and cruel, such persons often greatly value their physical strength and martial expertise, honing their craft. In fact, the demoniac soldiers often spend more energy and focus on their abilities and warcraft than do the righteous. Those who are evil believe in the power of power itself for victory whereas the virtuous rely as much or more on the power of dharma.

However, power alone is not sufficient for victory because Kṛṣṇa has set up the world to favor the mode of goodness. The righteous need to violate dharma in order to lose. Yet what the demoniac value: prowess, strength, virility, potency, and vitality, are the various aspects of one of Kṛṣṇa's six opulences – *vīrya*. As such, the demoniac soldiers represent Kṛṣṇa's *vīrya* itself. In Kṛṣṇa, however, such *vīrya* exists in an unlimited perfect form as part of unlimited wisdom and unlimited *yaśas* – the fame that comes from following dharma. So, while the demoniac rely on *vīrya* alone, Kṛṣṇa's *vīrya* is connected to dharma and is therefore perfect and complete.

Kṛṣṇa often appears in the material world as a *kṣatriya*, a member of government and a warrior. As a warrior, He is a gallant and an exceptional fighter who cuts down the wicked effortlessly and playfully. Even as a cowherd boy, He expertly defeats demoniac wizards who assume various gigantic and frightening forms to threaten His devotees. The strength of the cruel, therefore, represents one aspect of Kṛṣṇa – an aspect that, as part of His whole glorious character and personality, is splendid and perfect.

Meditation 65: *Vaiśyas*: The Lord's Thighs

His thighs are the *vaiśyas* (*Bhāgavatam* 2.1.37)

Thighs move the body and hold it up, and thus we may see Kṛṣṇa in those who manage the natural resources of this world as their occupation. The people who work with animals, land, water, and air to produce society's wealth in terms of food, clothing, medicine, and materials for building, furniture, and jewelry – or whatever we need – are the mighty thighs of the universal form. They are the only ones who truly generate all the resources of society. Others transform these elements or move them around. The *vaiśyas* who work in this field of resources – the farmer, trader, businessperson, banker, entrepreneur, and so forth – give power, strength, health, and vitality to society, just as our thighs give us foundational power.

Meditation 66: Śūdras: The Shelter of the Lord's Feet

The *śūdras* are under the protection of His feet (*Bhāgavatam* 2.1.37)

Those who provide all of society's beauty and functionality are the foundation of the social order and are thus sheltered by the Lord's feet. All jobs and careers in this area allow for health, cleanliness, record-keeping, assistance, arts, music, dancing, and athletics. Without the workers in these areas, there would be no pleasures in life, and life would come to a standstill. Just as our feet enable us to go from place to place, hopefully with grace, so those who work in these professions bring aesthetic pleasure, health, and the smooth flow of needed services. Thus, those in these jobs rest on the universal feet of the Lord.

Meditation 67: Evening: Under the Lord's Garments

Bali Mahārāja saw beneath the garments of the Lord, who acts wonderfully, the evening twilight (*Bhāgavatam* 8.20.24)

As day turns into night and we conclude our activities in this cycle of time, we chant the *gāyatrī mantra* reflecting on the sun. We remember the activities we did during the day by the grace of Kṛṣṇa, who is our ability, intelligence, and memory. The evening twilight is soft and soothing, gently and slowly moving from light into darkness. Gradually everything becomes hidden. The sun is there beneath the twilight, but we can't see it. Just as the body of an ordinary person is hidden underneath garments, the Lord's beautiful, shining and attractive form is hidden under His garments, glowing like the sun.

The Lord here is called Urukrama, meaning someone who performs glorious or amazing actions. The evening twilight is generally gorgeous beyond the skill of any ordinary artist. Our rotating planet in relation to the sun, giving us day and night, is a wonderful phenomenon beyond human comprehension. This amazing cosmic dance of evening twilight is the swirling of the Lord's clothes, wonderfully hiding His glories.

Meditation 68: Sky: The Lord's Navel

In the Lord's navel he saw the sky (*Bhāgavatam* 8.20.24)

The whole creation comes from the Lord's navel. From His navel sprouts a lotus flower. Within the lotus stem are all the planets and the great sky. In Vṛndāvana, Lord Brahmā told Kṛṣṇa that the whole universe is within the Lord's belly.

Looking up at the expansive sky, we can feel ourselves within Kṛṣṇa's navel. Kṛṣṇa's navel is the symbol of His connection to us and nourishment of us. We are within His abdomen, like a child in the mother's womb. We are sheltered, nourished, and cherished. As the supreme mother, Kṛṣṇa holds the vast expanse of space within a tiny portion of His navel. Our navel indicates our previous connection to the womb, to our mother's body, and reminds us of our debt to her and our bodily origin. This origin exists in the space in Kṛṣṇa's navel – without space there is no definition of anything, no understanding of anything, no movement, and no cause and effect. The sky, or space, is the essential background of all subtle and gross matter. And that sky is situated as we would expect, where Kṛṣṇa originates everything.

Meditation 69: Upper Planets: The Lord's Head

The upper planetary systems [are] from the chest to the head of the Supreme Personality (*Bhāgavatam* 2.5.42)

The nature of the residents of the uppermost planets in the universe are places we can only imagine when looking at the night sky. We learn from śāstra that in such places reside great sages and saintly beings who direct the celestial beings who then manage the universe – and through them, us – by their wisdom. Such beings are experts in yoga, scripture, and meditation. They serve in a similar way as our eyes, ears, nose, and mouth serve our own body. They observe the state of the universe and then guide it accordingly, like the head and brain does for our bodies.

Even in this world, wise and pious people direct us individually and collectively by their careful observation and thought. How much more so do these great beings in the upper reaches of the universe sustain universal wisdom and truly act as God's head.

Meditation 70: Vidhi: The Lord's Eyebrows

On His eyebrows were the regulative principles (*Bhāgavatam* 8.20.25–29)

Our eyebrows are very expressive. Research indicates that the facial feature we notice in other people the most are their eyebrows. Moving our eyebrows can easily indicate our pleasure or displeasure, even without any further facial expression, body language, or words. And on the Lord's eyebrows rest the regulative principles. The regulative principles, the

In the Lord's
NAVEL
he saw the
sky

ON HIS
forehead
WAS
ANGER

vidhi, means the rules that govern which actions of the mind and body are favorable, and which are unfavorable. There are *vidhis* that direct how to live a life of piety to attain good karma, and there are *vidhis* for each of the yoga systems to attain transcendence. In bhakti-yoga, there are *vidhis* to enable us to awaken our dormant love for Kṛṣṇa. When we follow these *vidhis*, Kṛṣṇa's eyebrows express approval, and when we neglect them, His eyebrows express concern, or even a rebuke. Just as the eyebrows of people in this world show their opinions and emotions, Kṛṣṇa's eyebrows ultimately communicate our best path for spiritual realization.

Meditation 71: Anger: The Lord's Forehead

On His forehead was anger (*Bhāgavatam* 8.20.25–29)

Anger fills us, seemingly suddenly. An insult, an unexpected turn of events, a failure, an injustice – whatever the trigger, anger readies us for self-preservation. Whether in its mildest form of irritation or its most extreme form of blazing rage, anger narrows our focus and intelligence.

A frown is not just a facial expression shown by the mouth but can also be expressed with a wrinkling of the forehead. A powerful person's simple contraction of muscles in the forehead can instill fear in subordinates. There is nothing that spells anger or dissatisfaction like such a frown. It is so universal that even small babies can do it, and it is so much associated with anger that when we contract our forehead in that way, even when we are not angry, we may have people ask us if we are.

Anger sits on Kṛṣṇa's forehead in the universe. The mood of anger tensing our muscles, changing our bodily chemicals, and robbing our memory and intelligence places us in a furrow of the Lord's forehead. As in a valley one cannot see beyond the surrounding mountains, so in anger we fail to see the greater picture. Although in our anger we are on the Lord's form and in His form, we are stuck in a fold and wrinkle and so lose perspective of where we are and how close we are to our beloved.

For Kṛṣṇa, anger is a divine *rasa* of love, not something that bewilders Him. For Him, there is truly such a thing as righteous anger that has the same beneficial and wonderful effect on Himself and others as His tenderness. His forehead on which anger sits is also a half-moon, soothing and cooling in its softness and caring, unlike the heat of bewildering anger. When anger floods us and we sense that we are thus connected with the Lord's forehead, we can be reminded that all is well. We are part of Him, in His shelter, and cared for. In this connection, we can find the original anger of which our mundane anger is a twisted and distorted reflection. We can feel that Kṛṣṇa's divine energy of love-filled anger is simply another form of pleasure for Him and for awakened souls.

Meditation 72: Death: The Lord's Shadow

On His shadow was death (*Bhāgavatam* 8.20.25–29)

It is scary to go into a dark alley alone or into a dark, lonesome underground parking lot where every shadow makes us believe there's danger. On a sunny day, however, if we sight a bird of prey soaring on the wind currents, we may find it awe-inspiring or at least we look twice. But for the little mouse in the grass, that bird's shadow is most probably the last thing he will see. It's not surprising that death exists in Kṛṣṇa's shadow.

How can Kṛṣṇa have a shadow? He is the source of all illumination. The sun is a tiny fraction of His bodily rays. When we turn our backs to Kṛṣṇa, it is we who are in shadow. That turning away becomes like death to us. We forget our spiritual identity and our eternal life. From Kṛṣṇa's perspective, the material energy is simply another one of His energies. Like a child plays with His shadow without fear, for Kṛṣṇa there is no death and illusion in His own shadow.

On His
Shadow
WAS
DEATH

Meditation 73: Illusion: The Lord's Smile

In His smile was the illusory energy (*Bhāgavatam* 8.20.25–29)

Smiles can create illusion. Many people are dazzled into foolishness by a beautiful smile promising romantic love. Our hearts can pump at turbo speed at the sight of the smile of someone we believe loves us, a smile that inspires us to achieve seemingly great things. But often the charming smile and the actions it inspires comes with less than charming consequences. And then we think, "What happened? I'm not that foolish, am I?" So, what did happen? We were the victims of a perverted reflection of Kṛṣṇa's smile.

There is illusion in the smiles between parents and children, also. In the smile of babies, cuteness trumps naughtiness. Think of all the times we see small children do something naughty. Often, they are forgiven for their transgressions because of their adorable smiles. Likewise, a parent's smile can make a young child forget all fear or believe there is nothing to fear. The smile of a salesperson can charm a customer into parting with a large sum of money unnecessarily. A politician's smile can bewilder voters. A spy's smile confuses the enemy.

Some sorts of illusion are wonderful, however. *Mahā-māyā* puts the fallen souls under the spell of illusion so that they can forget Kṛṣṇa. But, in the spiritual world *yoga-māyā* makes the devotees forget that Kṛṣṇa is the Supreme Personality so that they can serve Him more intimately. For example, Mother Yaśodā is dazzled by Kṛṣṇa's smile, even if He just broke a pot of yogurt which she has been churning for hours. Śrīmatī Rādhārāṇī's temper is subdued by Kṛṣṇa's sweet smile. The cowherd boys joke and wrestle and laugh with Kṛṣṇa all day, and Kṛṣṇa smiles and admits defeat.

These pastimes would not be able to take place if the residents of Vṛndāvana constantly remembered that Kṛṣṇa is the Supreme Person. So, He smiles at them and they forget. We may pray to Him that we may fall in love with His smile and thus be under a transcendental illusion of love that counteracts the material illusion from which we suffer right now.

Meditation 74: The Lord's Entire Body

Throughout His entire body and senses were all living entities, moving and stationary (*Bhāgavatam* 8.20.25–29)

The whole universe is the body of the Lord. Each planet, and every living entity on every planet, are within that body. In one sense, we are like a living cell within the universal body with roles to play for the functioning health of the universe. We are thus very much part of the Lord in a literal sense, even materially speaking. Our awareness of being a part of Him, of being in His body and part of His body, gives everything we do meaning and purpose. We are meant to contribute to His happiness and His purpose for creation.

Finding Kṛṣṇa's Qualities in the World

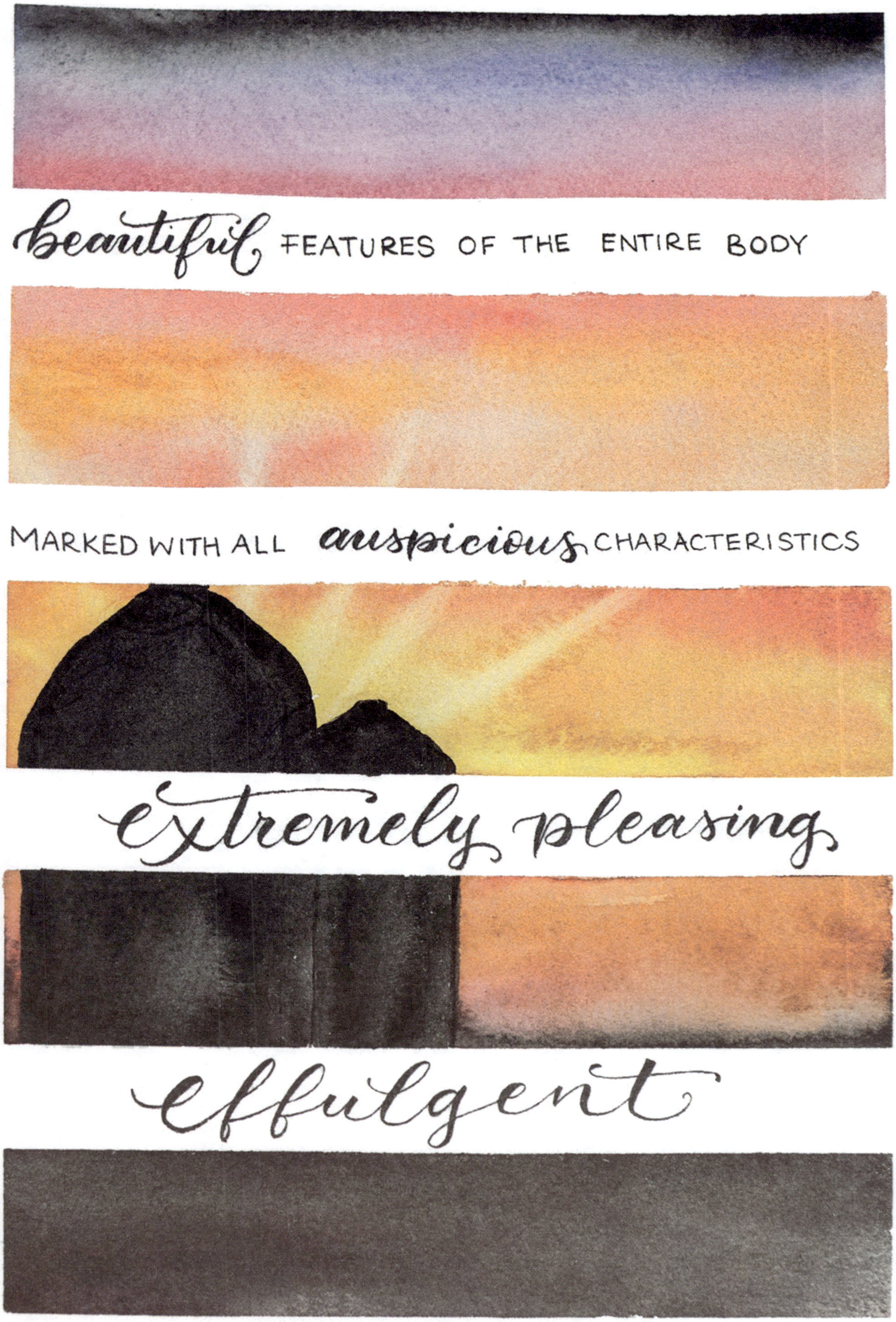
beautiful FEATURES OF THE ENTIRE BODY
MARKED WITH ALL auspicious CHARACTERISTICS
extremely pleasing
effulgent

Finding Kṛṣṇa's Qualities in the World

Unlike the other sections that start with what we perceive in the world and find Kṛṣṇa there, this section starts with the qualities of the person Kṛṣṇa and how we can find evidence of them in His creation. Rūpa Gosvāmī's descriptions of Kṛṣṇa's qualities in *The Nectar of Devotion* (Śrīla Prabhupāda's summary of Rūpa Gosvāmī's *Bhakti-rasāmṛta-sindhu*), Chapters 21 and 22, include being magnanimous, artistic, creative, and all-intelligent. He is truth and, therefore, truthful. Here we reflect on how we can see Kṛṣṇa's qualities in the world and the people around us.

Śrīla Prabhupāda says:

> Kṛṣṇa has created this nice world. Everything is very nice. The sun is rising just in exact time. It is setting in the exact time. The moon is rising. The seasons are changing. And we are getting nice food, nice fruit, nice flowers. So we are not so de . . . I mean to say, depressing agent. We won't discourage Kṛṣṇa. Why? Kṛṣṇa has created this nice world. How can I say it is *mithyā*? It is the by-product of Kṛṣṇa's energy. So Kṛṣṇa's energy cannot be false. It is eternal. Kṛṣṇa is eternal. Kṛṣṇa says in the Bhagavad-*Gītā* that this material world, *bhūmir āpo analo vāyuḥ khaṁ buddhir mana eva ca, bhinnā me prakṛtir aṣṭadhā* [Bg. 7.4]. 'These are eight kinds of separated energy of Me, Kṛṣṇa.' So Kṛṣṇa's energy . . . Kṛṣṇa is truth.
>
> (Lecture on *The Nectar of Devotion*, Vṛndāvana. October 17, 1972)

Meditation 1: Kṛṣṇa Has Beautiful Features of the Entire Body

The universe is also the body of the Lord, and all its features are full of beauty. The sky with its shifting colors is His navel; the oceans are His abdomen; the mountains with grasses, trees, and boulders are His bones; the glittering sun and the moon are His eyes; trees, herbs, and plants of all varieties and colors are His bodily hairs; and the sparkling and swirling rivers and streams are His veins.

Anything beautiful, wondrous, and glorious in this world is some reminder of the Lord's beautiful form. Golden flowers waving in the wind remind us of the golden hair on the Lord's chest, which is the form of the goddess of fortune. Ocean waves are like the beautiful three lines on the Lord's belly that disappear on His left side when He raises His hand to hold Govardhana Hill. Grayish rain-filled clouds make us think of Kṛṣṇa's complexion, lotus petals remind us of His eyes, red flowers and fruit help us visualize His reddish lips and the soles of His feet, peacocks take our minds to the feather on His crown, a lion's gait wraps our minds around His handsome waist, and the soothing light of the moon helps us contemplate His toenails. Nature is indeed bountiful, not just with its life-sustaining resources but with the exquisite variety of stimuli to fix our minds on the ever-youthful, flute-playing son of Nanda Mahārāja!

Meditation 2: Kṛṣṇa Is Marked with All Auspicious Characteristics

There are thirty-two auspicious symptoms on Kṛṣṇa's body as described in *The Nectar of Devotion*. Among them, Kṛṣṇa has a reddish luster in seven places on His body: His eyes, the ends of His hands, the ends of His legs, His lips, His palate, His tongue, and His nails. As the sun is Kṛṣṇa's eye, His auspicious reddish tint is visible in many a sunrise and sunset.

The universal body is full of auspiciousness. Every part of it is all good and all merciful. Even the seemingly difficult or painful experiences in life – when we accept them in a positive way – are ultimately auspicious, for they can bring us to our eternal life of bliss and knowledge. Seeing the good intentions of Kṛṣṇa behind everything fills us with peace, and perhaps paradoxically, with curiosity and anticipation to find out how the apparently bad things in life are truly all auspicious.

Meditation 3: Kṛṣṇa Is Extremely Pleasing

Kṛṣṇa's bodily features are called *rucira* because they are extremely pleasing. It is the "wow" factor of Kṛṣṇa's features. So many aspects of nature have forms we would call pleasing. As Brahmā addresses Kṛṣṇa, "This temporary existence of the material world appears to be pleasing and dear on account of its having evolved from Your body." (*Kṛṣṇa Book* 14: Prayers Offered by Lord Brahmā to Lord Kṛṣṇa). Therefore, whatever we find pleasing is due to the same quality present in the Lord. Whether it's someone's show-stopping eyes, dazzling smile, luscious hair, high cheekbones, or beautiful hands and feet, these features give us pleasure due to Kṛṣṇa's pleasing form being the source of all forms.

Similarly, whenever we find anyone's personality and company to be pleasing, that pleasure comes from Kṛṣṇa.

> Our husbands, friends, family members and children are all dear and pleasing to us only because of Your presence, for You are the Supersoul of all living creatures. Without Your presence, one is worthless. When You leave the body, the body immediately dies, and according to the injunction of the *śāstras*, a dead body must immediately be thrown into a river or burned. Therefore, ultimately You are the dearmost personality in this world.
>
> (*Kṛṣṇa Book,* Chapter 29: *The Rasa Dance: Introduction*)

Meditation 4: Kṛṣṇa Is Effulgent

The jewels on the chest of the Lord are so effulgent that they can make the sun look dim, but the same jewels look like one star in the sky when compared to the bodily effulgence of Kṛṣṇa. Yet His personal form is dark blue, like a raincloud. He is thus a seeming contradiction of being both a dark and a dazzlingly effulgent person.

Although the universe itself does not appear effulgent the Lord's universal form is full of brightness (*Bhagavad-Gītā* 11.17). Additionally, the sun, moon, and stars that light up the universal darkness indicate the brightness of the Lord (*Bhagavad-Gītā* 15.12). All effulgence comes from Kṛṣṇa – even the light of the screen on our phones or computers (*Bhagavad-Gītā* 13.18). The bright eyes of those in love or persons who seem to "light up a room" when they enter are a mere glimmer of Kṛṣṇa's brightness.

Meditation 5: Kṛṣṇa Is Strong

Kṛṣṇa's strength is often associated with His lifting of Govardhana Hill with His left hand or killing great demons. When the Lord exhibited many of these extraordinary acts of strength, He was apparently only a child or youth by human understanding. Each planet, indeed each universe, rests on the head of the Lord with as much significance to Him as a mustard seed would be on our head.

The world is filled with strength flowing from the infinite strength of the Lord. There is much power in all the elements – earthquakes, hurricanes and tornadoes, floods and tsunamis, wildfires, and various natural disasters. However, nature does not only show the Lord's strength through destruction but also through stability and protection. The earth does not only quake but also provides a solid strong base on which to build our houses. Strong winds roar powerful wind turbines into action, and roaring rivers convert the strength of water into electricity necessary for our everyday life. All the strength on this small planet is just the smallest indication of the unlimited strength of the Lord.

Meditation 6: Kṛṣṇa Is Ever Youthful

As the all-attractive Person, Kṛṣṇa is beautiful at all ages, but during His youth He is supremely beautiful since all His transcendental qualities have blossomed fully. At this youthful stage He is engaged in the most ecstatic pastimes with His devotees.

In *Bhagavad-Gītā* (10.35) Kṛṣṇa says that of the seasons He is the flower-bearing spring. Of the four seasons, spring is the ever-exuberant youth of the world, like Kṛṣṇa. Blossoms are the whispers of new, young life even after the most severe winter. Whether in nature, or displayed in the supermarket, or in flower stall on the street corner, we can see these tiny treasures of flowers, the little jewels of Kṛṣṇa's ever youthful quality.

STRONG
ever youthful
WONDERFUL LINGUIST
truthful

Youthfulness in anyone – human or animal – is attractive for its exuberance, innocence, idealism, hope, sensory strength and energy, and feeling of invulnerability. The way in which youthfulness draws our attention indicates how attractive is the Lord's eternal sweet youth.

Meditation 7: Kṛṣṇa Is a Wonderful Linguist

A wonderful linguist is able to speak many languages or use the subtleties of a language. In the scriptures we often find Kṛṣṇa's statements that have double, triple, or quadruple meanings. He is a master of language. He often speaks in layers of meaning, so that the more our consciousness advances, the more deep and intricate meanings we get. The expert poets and wordsmiths of this world give us the tiniest window into the expert abilities of the Lord. The pleasure we find in knowing languages, whether our own or of others, gives us the smallest hint of the pleasure Kṛṣṇa finds in His linguistic abilities. Furthermore, He can have separate conversations with everyone at one time, without mixing up what is being said to whom. We are bound to hear a variety of earthly languages at airports, train stations, or other places that draw an international crowd. How wonderful it is that Kṛṣṇa can speak all these languages and even the languages of the animals!

Meditation 8: Kṛṣṇa Is Truthful

One who keeps promises is truthful. Kṛṣṇa never breaks His word. He promised Queen Kunti that He would bring back her five sons from the Battle of Kurukṣetra and He did. Even when Kṛṣṇa, Arjuna, and Bhīma went to Jarāsandha disguised as *brāhmaṇas,* Kṛṣṇa told Jarāsandha who they were and that they wanted to fight with him. People who keep their word in their dealings reflect this quality from Kṛṣṇa, the most truthful person. The satisfaction we feel when we follow through with our own word and the happiness we feel when others keep their promise to us is a small indication of the happiness that comes from Absolute Truthfulness.

Meditation 9: Kṛṣṇa Talks Pleasingly

What is said can be completely lost to the listener because of *how* it is said. There is nothing as agonizingly sleep-inducing as a speaker who speaks in a monotonous voice, even when the message is important. Our eyelids fill up with lead and our neck vertebrae turn to jelly. Try as we might, we can't stay awake. In our relationships also we sometimes have difficulty accepting the point of view of our partner or friend because of how they convey it. When someone talks harshly, it immediately sends up the defensive walls of the other person. The best would be to convey a view in such a way that enables people to accept it. If a message is conveyed with a pleasant tone of voice, people are more likely to pay attention and accept what is said. Talented speakers who can convey their message tactfully and effectively are channels of Kṛṣṇa's quality of talking pleasingly. Kṛṣṇa is the expert of the *what* as well as the *how*; He could send even His enemies away with a smile.

Meditation 10: Kṛṣṇa Is Fluent

The *Nectar of Devotion* (Chapter 21) describes a fluent person as one whose speech is meaningful and polite. Although Kṛṣṇa asked His father, Nanda Mahārāja, to stop the worship of Indra and instead worship Govardhana Hill, He spoke with such politeness and gentleness that all those who heard Him felt like He was pouring nectar into their ears. As we teach our children – or even as we ourselves practice daily – to speak politely, gently, and in ways that take into consideration the feelings of others, we may remember how Kṛṣṇa's speech is always laden with both meaning and consideration of others' feelings.

Of course, our meaning and politeness is not only in our words but also in our intentions, motives, and desires. Even if others don't understand our intentions, Kṛṣṇa does. Indeed, He knows us better than we know ourselves and hears subtle nuances of our thoughts and spoken words that even we miss. Let us be aware that He is listening carefully to all we say and think. When both our words and intentions are valuable, beneficial, and caring, we are in sync with Kṛṣṇa's transcendent quality of fluency.

TALKS PLEASINGLY

fluent

HIGHLY *learned*

HIGHLY *intelligent*

a genius

ARTISTIC

extremely clever

EXPERT

Meditation 11: Kṛṣṇa Is Highly Learned

Being educated and having sound morals constitute learnedness. Being learned is therefore not just about what we know but also how we align our actions with moral principles. We work hard to learn new things, be it information from the scriptures, new skills, or languages and, hopefully, we try to use our learning in ways that benefit ourselves and others in fairness. Whatever we try to learn, Kṛṣṇa already knows without limit. When we contemplate, even slightly, that Kṛṣṇa knows everything and applies all His knowledge in a way that is always kind and fair, our sense of security and peace is very deep.

Sometimes in our daily lives we see clear evidence of Kṛṣṇa's unlimited knowledge applied in a moral and fair way. Yet, at other times we may feel confused as it seems that life is chaotic and immoral, when people sometimes use their knowledge to exploit others. But as we tiny beings try our best to be both knowledgeable and good, we can have deep faith that our source is unlimitedly both.

Meditation 12: Kṛṣṇa Is Highly Intelligent

Intelligence constitutes having a sharp memory and fine discretion. Whenever we are trying to memorize verses from the scripture or learning a new service or skill, we are likely not the done-and-dusted kind of learners. We have to consult the manual a few times or ask for help. Kṛṣṇa doesn't have to do that. His memory is infallible; as a student in Sāndīpani Muni's school, He would completely master a particular subject by only once being instructed in it.

When we have to apply our discretion in a situation, especially when we need to balance two or more important – and apparently contradictory – concerns, our discretion comes from Kṛṣṇa's intelligence.

Kṛṣṇa's memory and discretion can be noted in our own memory and intelligence even though we only possess them to a limited degree. His intelligence is also evident when He fulfils our desires or prayers in a magical way. Of course, Kṛṣṇa's memory and discretion do not only span this life but infinity. He can remember all the desires and hopes that we have ever had in previous lives and this one, and He fulfils them at the perfect time. How comforting it is that Kṛṣṇa never forgets and that He knows exactly what to give us at any given time so that we may learn to remember Him, as He remembers us.

Meditation 13: Kṛṣṇa Is a Genius

"Having the last word" is a concept that appeals to most people. Whenever we have a friendly conversation, a formal debate, or an argument, very few people want their viewpoints and statements defeated by the other person. *The Nectar of Devotion* (Chapter 21) explains that having the ability to refute all arguments with novel ones is called being a genius. Kṛṣṇa is the ultimate genius, but His defeating arguments benefited all who listened and, besides the demonic personalities He dealt with, the other person enjoyed being defeated by Kṛṣṇa. For example, Śrīmatī Rādhārāṇī derives immense pleasure when Kṛṣṇa plays clever word games with her and defeats her.

Similarly, engaging in a good, lively discussion in a sportive mood – thinking of newer ways to bring up points and come to an understanding with others – brings satisfaction. This pleasure is a little taste of the happiness Kṛṣṇa feels from being an absolute genius.

On almost any topic in this world, there are multiple logical options. Such is also due to the genius of Kṛṣṇa. Indeed, His ability to make His own existence neither proven nor disproven to us in this world, so that various views – even atheism – can find support is particularly evidence of His genius.

Meditation 14: Kṛṣṇa Is Artistic

Art naturally tends to attract our minds and senses, and people can spend hours staring at paintings or sculptures, watching dancers, or listening to music. Kṛṣṇa is the ultimate and consummate artist. The art we humans create in this world is a small glimmer of how attractive and absorbing Kṛṣṇa dresses, sings, speaks, or plays His flute. His artistry inspires the artists of this world.

We see Kṛṣṇa's artwork in nature on this planet when Kṛṣṇa paints a rainbow, a sunrise, or sunset on the canvas of the sky. The pearl of the moon sends rays of diamonds to dance on the waves of ever-changing hues of blue and green on rivers and oceans. The many forms and colors of living beings run, jump, swim, and fly in various dance-like movements through a variety of landscapes of forests, deserts, plains, mountains, and oceans. Sounds of birds, animals, whales, and humans mix with wind and water to form harmonies. Kṛṣṇa's love of art and His sense of creating fascinating beauty is evident everywhere on earth, which scripture describes as the lowest of the middle planets. So how amazing the Lord's art must be in His own abode!

Meditation 15: Kṛṣṇa Is Extremely Clever

A clever person is one who can perform various types of work at once, an expert multi-tasker. On some days we manage to execute our daily activities as planned; everything goes smoothly, and everyone is relatively happy. At other times, however, we don't manage to do all urgent tasks the way we would like. Then we multi-task and rearrange our day as we go, trying to attend to different things simultaneously.

Parents often have to multi-task, doing chores at home while taking care of small children. Sometimes our capacity to multi-task is stretched to the limit and with it our capacity to remain focused and calm. Kṛṣṇa's cleverness, however, is unlimited. He performs His multiple pastimes without getting stressed or rushed by anything. He charms the *gopīs* with His glances while He fights demons at the same time, or He composes songs about the cowherd boys while simultaneously herding the cows. His cleverness is endless and always pleasing.

Meditation 16: Kṛṣṇa Is Expert

An expert is someone who can quickly execute a very difficult task. Kṛṣṇa is the master of masters. He is, in a sense, "self-taught" and the teacher of everyone. His expertise flows effortlessly from His full knowledge of everything. He is the warp and weft of the cloth of everything, the rule-maker, the essence of everything. He is the master of time and is time itself. So, naturally, no task is "difficult" for Him, and He can accomplish any task instantly. Yet in His pastimes He finds satisfaction in displaying expertise as if He were merely an extraordinary human rather than the Supreme Lord.

There is something mystical in watching any expert using their skill. Whether a devotee is quickly and gorgeously dressing the Deities on a festival day, cooking tasty preparations quickly, or conveying tremendous inspiration to an audience in a short speech, we are, in fact, witnessing a fraction of Kṛṣṇa's expertise manifesting through them. Similarly, we are sometimes amazed when we face a daunting job and know how to do it intuitively, such as solving a problem that a team agonized over. Or we accomplish something perfectly in moments that we thought would take weeks. Often such expertise is the result of years of study under the expert guidance of a great master, yet in the ultimate sense the supreme expert is always giving us that guidance.

Meditation 17: Kṛṣṇa Is Grateful

When someone does something beneficial for us, especially out of affection, it is natural to be grateful for it. As stated in *The Nectar of Devotion* (Chapter 21), being grateful means to be always conscious of how others' activities are benefitting us and to never forget their service. We also feel indebted to them, even long after they have helped us. Kṛṣṇa, being a person, similarly becomes grateful to anyone who renders even a little service to Him, what to speak of His gratitude toward devotees who feelingly call out to Him and chant His holy names constantly. Indeed, the Lord is unable to forget such devotees and feels obliged toward them.

We experience Kṛṣṇa's gratitude when He reciprocates with us by filling us with joy whenever we serve Him or when He gives us interesting and fulfilling service to do. We feel His gratitude when he magically fulfils our desires, whether big or small. Kṛṣṇa's gratitude is evident in everything we have beyond the bare necessities of life – flowers, beautiful scenery, loving friends, delicious meals, and varieties of clothes. His gratitude surrounds us.

grateful
FIRMLY DETERMINED
AN EXPERT JUDGE OF
time and circumstances
SEES AND SPEAKS ON THE AUTHORITY
OF VEDAS OR SCRIPTURES

Meditation 18: Kṛṣṇa Is Firmly Determined

Being determined, according to Rūpa Gosvāmī, means undertaking practical activity to fulfil one's promise. Kṛṣṇa is determined to keep His promise. He promised His queen Satyabhama a pārijāta flower and waged a war to get it for her. He promised to repay Draupadī's kindness for bandaging His finger and thus saved her from being disrobed in the Kaurava assembly. He also kept His promise to Queen Kunti to bring back her sons from Kurukṣetra.

Most of the ways in which we see the Lord's determination in this world may fade into the background of our awareness because they are so much taken for granted. We rely on the sun to rise every day at a set time, and we rely on the seasonal changes. In this way, Kṛṣṇa shows His determination that we can rely on.

To illustrate the Lord's determination, Rūpa Gosvāmī cites the *Bhagavad-Gītā* (9.31), where Kṛṣṇa promises that His surrendered devotee will never be vanquished. Such is His determination to protect His devotees. We see that He does so in our lives and in the lives of our loved ones who are devoted to Him. Sometimes externally things may appear otherwise when devotees appear to suffer, but we can see in the long run that Kṛṣṇa's dealings with His devotees is always based on love. We can also remember Kṛṣṇa's determination when people are loyal and keep their promises to each other.

Meditation 19: Kṛṣṇa Is an Expert Judge of Time and Circumstances

Kṛṣṇa is the most expert person when it comes to dealing with others according to time, place, and circumstances. He knew the most opportune time for engaging in the *rasa* dance, herding cows, or pleasing His parents. He knows the perfect place to perform specific pastimes according to His desire and the desires of His intimate associates. This quality of Kṛṣṇa also manifests in His arrangements for His practicing devotees in this world. We can reflect when, in reciprocation with our sincerity, the timing was perfect to meet just the right person, find the right item, or connect with exactly what we needed for our spiritual advancement. Especially in these types of situations we become aware of the hand of the Lord acting in our life. Even when this divine planning is not visible to us, we can stop and recall that everything is being perfectly arranged by Kṛṣṇa.

Meditation 20: Kṛṣṇa Sees and Speaks on the Authority of Vedas, or Scriptures

Kṛṣṇa, the topmost guide, chooses to explain things through the Vedas and scriptures to show us how we should follow śāstra. The Vedic scriptures are a roadmap to help us when we are spiritually lost. Very few people can boast that they have never been lost, literally or figuratively. People with no sense of direction know how much they need a map or GPS. Tourists know that although a museum, castle, or national heritage site may be awesome to behold, it gains more significance when a guide is there to explain the context of the site. On an emotional level, no matter how good our sense of direction and how well-traveled we may be, we all have been in a proverbial jungle of life, entangled in the creepers of life's problems, and blocked from the sun. In any of these instances we understand the value of a GPS, a road sign, a tour guide, a brochure, or a friend that helps us climb out of the valley onto the mountain, just as Kṛṣṇa guides through scripture.

Meditation 21: Kṛṣṇa Is Pure

Kṛṣṇa possesses two kinds of purity: 1) the ability to deliver a sinful person, and 2) to never do anything impure, by which to get contaminated. The sun is evidence of Kṛṣṇa's purity in this world. It can purify even a dirty place, yet it never gets contaminated. Even the ordinary fire we use in our cooking has the same quality. Places that give us access to clean air, clean water, and uncontaminated soil, certainly remind us that the original state of nature is purity, and ability to purify that which is impure. When we associate with Kṛṣṇa daily through chanting His holy names, we directly experience becoming purified and insulated from impurity.

pure
SELF-CONTROLLED
STEADFAST
forebearing

Meditation 22: Kṛṣṇa Is Self-controlled

Will I go to sleep on time, or will I cruise the internet a bit longer? Will I eat three scoops of ice cream or only two? Will I entertain romantic thoughts about my attractive colleague, or will I ignore them? I need a new car because . . . We have so many impulses coursing through our thoughts during the day. Each of us has areas of weaknesses and desires to deal with. Sometimes they seem innocuous as extra ice cream, but sometimes they start as little as a playful glance and end in a broken relationship.

According to *The Nectar of Devotion* (Chapter 21), a self-controlled person can control his senses fully. Lord Kṛṣṇa's sixteen thousand queens possessed exquisite beauty and other wonderful qualities, which captivated the minds of even great demigods. Although each of the queens thought that Kṛṣṇa was captivated by her feminine beauty, factually He was not. The Lord always remains materially unagitated and is thus the supreme controller of the senses. Of course, Kṛṣṇa is attracted to the pure love of His devotees!

Whenever we look upon mountains in nature, the large, solid, immovable masses of rock may help us remember Kṛṣṇa's self-control. No matter how heavy the rainfall or strong the wind, mountains are not swayed from their position. As we try to keep our minds and senses under control while executing devotional service, we can pray to Kṛṣṇa, the master of the senses, to help our senses remain positively and constantly engaged in His service. We can remember *Bhagavad-Gītā* 2.64, where Kṛṣṇa tells us that that He gives mercy to those who practice freedom from attachment and aversion along with physical regulation of the senses. We can thus become, like Kṛṣṇa, a great hero in mastering our senses and mind. (*Śrīmad-Bhāgavatam* 4.25.25)

Meditation 23: Kṛṣṇa Is Steadfast

To persevere until a desired goal is reached is called steadfastness. When Kṛṣṇa was searching for the Syamantaka jewel, He traced Prasena to the dead lion and traced the dead lion to Jāmbavān with whom He fought for many days until He regained the jewel. Kṛṣṇa also is steadfast in delivering His devotee from illusion. Once a soul surrenders to Him, Kṛṣṇa keeps helping the devotee even if the devotee falls from the path or takes many lifetimes to achieve spiritual success.

Nature often displays Kṛṣṇa's quality of steadfastness. In the spring, we see new plants peeking from the ground. Weeks or months before they become visible, they begin to grow roots downward and then start pushing up through the hard, dark soil to finally break free into the light of day. Many plants can push through asphalt by growing steadily, persevering until they break through the hard surface. Similarly, no matter how hardened our heart, Kṛṣṇa is steadfast in His mission to push us to grow, to win us back and take us home to the spiritual sky when we take even the smallest step toward Him.

Meditation 24: Kṛṣṇa Is Forbearing

A forbearing person tolerates all kinds of trouble, even if the trouble appears to be intolerable. In His childhood, even though His transcendental body was very soft and delicate, Kṛṣṇa voluntarily took all troubles to serve His spiritual master. The earth is often cited in scripture (such as *Śrīmad-Bhāgavatam* 4.16.7) as exhibiting this quality of the Lord. She is walked upon and mistreated in many ways, yet she continues to supply life's necessities and carry us. Trees also exemplify forbearance. When they are thirsty, they silently wait until water arrives; when someone cuts or breaks them, they do not protest.

We experience a small part of Kṛṣṇa's forbearance whenever we tolerate any type of taxing activity; to strengthen the body and mind, we have to tolerate some difficulty and pain. Similarly, in taking up any mission in daily life we may have to tolerate inconveniences. The ability to withstand such difficulties comes from Kṛṣṇa as the unlimited source of forbearance.

Meditation 25: Kṛṣṇa Is Forgiving

A forgiving person is one who can tolerate all kinds of offenses from an opposing party and not feel resentment toward them. An extraordinary instance of Kṛṣṇa's forgiveness was when Bhṛgu Muni kicked the Lord's chest. Rather than getting angry at Bhṛgu, the Lord apologized for the hardness of His chest and His failure to greet Bhṛgu properly.

Often our parents forgive us just as Kṛṣṇa forgave Bhṛgu; they are so focused on our happiness that they hardly notice our offenses. Brahmā gives the example of how a pregnant woman never takes offense when the child in her womb kicks her by stretching. The grass we trample shows this quality of forgiveness in the Lord's universal form (*Bhāgavatam* 2.6.5). Although we press it with our feet, it cushions our feet and happily bounces back. A cork in water has the same forgiving nature; no matter how many times it's pushed into the water, it bounces back.

When we appreciate being forgiven by those we love, and we find peace and freedom in forgiving others, we can meditate on how glorious, compassionate, and liberating is the forgiveness of Kṛṣṇa.

Meditation 26: Kṛṣṇa Is Grave

One who does not reveal his mind to everyone and whose thoughts and intentions are difficult to understand is said to be grave. When Lord Brahmā prayed to Kṛṣṇa to be forgiven for having stolen the cowherd boys and calves and keeping them captive for an entire year, he could not understand whether Kṛṣṇa was satisfied or remained dissatisfied.

Sometimes as we make plans that depend on the weather conditions, an overcast sky can remind us of Kṛṣṇa's gravity. Clouds may or may not portend rainfall; there is no way to know for certain what the movements of material nature will be in the coming hours or minutes. Even the experienced weather forecaster cannot always understand the cloud's intentions. Similarly, we cannot always understand or predict Kṛṣṇa's intentions for our life.

While we greatly value those who keep our confidences sacred, we may feel frustrated with Kṛṣṇa's keeping His thoughts and intentions for our life so private. Our trust and surrender to His will may mature when His plans and desires are gradually revealed to us as our life unfolds. Of course, for His devotees, Kṛṣṇa's overall thoughts and intentions are always clear, even when He hides the details to create mystery and adventure. But for those who do not love Him, the workings of God and His energies remain a closely guarded secret between the Lord and His servants, such as the devas, who personify the material energies.

Meditation 27: Kṛṣṇa Is Self-satisfied

One who is satisfied within, who does not hanker for anything, and who does not get agitated even when there is a serious reason for being distressed, is known as a self-satisfied person. When Kṛṣṇa, Bhīma, and Arjuna challenged Jarāsandha, Kṛṣṇa gave all credit to Bhīma for killing Jarāsandha. This is because Kṛṣṇa does not care at all for fame, although no one is more famous than He. When Śiśupāla called Kṛṣṇa ill names, the Lord was not disturbed at all, further illustrating His quality of being self-satisfied.

Cactus plants may help us remember this quality of Kṛṣṇa. Compared to other plants, the cactus appears to be quite satisfied. Despite the lack of rainfall, it does not seem to hanker for being watered because it preserves water within itself. In fact, desert travelers open a cactus in an emergency to derive life-saving fluids to quench their thirst. In addition, the cactus can withstand the harshness of desert climate – extreme heat during the day and extreme cold at night – without any disturbance, even though such conditions would be distressful or unbearable for most plants, animals, and humans. Like Kṛṣṇa, they don't find external situations distressing.

Meditation 28: Kṛṣṇa Possesses Equilibrium

Possessing equilibrium is defined in *The Nectar of Devotion* (Chapter 21) as being unaffected by attachment and envy. When Kṛṣṇa chastised the Kāliya serpent, Kāliya's wives praised Kṛṣṇa with beautiful prayers with which they con-

forgiving
GRAVE
self-satisfied
POSSESSING
EQUILIBRIUM

veyed their realization that Kṛṣṇa was chastising the serpent with its future welfare in mind. Kṛṣṇa's dealings are thus without envy and always beneficial for the recipient, whether it is chastisement or reward. Cows can remind us of Kṛṣṇa in that they are among the most beneficial animals on earth. Cows are generally peaceful and graze upon a little grass but offer so much in return. Even when they are ill-treated, they supply not only nutritious milk but also dung and urine, which are greatly purifying and essential for the performance of Vedic sacrifices. Even after their death the skin of cows and bulls can be used to make instruments such as the mṛdaṅga drum.

Regarding equilibrium, Kṛṣṇa is also glorified in the scriptures as impartial, being without attachment; He treats all living entities equally and simply reciprocates according to how they choose to interact with Him. Kṛṣṇa cites rainfall as evidence of impartiality when He speaks to Nanda Mahārāja (*Kṛṣṇa Book,* Chapter 24). When clouds pour rain in a particular area, they shower every square inch without discrimination. How the rain is received depends on the makeup of the ground it falls upon but not upon the clouds themselves; solid rock does not absorb rainwater in the same way that soil does. So when we see clouds indiscriminately showering rain, we can think of Kṛṣṇa's impartiality or equilibrium. In fact, the *gopīs* say that the clouds are Kṛṣṇa's friends because they share this quality with Him. (*Śrīmad-Bhāgavatam* 10.21.16 and 10.33.7)

Meditation 29: Kṛṣṇa Is Magnanimous

To be magnanimous is to be very charitably disposed. The amount of charity Kṛṣṇa gave daily when He reigned as king of Dvārakā is inconceivable. It is said to have even surpassed the opulences of the spiritual kingdom.

A mother's love gives us remembrance of Kṛṣṇa's magnanimity in this material world. She gives her body in pregnancy and breastfeeding. She gives her time, energy, love, and resources until the child is grown and often beyond. Her time and resources are limited, but a mother's consciousness is so magnanimous that even her limited efforts of love may seem limitless.

Aside from charitable people such as mothers, Kṛṣṇa's magnanimous nature is seen throughout creation. He gives abundantly, exceeding our needs. Most of us have more clothes, food, and space than we absolutely require to remain alive. We have opportunities to do what we love, and we have friends and associates. Fruit trees and vegetable gardens can give so abundantly that we cannot possibly use all the bounty and even struggle to find friends who will share the overflowing harvest. Yet the scriptures compare this world to a prison. Surely there is no earthly government that gives so generously to its prisoners.

We have a natural tendency to focus on the lacks in our life. We then may feel that God has not given us enough. Focusing on how Kṛṣṇa's magnanimity is flowing through our lives leads to gratitude and joy.

Meditation 30: Kṛṣṇa Is Religious

Being religious is described as having two components: practicing religious principles as they are given in śāstra and teaching these principles to others. Kṛṣṇa did both perfectly and is thus known to possess the quality of religiousness. By His example He showed how to conduct household life according to the śāstra and spoke the profound truths of the *Bhagavad-Gītā* simply and eloquently for our benefit. Thus, whenever we are learning the principles of religion, especially with a qualified and giving teacher, we may remember Kṛṣṇa as the perfect embodiment of religiousness.

Those who act and teach in accordance with scripture and moral codes exemplify the religious quality of the Lord. In nature, the movements of the stars demonstrate religiousness in the universal body of God. The stars and planets only move in strict obedience to cosmic laws; their movements can be calculated for thousands of years, both past and future. And the placements of those heavenly bodies indicate our dharma and right path of action in the form of astrological readings.

MAGNANIMOUS

Religious

HEROIC

compassionate

Meditation 31: Kṛṣṇa Is Heroic

Heroism refers to someone who is enthusiastic in battle and expert at releasing weapons. Kṛṣṇa would kill opposing military forces with the ease of an elephant destroying lotus stems by swinging its trunk. He was so expert at releasing weapons that even when Jarāsandha attacked Kṛṣṇa's army with thirteen divisions of soldiers, not a single soldier on Kṛṣṇa's side was hurt.

Kṛṣṇa's heroic quality manifests in His devotees who fortify themselves with the *mahā-mantra,* taking up the sword of śāstra, and riding the horse of truth through life. Our most recent hero was Śrīla Prabhupāda, who overcame many opposing elements to victoriously spread the movement of Lord Caitanya. He was undeniably the greatest hero of our time.

Regarding literal warfare, expert martial artists, police officers, and soldiers of our time still exist who have a little spark of Kṛṣṇa's heroism. We may hear in the news of their heroic measures to take down a criminal. The soul's eagerness to hear about Kṛṣṇa, the real hero, is reflected in the material world as the desire to hear and see modern entertainment where fictional characters – often with superhuman powers – are enthusiastic and expert in battling evil and acting heroically.

Even in nature predatory animals reflect Kṛṣṇa's quality of heroism in His universal form. While our sympathy and compassion usually rest on prey animals, we generally revere and admire the predators – eagles and hawks, sharks and jellyfish, lions and tigers, and grizzly and polar bears. The mongoose or peacock who fearlessly and dexterously captures a poisonous snake with its natural weapons of claws or talons, beak or teeth, shows a spark of Kṛṣṇa's heroism.

Meditation 32: Kṛṣṇa Is Compassionate

A compassionate person cannot bear to see another's distress. We read about the many times Kṛṣṇa showed compassion by alleviating someone's suffering. He delivered the kings imprisoned by Magadhendra, rescued Rukmiṇī from marrying Śiśupāla, and appeared before Bhīṣmadeva when he was lying on a bed of arrows. Upon seeing the painful situation of Bhīṣma, Kṛṣṇa became overwhelmed with compassion and shed tears profusely. His ultimate compassionate nature is represented by Śrīmatī Rādhārāṇī; therefore, devotees do not offer obeisances to Kṛṣṇa directly. They pray to Śrīmatī Rādhārāṇī first to access the compassion of the Lord.

It is easy to think of Kṛṣṇa's compassion when we see small children running to their parents when they are hurt or want empathy, and the parents or relatives doing everything to comfort them or remove their distress. Kṛṣṇa's compassion is evident all around us in such small everyday acts of kindness we give and receive. It is evident in the large, comprehensive philanthropic organizations to which people give their wealth, time, and expertise to help those less fortunate. Ultimately, we remember Kṛṣṇa's compassion when we contact persons such as Śrīla Prabhupāda who dedicate themselves to bringing others the ultimate joy and alleviating the existential suffering of forgetfulness of the Lord.

In nature, parents in many species sacrifice to aid their dependent children, often risking their lives. Herd animals attempt to help their weaker members. Creatures such as dogs and dolphins show care to humans in distress. An urge to comfort and alleviate the suffering of others exists even in the plant kingdom, where trees will share their food underground with a stump until new foliage grows.

Meditation 33: Kṛṣṇa Is Respectful

Although Kṛṣṇa is the Supreme Personality of Godhead, He always followed social etiquette, by paying obeisances to His spiritual master, parents, and His older brother, Balarāma.

In any kind of gathering of people, mutual respect creates a safe atmosphere for everyone, facilitates even the most difficult conversations, and allows for open and healthy discussion, even among people who may not agree with one another. Experiencing such respectful dealings deepens our love for this quality in the Lord. And when we are respectful to our elders, friends, and subordinates, we appreciate that some of Kṛṣṇa's own quality is shining through us.

Respect abounds in Kṛṣṇa's universal body. The ocean and shore respect each other's boundaries. Animals smell the scent of others in their group and respect territorial markers. The stars and planets cede the sky to the powerful sun in the daytime. Yet the sun also respects the jurisdiction of the night and leaves the stage of the sky. Bees and ants obey their queen. Elephants and wild horses obey their matriarch. In the lion's pride or the wolf pack, the group respects the dominant male.

Meditation 34: Kṛṣṇa Is Gentle

Śrīla Rūpa Gosvāmī describes a gentle person as one who does not become impudent or proud. (*The Nectar of Devotion,* Chapter 22) Kṛṣṇa, even though the Supreme Personality of Godhead, followed social etiquette and showed King Yudhiṣṭhira all due respect at the Rājasūya sacrifice by getting down from His chariot and falling at the king's feet.

Lord Caitanya gives the example of fully laden fruit trees to show gentleness. (*Caitanya-bhāgavata, Ādi-kāṇḍa* 13.14) Although they are bountiful with many fruits and thus have good cause for pride, they are not arrogant and thus bend low under the weight of their fruits. The beautiful ocean creatures also show this gentle quality. They do not parade or exhibit their beauty of form and movement; rather, hiding in the depths, they eschew arrogance.

Gentleness is in the workings of our own bodies, too. Our bodies perform miracles, moment by moment, of digestion, respiration, growing of hair, or forming a new human in the womb. All this greatness happens nearly automatically and without announcement or fanfare, the mark of gentleness free from pride.

Meditation 35: Kṛṣṇa Is Liberal

We may think of *liberal* in terms of political, moral, or religious views, but Śrīla Rūpa Gosvāmī describes *liberal* as a person who is mild-mannered and generous with compassion and gentleness. In this connection Śrīla Prabhupāda explains in *The Nectar of Devotion* that Kṛṣṇa is so kind that even if His servitors are accused of committing offenses, He overlooks their shortcomings and simply considers their service. We see this when Pūtanā tried to kill baby Kṛṣṇa by offering Him her poisoned breast to suck on, and instead of condemning her to hell, Kṛṣṇa liberated her and promoted her to the position of one of His mothers in the spiritual world – He took her offering of breast milk as motherly although her intention was to kill Him. This deceitful guise of a mother may be considered a further offense of betrayal, yet Kṛṣṇa is so liberal that he counted her behavior as service.

We can also be reminded of Kṛṣṇa's liberal nature when we see a mother watching her young child using a spoon to eat a mixture of yogurt and fruit. "He is so good eating with a spoon!" she says with love and pride, watching him scoop some yogurt onto the spoon and shoving it into his mouth. And, when asked if she noticed the yogurt smeared around the child's mouth, hand, spoon handle, and the tray, she realizes that she did not pay heed to the mess at all, only his budding skill. We can find such liberality and gentleness that focuses on the good and overlooks fault not only in similar dealings between parents and children, but also between spouses, employers and employees, or judges and the accused.

We see further liberality, as demonstrated by Kṛṣṇa with Pūtanā, when someone reframes another's fault as a good quality. Examples of people exhibiting this aspect of Kṛṣṇa's liberal nature, are a wife who is grateful for her husband working hard to maintain the family when he regularly comes home late from work, and a person who considers blunt speech by another as honest rather than rude.

We may see Kṛṣṇa's liberal quality in His universal body in gemstones. Rocks containing gems are forcibly removed with sharp tools and then cut and polished in various ways. From the stone's perspective, the miners and gemmologists' actions could be understood as damaging and harmful, yet the jewel accepts the cutting and cleaning process as kindness to reveal its beauty and splendor to the world.

RESPECTFUL
gentle
LIBERAL
shy

Meditation 36: Kṛṣṇa Is Shy

Shy persons do not want to draw attention to themselves or their achievements or actions. We can see this quality in Kṛṣṇa when Lord Brahmā steals the cowherd boys and calves. Kṛṣṇa expanded Himself into each cowherd boy and calf for one year until Lord Brahmā brought them back to Vṛndāvana. Only Lord Balarāma knew the truth after some time, and Kṛṣṇa also did not proclaim it to everyone. Śrī Caitanya Mahāprabhu was also very shy. Whenever someone called Him the Supreme Lord, He would cover His ears, not wanting to attract attention to His supreme status. Sudāmā Brāhmaṇa, Kṛṣṇa's friend, was extremely shy. Even though he went to visit Kṛṣṇa to ask Him for help to save him from his poverty-stricken condition, he didn't ask for help; Kṛṣṇa nonetheless blessed Him with more riches than he could have dreamed of. Śrīla Prabhupāda was always shy about accepting praise for his achievements and ascribed his success to the mercy of his spiritual master, Śrīla Bhaktisiddhānta Sarasvatī Ṭhākura.

The Lord is also modest as the creator and maintainer of this universe. While His glorious deeds are evident everywhere, He keeps Himself hidden such that people praise nature as if there were no creator at all. While it may frustrate those looking for clear evidence of God by not directly seeing Him painting the sun setting into the ocean on His easel, it is Kṛṣṇa's gentle modesty that keeps Him hidden – He sees our admiration but doesn't take credit.

In fact, Kṛṣṇa's modesty can be found in all aspects of nature that appear to happen "automatically" by scientific law or random forces. Sea turtles show modesty in laying their eggs and then disappearing into the ocean so that baby turtles seem to hatch later without an obvious cause. Among plants, those that produce wind-borne seeds have offspring that grow so far from the parent plant that they appear to have no source at all.

In our own lives we sometimes experience synchronicity of events that seem almost magical. We may miss the bus only to meet our future spouse while waiting for the later one. Right when we desperately need money, we find unclaimed cash on the street in the exact amount we required. A desire arises in us for something, and moments later someone gives us the very thing we desired. Such moments are evidence of Kṛṣṇa's hand, yet He modestly keeps Himself hidden.

Rūpa Gosvāmī also describes a shy person as one who thinks others are aware of His secret love affairs. We see this in Kṛṣṇa's modesty or unfathomable shy dealings with the *gopīs*. During the lifting of Govardhana Hill, Kṛṣṇa became shy when He thought Balarāma had caught Him staring at the *gopīs*. We may also come across people whose behavior demonstrates this type of shyness. In some cultures, ladies cover their heads with a veil out of shyness – a quality that Śrīla Prabhupāda says commands respect. Kṛṣṇa's love for the living entity is often private and secret, and it is common among people to keep intimate loving dealings private, thus showing some of Kṛṣṇa's gentle and modest quality.

Meditation 37: Kṛṣṇa Is the Protector of Surrendered Souls

Sons and daughters don't always walk the straight and narrow path; they sometimes cross swords with their parents and commit mistakes. This hurts the parents, but when the child genuinely acknowledges the mistake and asks for protection and help, the parents will readily help out of unconditional love. Aside from family, stories abound of criminals who receive government protection in exchange for providing evidence to arrest other criminals. Some of the most popular stories, both truth and fiction, are of people who regret their wrongdoing and find redemption in the shelter and acceptance of another person.

Rūpa Gosvāmī says this quality of Kṛṣṇa's giving shelter to the surrendered souls is evident when He protects even demons who surrender. A prime example is of Rāvaṇa's brother, Vibhīṣaṇa, who was born and raised in a demon family but tried to persuade Rāvaṇa to give Sītā back to Rāma. After failing in his attempts, he chose to fight for Rāma. Naturally his family lineage engendered doubt in the monkey army as to his fidelity to Rāma. Yet Rāma declared that surrender is His criterion for protection, not a person's previous activities or country of origin.

To illustrate this quality in nature, Rūpa Gosvāmī gives an example of the moon that gives light to anyone regardless of that person's behavior or character. In the animal kingdom this quality of giving protection to the surrendered is seen when males fight over territory or mates, but when one male surrenders, the other stops the fight and walks away.

Meditation 38: Kṛṣṇa Is Happy

Śrīla Rūpa Gosvāmī describes a happy person as someone who is always joyful and untouched by distress. The opulences enjoyed by Kṛṣṇa – His ornaments, beautiful queens, and unlimited wealth – cannot be imagined by even the demigods. We can meditate on true and eternal happiness residing in Kṛṣṇa particularly when we see an advertisement for jewelry, some beauty product, or an expensive residence. While people think they can achieve an inner state of joy by imitating Kṛṣṇa's opulences, real joy is in the personal exchange Kṛṣṇa has with His energies.

There is much in our lives and nature that is joyful, from beautiful birds dancing in courtship, to children running in the ocean's waves, to flowers opening in daytime to greet the sun. The music and dancing among humans, birds, and even insects, such as bees, show that the true nature of a living being is to seek and feel joy, as our source is supremely joyful.

Meditation 39: Kṛṣṇa Is the Well-wisher of His Devotees

We may be fortunate to have one, if not a few, people in our lives who genuinely care about our well-being. We may have done something for them which inspired their care for us, or they may be our well-wishers simply because we happen to know them. Such kind-hearted souls can help us remember Kṛṣṇa's quality of being the well-wisher of His devotees. Whenever we encounter people who especially care for their employees, customers, students, friends, or family, we find a little glimmer of this quality of Kṛṣṇa. Cows will give a greater quantity of milk and for a longer time to those who treat them with love, and dogs will sacrifice their lives in loyalty to a human who feeds them and pets them. Sometimes Kṛṣṇa's quality as a well-wishing friend is understood as the most glorious among all His qualities. He is known as *bhakta-vatsala*, meaning that He is always favorably inclined to His devotees, even at the risk of breaking His promises. Even for a little bit of service rendered with devotion, the Lord feels so grateful and becomes indebted to His devotee.

Meditation 40: Kṛṣṇa Is Controlled by Love

Śrīla Prabhupāda explains that it is the loving attitude of the devotee that controls Kṛṣṇa and not exactly the service rendered. Kṛṣṇa is not in need of the things we offer Him, but being the supreme conscious being, He has the deepest desire to have loving exchanges with His parts and parcels who lovingly serve Him out of their free will.

Parents know how their heart is touched when their children buy them a birthday present or cook something for them. Most likely the money used to buy the presents or ingredients comes from the parents themselves, so it is not that the children are really giving anything tangible; they are giving love and affection.

Putting ourselves voluntarily under the control of love without wanting anything in return happens from time to time in friendship, romantic relationships, and service to our country or to some mission or goal. One of the most pleasurable feelings is to be in love and to let that love control us such that we find great joy in willing self-sacrifice. We experience that self-sacrifice as a gift we are giving rather than a "payment" with expectation of a return.

Animals can also be controlled by love and serve loyally just for the joy of giving to their human masters. Plants respond to the mood of those around them and yield more when talked to and treated with affection. Nearly every day we encounter the sweet control of love, and stories of such love abound in society. How fitting that this sweet quality of Kṛṣṇa can be found throughout His creation.

Meditation 41: Kṛṣṇa Is All-auspicious

Kṛṣṇa is known as all-auspicious because of always being engaged in auspicious welfare activities for everyone. He incarnates countless times to bestow mercy on the fallen souls of the age. As Varāha He saves the earth from the depths of the primordial ocean, slaying Hiraṇyākṣa, one of the greatest demons of the *yuga*. As Lord Nṛsiṁhadeva He saves the little boy Prahlāda from his brutal father, Hiraṇyakaśipu. As Kṛṣṇa He plays with His cowherd friends, providing them

THE PROTECTOR OF
surrendered souls

HAPPY

THE WELL-WISHER OF DEVOTEES

CONTROLLED BY *love*

with joy and adventure when He slays the demons who come to Vṛndāvana to kill Him. He showers the *gopīs* with love during the *rasa* dance, and He protects the residents of Vṛndāvana from Indra's flood, crushing Indra's pride and restoring Indra's devotion to Him. Without fail He saves the Pāṇḍavas from their trials and tribulations and brings them safely through the war. As Lord Caitanya He inundates the world with the holy names of the *mahā-mantra,* bringing joy and love that we are looking for in our everyday activities.

Much in nature is all-auspicious, which is shown in the Lord's universal form. What seems harmful or destructive in nature leads to the good and is therefore auspicious. For example, the death of plants and animals fertilizes the ground to bring new life, providing food for other creatures; the death of one creature is thus the life of another. The presence of predator animals keeps prey populations in balance, leading to a healthy and thriving ecosystem. Floods bring rich earth from the mountain tops to the fields and form deltas of new land. Winter cold destroys diseases and pests. In these ways all the actions in the universal body, even those that seem destructive, are all-auspicious.

Thinking about how the earth naturally gives prosperity and success can invokes our appreciation of Kṛṣṇa's auspiciousness. Land ownership is one of the prime types of wealth and supplies nearly everything we count as riches – food, clothing, jewels, metals, and so forth.

Meditation 42: Kṛṣṇa Is Most Powerful

In different contexts people have different levels of power. Bosses have power over their employees, teachers over their pupils, governments over their citizens, and parents over their children. Even in friendships there are sometimes power-relationships. We may be considered powerful, but Kṛṣṇa is the most powerful. Śrīla Prabhupāda describes how Kṛṣṇa's power causes calamity to His foes and strikes fear in their hearts.

Rūpa Gosvāmī gives an example of Kṛṣṇa's power in nature as the sun, which causes darkness to hide in mountain caves. Kṛṣṇa's power can also be heard in the roar of a lion, the trumpet of an elephant, the rumble of thunder, and the flow of a mighty river. Generally, when people encounter the power of other beings or natural forces, they become afraid or perhaps full of wonder. But when those same examples of power remind us that Kṛṣṇa is the most powerful, our awe can include how we feel safe and comforted.

Meditation 43: Kṛṣṇa Is All-famous

Śrīla Rūpa Gosvāmī describes an "all-famous" person as one who becomes well known because of spotless character. We find opportunities to remember Kṛṣṇa's fame through the many people we know or hear about who have righteous renown. Even in nature we can be reminded of Kṛṣṇa's fame: Animal species, such as dolphins and horses, are well known for good qualities and high character; the Ganges River in India and the spring in Lourdes, France, are famous for bringing physical and spiritual healing. Rūpa Gosvāmī describes Kṛṣṇa's fame to be like moonlight, which illuminates everything and drives darkness away. Glancing at the moon can deepen our conviction that preaching Kṛṣṇa's glories can replace the ignorance and resultant suffering of our dark world with the peacefulness and prosperity that come from living God-centered lives.

Meditation 44: Kṛṣṇa Is Popular

Being popular generally means to be dear to people. We may know individuals whose presence brings joy to others and wins the favor of everybody they meet. They are the life and soul of communities. Such people can help us remember Kṛṣṇa, whose popularity knows no limits. Rūpa Gosvāmī gives examples of Kṛṣṇa's popularity: When Kṛṣṇa returned to Dvārakā after the battle of Kurukṣetra, the Dvārakā citizens related how they endured the unbearable separation from Him. Similarly, when Kṛṣṇa entered Kamsa's wrestling arena, He was met with cries of victory, the blessings of sages, the prayers of demigods, and the joyful glances of the ladies and girls.

ALL auspicious
most POWERFUL
All~famous
POPULAR

Such popularity is also seen in the universal form when the sun appears in winter or in the midst of a cold, rainy day. On a hot day a place to drink cool beverages and to swim in cool water is eminently popular, and a fire is popular with everyone on a chilly, dark night.

Meditation 45: Kṛṣṇa Is Partial to His Devotees

Natural and inherent to being a person is to be affectionately inclined to those who act in our interest. Kṛṣṇa, being a person, also feels affection for those who serve Him with love. He is equal to everyone, but His devotees especially attract His favor by their loving reciprocation. Whenever we associate with those who hold a special place in our hearts, we can remember Kṛṣṇa's partiality toward His devotees.

Those who are devoted to God, regardless of faith or religion, have a sense of purpose and comfort in their lives unlike those who perceive the world to be merely a mechanical arrangement, or springing from a force of chance. While Kṛṣṇa's devotees appear to have the same troubles as anyone else, their lives are joyful and meaningful because of their conviction that Kṛṣṇa is personally present, guiding them.

Meditation 46: Kṛṣṇa Is Very Attractive to All Women

Kṛṣṇa possesses all the special qualities that are attractive to women. Kṛṣṇa is, after all, the original "tall, dark, and handsome," and therefore women cannot help being attracted to Him. The damsels of Vraja are attracted to Him just like shards of iron to a magnet, which are constitutionally attracted to each other. So, whenever we use a magnet, we can think of how Kṛṣṇa is very attractive to all women and how we may also uncover our innate attraction for Him, as ontologically speaking all living beings are considered "female" in relation to Kṛṣṇa, the supreme male.

Meditation 47: Kṛṣṇa Is All-worshipable

Kṛṣṇa is eternally respected and worshiped not only by the living entities who are His parts and parcels, but even by His own plenary expansions. For example, there is the story in the *Śrīmad-Bhāgavatam* where Mahā-Viṣṇu reveres Lord Kṛṣṇa.

Worship means to revere and adore. Driving by a church or mosque, for example, can remind us of how the all-worshipable Lord is addressed as Jehovah, Allah, and other divine names according to time, place, faith, and culture.

Kṛṣṇa is the most beautiful, the wealthiest, the most famous, the strongest, the most renounced, and the most knowledgeable. He is therefore worthy of our worship. When humans possess fractions of these opulences, others often revere them. However, we may forget the source of all opulences and have started to worship the opulences only.

In nature we can be reminded of Kṛṣṇa's quality of being worshipable when we see the sunflowers adore the sun and turn their faces towards him as they bask in his warmth and light. The wild animals revere the strength and power of the lion, tiger, and elephant. The earth worships the rain clouds and soaks up the rain after the dry season.

Meditation 48: Kṛṣṇa Is All-opulent

Kṛṣṇa possesses all six opulences – strength, wealth, fame, beauty, knowledge, and renunciation – without limit. Any of these opulences, when found in abundance in human society or in the natural world, can help us remember this transcendental quality of Kṛṣṇa. We see Kṛṣṇa's beauty in soothing sunsets, His strength in hurricane winds, and His wealth in the unending torrents of life-sustaining rivers. His fame is spread like the sky that covers everyone, His knowledge is like the air that pervades everything, and His renunciation is like the ocean that is unaffected by the hundreds of rivers pouring water into it at every moment.

PARTIAL TO DEVOTEES

VERY attractive TO ALL women

ALL worshipable

ALL opulent

Meditation 49: Kṛṣṇa Is All-honorable

Kṛṣṇa is the foremost among important persons and is therefore all-honorable. We may think of this quality whenever we find ourselves in the company of esteemed people to whom we feel the inspiration, need, or obligation to pay respects. Just as guests pay respects to the hosts of an event, or a master of ceremonies honors important guests by thanking them for their presence, devotees always pay obeisances to a spiritual teacher, be it a spiritual master, a *śikṣā* guru, *sannyāsī,* or any other senior devotee. In whatever way we pay respects or show honor to someone, we can meditate on how we are honoring the Supersoul – who is all-honorable – within the person's heart.

Rūpa Gosvāmī gives an example as evidence of Kṛṣṇa's being all-honorable – the demigods need to wait to see Him and are sometimes told to pray silently or come back another day. We often show honor by waiting for someone with more importance, power, or expertise than we have. Standing in line, sitting in a doctor's waiting room, having secretaries and receptionists put us on hold, having to schedule appointments months in advance – how willing we can be to wait for Kṛṣṇa to call us and want to see us!

Meditation 50: Kṛṣṇa Is the Supreme Controller

Śrīla Rūpa Gosvāmī tells us that Kṛṣṇa is the supreme controller because of two things: He is completely independent, and His orders cannot be neglected. Forces of nature, especially in their extreme manifestations, can easily remind us that Kṛṣṇa is the supreme controller. Excessive heat or cold, rain or sunshine, and so on, manifest independently of our will. We may plan to have a picnic outdoors, but whether it will rain or not is something beyond our control. Moreover, we are unable to refuse the conditions that natural forces impose upon us and can only learn to adapt and tolerate; if it's cold, we have to wear extra clothing to safeguard our health. Even our spiritual life depends not just on our sincerity and our practices but also on Kṛṣṇa's mercy and grace. We thus can easily see Kṛṣṇa's supreme control in all areas of our life and in the world.

Meditation 51: Kṛṣṇa Is Changeless

We live in a world in which change is the general currency. Stock markets show how shares change in value every day; governments' currency changes in value almost every day. Presidents or prime ministers change, and even dictators die at some stage. In spring all plants show magnificent arrays of colors in blossoms and new foliage. In autumn the natural world is set ablaze with hues of red, yellow, green, and orange. Our personal lives are a constant seesaw of ups and downs; the babies grow up and the grownups get old.

In our lives and in the world, change is thus the only constant. But Kṛṣṇa is truly changeless. He never changes His position or body when He enters the material world and is never touched by the modes of material nature. He never forgets that He is Kṛṣṇa (except in His dealings with His intimate devotees when *yoga-māyā* covers Him to increase the mellows of love), and although His form changes from *avatāra* to *avatāra*, it's more like showing a different side of His personality than a completely new body. In essence, He always remains as Kṛṣṇa.

Although our world, by its very design, is under the influence of time and therefore subjected to transformation, it can still remind us of the Lord's changelessness. For instance, we can see Kṛṣṇa's changelessness in the constancy of the lunar cycles and in how sunrise and sunset happen in their respective directions everyday. We can see this quality in the constant cycle of birth and death. Kṛṣṇa is, however, the pivot that keeps all changes together. He is the fulcrum of the seesaw that never moves or changes position. He is our anchor that keeps us grounded in the sea of changes around us.

Meditation 52: Kṛṣṇa Is All-cognizant

Kṛṣṇa is all-cognizant because He knows everyone's thoughts and everything that is happening at all times and in all places. He saved Draupadī twice – when the Kurus attempted to disrobe her in their assembly, and when she was in exile in the forest and had nothing to feed the sages. In both cases Lord Kṛṣṇa was far away in Dvārakā yet he fully heard her and responded immediately.

ALL honorable
the SUPREME controller
CHANGELESS
ALL cognizant

He knew that Lord Brahmā had stolen the cowherd boys and calves. He knew that Karna was the son of Kunti even though she tried to hide it. Kṛṣṇa knew that Bhīṣma had empowered five arrows with which to kill the Pāṇḍavas. He knew that Dhṛtarāṣṭra had a yearning to see His universal form, and so He gave him sight just for that instant.

Small reflections of Kṛṣṇa's quality of all-cognizance are all around us. When we're sometimes able to complete a loved one's sentences for them, it's because we are somewhat "tuned in" to their nature and inner workings. Sometimes we are keenly aware when a loved one dies or is in danger in a distant place although no overt communication has taken place. Most of us can perceive that an argument has just occurred when we walk into a room, even if the parties go silent upon our entrance. And many managers and leaders are aware of a broad scope of the domain they supervise. Modern governments and some companies try to imitate Kṛṣṇa's all-cognizance with detailed records of phone calls, social media posts, movements, and shopping history. Yet only Kṛṣṇa's understanding is total.

Often, we feel Kṛṣṇa's cognizance in our lives when we silently wish for something only to receive it a little later. How often have we been critical in our thoughts of others' actions only to land in the same situation ourselves and thus re-evaluate our judgments. We can marvel at how Kṛṣṇa's knowledge of every living being's desires and destinies brings together all the billions of living entities to experience their karmic reactions, good and bad.

Meditation 53: Kṛṣṇa Is Ever Fresh

Living beings by their constitutional nature are spiritual and not meant to be the enjoyers of matter. The proof is that their enjoyment of a particular sense object cannot be sustained indefinitely; they tend to get satiated and need to step away from the object of enjoyment to regain enthusiasm for it. In contrast, Kṛṣṇa is ever fresh.

It is said that fortune is fickle and restless, but Rūpa Gosvāmī explains that in Dvārakā, Kṛṣṇa's queens, who are goddesses of fortune, are unable to leave Kṛṣṇa's company because of His ever-fresh attractiveness. Since time immemorial countless devotees have been hearing, chanting, and remembering Kṛṣṇa's name, fame, and qualities without getting satiated. In fact, they get renewed impetus and ever-increasing inspiration to continue the same process. Whenever we become so fortunate as to absorb ourselves in *kīrtana* for hours on end, we may remember that this is due to Kṛṣṇa's quality of being ever-fresh.

We see Kṛṣṇa's ever-fresh nature in the fact that even though springtime occurs every year, we find each spring refreshingly beautiful after the long winter. Similarly, the winter sun is always welcome on a cold day, as is a cool breeze on a warm day. A shower refreshes tired nerves. These are tiny sparks of Kṛṣṇa's ever-freshness. Yet when we bring our awareness to Kṛṣṇa's presence in the world, we find that even within creation the Lord's artistry, intelligence, design, and plan are unlimitedly fascinating and glorious.

Meditation 54: Kṛṣṇa Is *Sac-cid-ānanda* (Possessing an Eternal Blissful Body)

We can see Kṛṣṇa's *sac-cid-ānanda* feature in separate. parts. Śrīla Prabhupāda explains that Kṛṣṇa's sat quality refers to His eternal and all-pervading existence. We can think of this feature wherever we feel the wind, which brings to our awareness the ever-present air. Cit means to be full of knowledge. We can think of this quality whenever we search for information on the Internet or in a library and remembering that Kṛṣṇa is infinitely more knowledgeable than any computer search engine can ever be. Kṛṣṇa is also the reservoir of *ānanda* or bliss, so whenever we feel relief from pain or discomfort, we can think of this feeling as a dim reflection of the happiness of merging into the Brahman effulgence, which is itself hardly a minute fragment of the true bliss that characterizes Kṛṣṇa, His spiritual energies, and the liberated souls who unite with Him in pure devotional service.

Meditation 55: Kṛṣṇa Possesses All Mystic Perfections

Śrīmad-Bhāgavatam (11.15.4–5) lists eight primary mystic perfections: (i) becoming smaller than the smallest, (ii) becoming greater than the greatest, (iii) becoming lighter than the lightest, (iv) acquiring whatever one desires, (v)

ever fresh
sac-cid-ananda
POSSESSING AN ETERNAL BLISSFUL BODY
POSSESSING
ALL MYSTIC PERFECTIONS
HE HAS inconceivable potency

experiencing any enjoyable object, (vi) manipulating the sub-potencies of maya, (vii) being unimpeded by the three modes of nature, and (viii) being capable of obtaining anything from anywhere to the highest possible limit. Kṛṣṇa is known as Yogeśvara, the supreme mystic, because He possesses all material and spiritual perfections in full.

Kṛṣṇa is smaller than the tiniest insect that crawls across the page of our book or our desk. He is, indeed, the Supersoul within the insect. He is also infinitely larger than the greatest mountain, because as Varāhadeva He picked up the entire earth planet from the nether regions of the universe. Kṛṣṇa is lighter than any helium balloon floating in the air, which is itself so light that we don't even feel it when it's still.

Sometimes we are fascinated by people who appear to do mystical things, such as seemingly impossible athletic feats or magic shows. How amazing is the mystic perfection of the supreme magician, Śrī Kṛṣṇa!

Meditation 56: Kṛṣṇa Has Inconceivable Potency

Among Kṛṣṇa's inconceivable potencies is His omnipresence, whereby He expands Himself to enter every atom and heart of every living entity. He can simultaneously perform pastimes in His own abode while hearing and answering the prayers of His devotees from every corner of His creation and protecting surrendered souls from sinful reactions. He incarnates in material universes in multifarious forms to perform pastimes for His own internal reasons as well as for attracting conditioned souls back to His abode.

Inconceivable potencies abound in the universe that can spark meditation on this quality in the Lord's personal form. One grain of sand can be transformed into a pearl inside an oyster. One man's forgiveness has the power to unite a divided country. One man's faith and love for God can elevate millions of people spiritually.

Śrīla Prabhupāda, on a morning walk in Māyāpur, April 3, 1975, talked of inconceivable power in our lives as follows:

Prabhupāda: That is their foolishness. They are thinking God a person like me, like himself. That is foolishness. They cannot conceive that a person can become so powerful than myself. That is the defect. A person has *acintya-śakti, acintya-śakti,* inconceivable power. Now, just like you are person, you cut your hair, it is growing. Do you know how it is growing?

> Haṁsadūta: No.
>
> Prabhupāda: Then? Even it is beyond your conception, what to speak of others. But it is growing. If there is any scar or if the nail is broken some way or other, it will come out. You cannot manufacture it by conceiving. But it is coming out. That means within you there is an inconceivable power. So if you have got, an ordinary human being, so much inconceivable power, how much God has got inconceivable power. That is God.
>
> Haṁsadūta: In Los Angeles you called it mystic power, that every living creature has some mystic power.
>
> Prabhupāda: Yes. Every living creature.
>
> Trivikrama: You gave the example of a lemon tree.
>
> Prabhupāda: Yes. The mystic power producing tons of citric acid.
>
> Trivikrama: Citric acid.
>
> Prabhupāda: Yes, lemon juice. *Acintya-śakti*, inconceivable power. [pause] The cow eating grass, producing milk – this is inconceivable power. Can you produce milk from the grass? But how the cow is producing? Hmm? Answer this. You eat grass and produce milk. Give your wife grass and let her produce milk.

Meditation 57: Kṛṣṇa Has Uncountable Universes Generating from His Body

Anything we encounter in vast numbers in this world – grains of sand on a beach, raindrops in a cloud, or mustard seeds in a bag – can remind us of Kṛṣṇa's gigantic form of Mahā-Viṣṇu, who lies down in the causal ocean and breathes out innumerable universes from His pores. Each of these universes also contains innumerable planets. All the planets and stars we see in the night sky fill only one of many universes. With the naked eye we see so little of even this universe! Yet, to the Lord, this whole universe is like one tiny mustard seed among a bag of seeds, effortlessly generated and later destroyed in His blissful yogic sleep-like trance. How great the Lord is!

Children blowing bubbles that dance in the sunlight may remind us of the great form of the Lord who breathes out bubble-like universes. Spiders lay egg-sacs, which, when they hatch, send out uncountable baby spiders floating on web parachutes. Dandelion plants send out dozens of air-borne fluff seeds, businesses open chain stores throughout the world, and a speech inspires millions of people to improve their lives. Surely, then, the Lord can breathe out uncountable universes.

Meditation 58: Kṛṣṇa Is the Original Source of All Incarnations

We cannot possibly count the number of ocean waves reaching the shore. Likewise, the number of incarnations emanating from Kṛṣṇa is endless. The waves of the ocean or a river, which the scriptures compare to Kṛṣṇa's incarnations, also never stop. The Lord's incarnations are also compared to actors, who take on many roles, forms, voices, and purposes. The actor as the origin of all these characters reminds us of Kṛṣṇa, the source of all incarnations. Even a person who plays many roles such as wife, mother, daughter, and teacher can spark remembrance of Kṛṣṇa who is the fountainhead of unlimited manifestations. Of course, much in our lives remind us of the Lord's specific incarnations. Heroes remind us of Lord Rāma; those who root out corruption, of Paraśurāma; teachers of peace and nonviolence, of Buddha; protectors of children, of Nṛsiṁhadeva; quiet, peaceful supporters, of Kūrma.

Meditation 59: Kṛṣṇa Is the Giver of Salvation to the Enemies Whom He Kills

The law of karma states that if a person kills someone in this life, he or she will be killed in a next life. When a government gives the death penalty to a murderer, the karmic payment is accomplished and the killer can be spared having to be killed in his next life.

Of course, such actions from governments do not give ultimate salvation. Human beings can under no circumstances give salvation to people they kill. Kṛṣṇa is the only person who can give salvation in this way, and He is so merciful that He gives liberation from the cycle of birth and death even to His enemies.

In addition to the proper use of the death penalty, we can remember this quality of Kṛṣṇa whenever we forgive someone from an offense, or someone forgives us. In a sense such forgiveness liberates us from the natural reaction to the offense. To accept being forgiven we need to "kill" the selfish or cruel motives that caused us to offend. Additionally, some programs to reform criminals or drug addicts may seem harsh, but the motive is to save and purify the person of their harmful mentalities and actions. Similarly, Kṛṣṇa's punishments are meant to reform and ultimately liberate us.

Meditation 60: Kṛṣṇa Is the Attractor of Liberated Souls

Liberated souls can be in this world but not of it; they are completely free from desires for sense gratification. Yet, despite being situated in such peace, they hanker to hear about the pastimes of Rādhā and Kṛṣṇa, for such is the wonderful all-attractive nature of Their names, forms, qualities, and activities! The only purpose and pleasure of liberated souls is to whole-heartedly love the source of their freedom: Kṛṣṇa. They are like birds aiming straight for the sky after being set free from their cage.

There are many examples in this world of attraction on a platform of freedom rather than necessity. While people generally work because they need an income, hobbies are done purely out of attraction, using one's free time for no reason other than love. Anything done not out of obligation, but simply out of joy and love, hints at the liberated soul's attraction for Kṛṣṇa and His activities.

UNCOUNTABLE UNIVERSES
generate FROM HIS body
HE THE ORIGINAL SOURCE
IS OF ALL incarnations
HE THE GIVER OF salvation
IS TO THE ENEMIES WHOM HE KILLS
HE THE attractor OF
IS liberated souls

Meditation 61: Kṛṣṇa Is the Performer of Wonderful Varieties of Pastimes

The scriptures describe the material creation as a perverted reflection of the spiritual world. In God's spiritual abode, He is the sole enjoyer, and His liberated associates are the enjoyed. Kṛṣṇa constantly performs wonderful pastimes, during which His loving devotees serve Him in five kinds of relationships – neutrality, servitorship, friendship, parental affection, and conjugal love – and in which they experience unlimited happiness. Out of all the manifestations of Godhead, Kṛṣṇa has the widest and deepest variety of playful pastimes.

In human society, we find conditioned souls seeking enjoyment in various activities: being attended to by a restaurant waiter or in serving a customer; in sporting activities with their peers; in nurturing their offspring; and in the hope of being loved unconditionally by their spouse. But herein also lies the devotee's key to remembering Kṛṣṇa as the performer of wonderful pastimes! The perverted reflection of something can be a powerful impetus to remember its original manifestation. A chauffeur driving an important businessman can help us remember Garuḍa, the carrier of Viṣṇu. Children absorbed in play can inspire us to meditate on the pastimes of Kṛṣṇa, Balarāma, and the cowherd boys. Parents taking their children out for entertainment are reminders of Nanda Mahārāja and Mother Yaśodā, Kṛṣṇa's eternal parents, who entertain Kṛṣṇa in various ways. And young couples walking together can inspire our remembrance of the intense ecstatic moods of Rādhā and Kṛṣṇa in Their conjugal pastimes.

Meditation 62: Kṛṣṇa Is Surrounded by Devotees Endowed with Wonderful Love of Godhead

Browsing through the news, one inevitably comes across images of important political figures or celebrities who are surrounded by people. A president is always surrounded by his bodyguards or ministers. Actors almost always have an audience or a camera crew, or more unpleasantly, the paparazzi around them. Teachers have their students. Similarly, Kṛṣṇa is never alone. He is always surrounded by His loving devotees, since real enjoyment is experienced not in isolation but within relationships.

Kṛṣṇa, the true possessor of all opulences, is always surrounded by His devotees, who desire nothing other than to please Him by their love-imbued service. They are like bees attracted to the sweetest-smelling flower. The Absolute lovable person will always be surrounded by His loving devotees.

Meditation 63: Kṛṣṇa Attracts Everyone by Playing on His Flute

The sound of Kṛṣṇa's flute is not of this world. It is nondifferent from Him and is therefore pure and spiritual, composed of eternity, cognizance, and unadulterated bliss. *The Nectar of Devotion* describes that great demigods become completely captivated when they hear Kṛṣṇa's flute song; they stop everything they are doing and absorb themselves in hearing the captivating vibration of this most fortunate instrument. Could we think of Kṛṣṇa's all-attractive flute-playing in our daily lives even though unable to hear it yet? Certainly, seeing a flute or witnessing a flute being played can be a reminder, but in a broader sense, any instance of our being attracted by particular sounds of this world can help us reflect on our relationship with spiritual sound.

There are certain pleasant sounds that instantly attract our attention: bird songs, ocean waves, tinkling bells, rustling leaves, or the crackling of a wood fire. The sounds our ears are easily attracted to can remind us of our real connection – to spiritual sound, which is most attractive and satisfying to the heart.

In addition to the sounds that attract our attention, the music that attracts us in this world can stimulate our remembrance of Kṛṣṇa's attractive flute sound. Musicians attract a crowd on a street corner, and thousands of people pay money and wait in line to have the experience of their emotions syncing with the music of their favorite performers.

Meditation 64: Kṛṣṇa Is the Possessor of Exquisite, Unrivaled Beauty

The very first quality of Kṛṣṇa that Rūpa Gosvāmī gives is that His form is beautiful. A further quality, beyond beauty in general, is that Kṛṣṇa has a wonderful excellence of beauty which cannot be rivaled anywhere in the creation. So how could anything in our experience spark appreciation of this quality?

Of course, anything or anyone we call "unrivaled" is relative to our experience, or at least to our planet. But the concept of celebrating the best, the topmost, superlative beauty, is certainly prevalent around us. Beauty contests in which young women compete speak to the desire within us to find an unrivaled beauty. Such is also the case in competitions for beauty in motion, as in dance contests and athletic sports, such as gymnastics and synchronized swimming. Artwork that is auctioned for the highest price are the "most beautiful" pieces. Museums, too, ostensibly aim to display unrivaled beauty. Fairy tales, such as Snow White, deal with the dark side of wanting to be the most beautiful without a rival. Fashion designers compete for a presentation of the most attractive. While all these attempts to find the summit of beauty are certainly insufficient and flawed, they can awaken in us the sweet understanding that we are all looking for Kṛṣṇa.

Appendix 1: Benedictions for the Soul

May your ears hear the notes of the Lord's flute-song, and may your heart listen to its message.

May the Lord's love be your shelter today, and always.

May the white lotus of your heart open in Kṛṣṇa's moonlight.

May Śrī Śrī Rādhā and Kṛṣṇa shower mercy on you like the monsoon and keep you grounded like the mountain. May your love for Them be deep as the ocean and your enthusiasm as constant as the rising sun.

May you be blessed with rock-solid inner control and oceans of enthusiasm and compassion.

May the river of life only carry you to more mercy and love for Śrī Śrī Rādhā and Kṛṣṇa.

May the rays of the sun warm your heart and may the Lord's light guide your way.

May Śrī Śrī Rādhā and Kṛṣṇa bless you with blossoms of their love today.

May the Lord plant in your heart the seed of ever-lasting love and humility, and may it grow like a beanstalk that takes you back to Him.

May Śrīmatī Rādhārāṇī's spirit of devotion and *bhakti* sweep over your soul like a cool breeze.

May you swim in the love of Śrī Śrī Rādhā and Govinda today, and always.

May Śrī Kṛṣṇa's love and mercy make your heart unfurl like *kairava-candrikā*.

May the mercy of Śrī Śrī Rādhā and Kṛṣṇa transform the current of your life into a soothing stream to carry you to Them.

May the Lord's love be a buoy to keep you afloat and safe in the rushing current of everyday life.

May Śrī Śrī Rādhā and Kṛṣṇa's mercy and love soak you like a celestial rainstorm today and always.

May you be given the eyes to see all the silver linings and the heart that is undaunted by any dark clouds.

May the realms of your heart and mind be peaceful, clear, and reflecting as a lake on a silent, windless, and moonlit night.

May every moment of pain, self-inflicted or otherwise, that you experience, by Kṛṣṇa's mercy, become a prism through which you can see and spread the beauty of *bhakti*.

May every moment of pain be a prism in Kṛṣṇa's hands through which He may show you the beauty of humility and surrender.

May Kṛṣṇa continue to use you as a prism through which others can see the beautiful colors of *bhakti*.

May your heart always be a fountain of love for chanting the holy names and that the echoes of Lord Caitanya's chanting resound in your mind and soul while you are following the path of His *līlās*.

May Kṛṣṇa grant you the vision to see His face in looming thunderclouds and also in the silver linings that go with them.

May you feel Kṛṣṇa's love and guidance like a cooling breeze in the heat of Maya's material realm.

May Kṛṣṇa be your lighthouse fortress in the madness of the material ocean that is forever trying to engulf us. May His light show you the way and may the walls keep you safe. I pray that Kṛṣṇa keeps His hand on your heart so that you may always perform your *sādhana* with steadfast sincerity in any raging storm.

When Maya throws you a mudslide, may it become the fertile soil from which the lotus of love and devotion grows even more in your heart.

When torrents of rain threaten to wash you away, may you seek the shelter of Govardhana Hill.

When Maya sends you a heat spell, may the Queen of Vṛndāvana grant you the shade of a *kalpa-vṛkṣa* tree.

May the thunderclouds of life remind you of Kṛṣṇa's complexion, may you hear His voice in the rolling thunder, and see the twinkle of His eye in the flashes of lightning.

May every pit of darkness become a source from which you draw deeply from the Reservoir of Mercy, so that you have more to share with others.

May you be blessed with faith and friendships that stand as firm as the giant redwood trees.

May the waves of the ocean play to you the rhythm to which your heart must beat like the *gopīs*, in separation of their beloved Kṛṣṇa.

May the fire of your mind be used only to illuminate the glories of Śrī Kṛṣṇa, may the power of your words be harnessed only for His pleasure, and may your body be a marionette in His masterful hands, just like Śrīla Prabhupāda's.

May Kṛṣṇa melt any shards of ice still left in your heart, and may you use the water from those shards to make the desert-like world flower in love of Kṛṣṇa again.

May your heart be a grove of Vṛndāvana where Śrī Śrī Rādhā and Kṛṣṇa can spend time together. May your words be the roses, jasmines, and gardenias that beautify that grove, and may your actions be the garlands you offer Them.

When the road gets thorny may you be able to see the roses that come with it.

When the dragons of Lust, Anger, or Greed assail you, may Love be your armor, Humility your weapon, and Contentment your steed.

In times of darkness, may you turn to your *gurudeva,* your guide, and may you follow the lamp of knowledge that he holds before you.

May you see Kṛṣṇa's beautiful color in the blue light of every new dawn, and may the shining rays of the young sun be His fingers that touch your eyes with new spiritual vision every day.

May Śrīmatī Rādhārāṇī watch over you. May Her glance be like a raincloud giving life to a parched desert. May She bestow on you the capacity to serve Her beloved Lord with a calm heart and peaceful, jubilant mind.

May Lord Balarāma's strength wash over you like the unending waves of the mighty ocean, and may His compassion inundate your heart, tomorrow and every day after.

May the *mahā-mantra* remain your anchor and the words of *śāstra* your sails in the ocean of material existence.

May your soul be set alight like the flame of the ghee lamps we offer to Lord Dāmodara. May the rope of your devotion and endeavor together with His mercy bind your heart to His even closer. May your very heartbeat be infused with Mother Yaśodā's love.

May your heart be like a night jasmine flower filling the air with sweet devotion and love of Kṛṣṇa!

May your heart burn at its brightest for Lord Kṛṣṇa, and may you find more and more ways to spread that light in the dark realm of maya around you.

May your heart and mind continue to be fertile ground in which Kṛṣṇa can make His *bhakti* grow.

May Kṛṣṇa continue to cultivate in your heart the pearl plant of love and devotion for the Divine Couple and your dearest Śrīla Prabhupāda.

May your road in Kṛṣṇa Consciousness always be alight with sparks of hope.

May you find the victory you pray for against the walls of pride around your heart. May the words of *sadhu* and *śāstra* be like a drenching rainstorm that turns these walls of pride to mud. May that rain turn to rivulets and overflow your heart's lake with their love and affection. May the mud, by Kṛṣṇa's mercy, be carried away to the great ocean of His love, where it can settle and never wash upstream again.

May any ripples on the lake of your mind be stilled to reflect only Śrī Kṛṣṇa's love, and if any ripples remain, may their source be only the rhythm of Kṛṣṇa's heartbeat.

May the compass needle of your heart continue to always point to Kṛṣṇa.

May the ocean of your mind be always cooling and calm so that the vessel of your intelligence can have a smooth crossing. May you continue to have unflinching faith in the captain of your ship and soul, Śrī Kṛṣṇa.

May you rejoice even in the darkest of nights, for they carry the brightest of stars.

May the gentle tendrils of the *bhakti* creeper enfold your heart with love and devotion for Śrī Śrī Rādhā-Kṛṣṇa. May they continue to produce the flowers and fruit of loving service for Them.

May Kṛṣṇa's loving light continually find its way through the cracks of your conditioning until you are filled and can reflect it to others from the inside out.

May the waves of your mind come to a restful reflection of that most beautiful blue boy, and may the sweet notes of His flute drift over its quiet waters into your heart.

May your life be like a new lotus, blooming with possibilities in Kṛṣṇa's loving sunlight. May each petal be a beautiful offering of love and devotion to Kṛṣṇa, who can extract beauty from the deepest material mire.

Appendix 2: Quotes on Seeing Kṛṣṇa in the World

From Nārada

Nārada Mahārāja said that "This world is Kṛṣṇa." *Idaṁ hi viśvaṁ bhagavān ivetaraḥ*. "But it appears like that it is different from Bhagavān." Actually, there is . . . For a *mahā-bhāgavata*, he has no such conception, material conception, because he sees everywhere Kṛṣṇa. *Sthāvara-jaṅgama dekhe nā dekhe tāra mūrti* [*Caitanya-caritāmṛta*, Madhya 8.274]. He's seeing one tree, but he is . . . he's forgetful of the tree. He's seeing energy of Kṛṣṇa. As soon as he sees the energy of Kṛṣṇa, he sees Kṛṣṇa. Therefore, instead of seeing the tree, he sees Kṛṣṇa. . . . As soon as he sees anything we call material, he sees this is the conversion of the energy. *Pariṇāma-vāda. Sarvedam akhilaṁ jagat. Parasya brahmaṇaḥ śaktiḥ* . . . Just like as soon as you see the sunshine, you see immediately sun. Is it not? In the morning, as soon as you see within your window the sunshine, immediately you remember sun and you are confident sun is there. Without sun, how there can be sunshine? Similarly, whatever we see, if we immediately see Kṛṣṇa, with reference to that particular thing . . . Because that particular thing is the manifestation of the energy of Kṛṣṇa. So those who have understood Kṛṣṇa along with His energies, he sees the energy, because energy is not different from the energetic, he sees immediately Kṛṣṇa. Therefore, he does not see anything except Kṛṣṇa. So therefore, for him, there is no material world. There is no material world. To a perfect devotee, there is no material world. Everything is spiritual. *Sarvaṁ khalv idaṁ brahma*. He sees everything Brahman. So we have to make our eyes to see Kṛṣṇa. *Tat-paratvena nirmalam*.

sarvopādhi-vinirmuktaṁ
tat-paratvena nirmalam
hṛṣīkeṇa hṛṣīkeśa-
sevanaṁ bhaktir ucyate

[Caitanya-caritāmṛta, Madhya 19.170]

Tat-paratvena. As soon as we are in Kṛṣṇa consciousness, our seeing, touching, smelling – everything become *nirmala*, purified. Then we can immediately see Kṛṣṇa. These eyes, so long it is not purified, we cannot see Kṛṣṇa. As soon as it is purified, you see Kṛṣṇa. As soon as it is purified, you see Kṛṣṇa, nothing but Kṛṣṇa.

(Lecture on *The Nectar of Devotion*, Vṛndāvana. November 11, 1972)

From Jīva Gosvāmī

Following the order of guru, Kṛṣṇa and Balarāma quickly went to the ocean near Prabhāsa on a chariot with a driver. They arrived quickly. Then, seeing the broad expanse of the ocean for the first time, in excitement They reflected. "Ah! The ocean which spreads out water spreads wide the beholder's eyes. It seems that the ocean is happy to see us and is offering respect.

"He is coming close to embrace us, by those rolling waves. He is smiling by His many balls of foam. He is spreading His nostrils wide to smell by the forms of *makaras in* the waves. Marked with thousands of turtles with raised backs, appearing to be eyes, He is looking at us. With the sound of millions of clouds rumbling, He is playing welcoming music.

He is dancing, expressing various emotions with His limbs, by the waves. The ocean is making an offering in his folded hands by the whirlpools which reveal gems rare for endeavoring kings who have conquered all enemies."

After making these analogies and looking at the ocean, the ocean, conforming to the description given, became visible.

The *gopīs* would continually see Kṛṣṇa in other objects, speak of Kṛṣṇa in other speeches, and hear Kṛṣṇa in other statements.

(Gopāla Campū)

From Bhaktivinoda Ṭhākura

Holy men to whom God have been pleased to show His spiritual form have often attempted to picture it to their fellow brethren. The picture, whether it be by pencil, chisel, or pen, is always made through the medium of matter, and hence a degree of grossness has all along attended the representations. This emblematic exhibition of spiritual impressions is far from being open to [the] charge of idolatry. Those who rationally conceive the idea of God, and by the assistance of the imagination create an image, are certainly open to the charge. There is one absolute truth at the bottom of this important question. It is this: Nature has indeed a relation to the spirit. What is that relation? As far as we have been instructed by the inner Tutor, we may safely say, that spirit is the perfect model and nature is the copy which is full of imperfections. Draw inferences from the side of nature and press them upon the Deity, they will ever remain gross and imperfect. Draw from the spirit inside and push your impressions at first to the mind and then to the body, you simply spiritualize them both. Here is [the] advent of God on the scene of nature. It is then that the model is to be found represented by the corresponding copy in nature. God's transcendental form also finds its corresponding reflection in nature, and when we worship the Deity, in pure love, in the reflected scenes of Vṛndāvana. Here the imagination has no play. It is the soul which sees and makes a description in the corresponding phenomena in nature. The spiritual form thus conveyed to us is none but the eternal form of God. The grossness is simply apparent, but all the actions and consequences are fully spiritual. The man who weeps and dances in felicity when he spiritually sees the beauty of God is certainly translated to the region of spirits for the time and the gross action of his body is but a concomitant manifestation caused by a current of spiritual electricity. Here we find the absolute in the relative, the positive in the negative and spirit in matter. The spiritual form of God is therefore an eternal truth and with all its inward variety, it is one Undivided Unity. What appears to be a contradiction to reason is nothing but the rule of spirit. And the greatest surprise arises when we see full harmony in all these contradictions.

(*The Seventh Goswami: A Biography of His Divine Grace Śrīla Saccidānanda Bhaktivinoda Ṭhākura*, by Rupa-Vilasa Dasa, Sitarama Deva Trust, 1993, Chapter 17, quoting an untitled essay of Bhaktivinoda)

From Śrīla Prabhupāda

This World is Not False

Brahma satyaṁ jagan mithyā. *Jagat* is not *mithyā*. To the Vaiṣṇava, to the devotee, we cannot accept that this *jagat*, this world is false. No. How it can be false? Suppose you enter in a very beautiful garden, very nicely trees, [indistinct] so many nice flowers, building. Everything is, they are nice. The proprietor of the garden takes you to show you. And if you say, "Oh, it is all *mithyā*," then how much depressed he becomes, just see. "I brought this friend to show the beauty of this garden, and he says it is *mithyā*." Similarly, we won't want to depress Kṛṣṇa. [laughter] That is not our business. Kṛṣṇa has created this nice world. Everything is very nice. The sun is rising just in exact time. It is setting in exact time.

The moon is rising. The seasons are changing. And we are getting nice food, nice fruit, nice flowers. So, we are not so de . . . I mean to say, depressing agent. We won't discourage Kṛṣṇa. Why? Kṛṣṇa has created this nice world. How can I say it is *mithyā*? It is the by-product of Kṛṣṇa's energy. So Kṛṣṇa's energy cannot be false. It is eternal. Kṛṣṇa is eternal. Kṛṣṇa says in the *Bhagavad-Gītā* that this material world, *bhūmir āpo analo vāyuḥ khaṁ buddhir mana eva ca, bhinnā me prakṛtir aṣṭadhā* [*Bhagavad-Gītā* 7.4]. "These are eight kinds of separated energy of Me, Kṛṣṇa." So Kṛṣṇa's energy . . . Kṛṣṇa is truth. So Kṛṣṇa's energy is also truth. Because form truth, false cannot come. If Kṛṣṇa is truth, this energy is also truth. But it is not false.

Therefore, we do not accept this *Māyāvādī* theory that the world is false, *jagan mithyā*. We say that *Brahman* is *satya*, and this world is also *satya*. The difference is that a devotee relishes a particular type of mellow, *rasa*, in this material world. But the . . . those who are not devotees, they do not feel any relish from this material world. They feel for some time, but when it becomes stale in their taste, they say, "It is false." Just like the same example: The jackal first of all tried to get the grapes, jumping, jumping, and when it was a failure, he said, "Oh, the grapes are sour. I don't require." So, except devotee . . . The non-devotees, the *karmīs*, *jñānīs*, *yogīs*, they actually do not relish the sweetness of the creation of Kṛṣṇa.

(Lecture on *The Nectar of Devotion*, Vṛndāvana. October 17, 1972)

Meditation on the Universal Form to Saturate the Mind with Spiritual Consciousness

When the mind is fixed upon the Supreme Personality of Godhead in His external feature made of the material modes of nature – the gross universal form – it is brought to the platform of pure goodness. In that transcendental position, one can understand the Supreme Personality of Godhead, Vāsudeva, who in His subtler form is self-effulgent and beyond the modes of nature. O my lord, please describe vividly how that form, which covers the entire universe, is perceived.

Purport

Mahārāja Parīkṣit had already been advised by his spiritual master, Śukadeva Gosvāmī, to think of the universal form of the Lord, and therefore, following the advice of his spiritual master, he continuously thought of that form. The universal form is certainly material, but because everything is an expansion of the energy of the Supreme Personality of Godhead, ultimately nothing is material. Therefore, Parīkṣit Mahārāja's mind was saturated with spiritual consciousness. Śrīla Rūpa Gosvāmī has stated:

prāpañcikatayā buddhyā
hari-sambandhi-vastunaḥ
mumukṣubhiḥ parityāgo
vairāgyaṁ phalgu kathyate
[*Bhakti-rasāmṛta-sindhu* 1.2.255–256]

Everything, even that which is material, is connected with the Supreme Personality of Godhead. Therefore, everything should be engaged in the service of the Lord. Śrīla Bhaktisiddhānta Sarasvatī Ṭhākura translates this verse as follows:

śrī-hari sevāya yāhā haya anukūla
viṣaya baliyā tyāge haya bhūla

"One should not give up anything connected with the Supreme Personality of Godhead, thinking it material or enjoyable for the material senses." Even the senses, when purified, are spiritual. When Mahārāja Parīkṣit was thinking of the universal form of the Lord, his mind was certainly situated on the transcendental platform. Therefore, although he might not have had any reason to be concerned with detailed information of the universe, he was thinking of it in relationship with the Supreme Lord, and therefore such geographical knowledge was not material but transcendental. Elsewhere in *Śrīmad-Bhāgavatam* 1.5.20, Nārada Muni has said:

> *idaṁ hi viśvaṁ bhagavān ivetaraḥ:* the entire universe is also the Supreme Personality of Godhead, although it appears different from Him. Therefore, although Parīkṣit Mahārāja had no need for geographical knowledge of this universe, that knowledge was also spiritual and transcendental because he was thinking of the entire universe as an expansion of the energy of the Lord.
>
> (*Śrīmad-Bhāgavatam* 5.16.3)

Not Inferior Energy

In the *Bhagavad-Gītā* the living entities have been described as *prakṛti. Apareyam itas tu vidhi me prakṛtim parā.* After describing the material energies – earth, water, air, fire sky, mind, intelligence, ego – Kṛṣṇa says *apareyam*, all these energies, separated energies, material energies, they are *aparā*, inferior. But that is also Kṛṣṇa's energies. Inferior means not actually inferior, because they . . . there cannot be anything inferior which is emanating from Kṛṣṇa. The inferior in this sense: by our absence of Kṛṣṇa consciousness. Because we have come here, in this material world, to enjoy, to satisfy, sense satisfaction, sense gratification, we have made it inferior. Otherwise, it is not inferior. One who knows how to utilize this energy, for Him, it is not inferior. *Nirbandha-kṛṣṇa-sambandhe yukta-vairāgyam ucyate.* One who does not know how to utilize this material energy for the purpose of Kṛṣṇa, for them, it is inferior. Otherwise, *advaya-jñāna*, absolute . . . *Idaṁ hi viśvaṁ bhagavān ivetaraḥ.* Nārada Muni has described before to Vyāsadeva: *idaṁ hi viśvaṁ bhagavān ivetaraḥ.* It appears like different, but actually Kṛṣṇa . . . This is the vision of *mahā-bhāgavata*, not ordinary man. *Mahā-bhāgavata . . . Sthāvara-jaṅgama dekhi tāra mūrti* [*Caitanya*-caritāmṛta, *Madhya* 8.274]. A *mahā-bhāgavata* sees a tree or an animal or a . . . He does not see the form, but he sees his *iṣṭa deva mūrti*; he sees there Kṛṣṇa. Actually, Kṛṣṇa is there as Paramātmā. So, he sees Paramātmā. He does not see the external body. So Kṛṣṇa's two energies . . . Inferior means where Kṛṣṇa consciousness is almost absent. That is inferior. When there is Kṛṣṇa consciousness, that is no more inferior; that is superior.

(Lecture on *The Nectar of Devotion,* Vṛndāvana. October 30, 1972)

No Material World

Material things means, as I have repeatedly explained, forgetful of Kṛṣṇa. Otherwise, there is nothing material. It is illusion. Illusion means actually there is nothing material. How it can be material? If the Supreme Lord is Supreme Spirit, everything is coming from Him, so what we call the material energy, that is also coming from the Supreme.

But the difficulty is that in this inferior energy . . . Inferior energy means where there is possibility of forgetting Kṛṣṇa. Actually, that is the fact. People are engaged in so many activities. We can see it very nicely in the Western countries. They are inventing so many modern facilities. But the result is they're forgetting Kṛṣṇa. That is material. Material means forgetfulness of Kṛṣṇa. Otherwise, there is nothing except Kṛṣṇa.

(Lecture on *The Nectar of Devotion,* Vṛndāvana. November 11, 1972)

Nothing Material

Actually, in pure Kṛṣṇa consciousness there is nothing material. I have several times explained. Material activities means activities without Kṛṣṇa consciousness. That is material activity. Just like we are speaking through this microphone. We do not reject it as material. We take it as spiritual. Because it is being used in spreading Kṛṣṇa consciousness. *Anāsaktasya viṣayān yathārham upayuñjataḥ. Yathā arhati*, as it deserves. Because this microphone is made of material elements, earth, water, fire, air . . . But this, if we remember that these material energies, earth, water, air, fire, sky, even mind, intelligence, ego . . . *Prakṛti me, prakṛti me bhinnā aṣṭadhā.* They're also energies of Kṛṣṇa. They're not separate from Kṛṣṇa. Therefore, if Kṛṣṇa is spirit, then these so-called material elements, they are also spirit. But it is used as material because we do not remember the relationship of these material elements with Kṛṣṇa. Therefore, the conclusion is when we are forgetful of Kṛṣṇa, then it is material. Otherwise, there is nothing as material. Everything is spiritual. Because *brāhmaṇaḥ śakti . . . Sarvaṁ khalu idaṁ brahma.* Everything that we experience, that is manifestation of the energy of Kṛṣṇa. *Sarvedam akhilaṁ jagat. Brahmaṇaḥ śakti. Śakti* and *śaktimān*, they are not different. So, if we accept everything as expansion of *brahmaṇaḥ śakti,* energy of Kṛṣṇa, and utilize it for Kṛṣṇa, then there is nothing, such thing as material. Everything becomes spiritual. So, if we think in that way, thinking, feeling, and willing, if we utilize our psychological activities in Kṛṣṇa consciousness, then we keep steady . . . attached with Kṛṣṇa. *Yukta-vairāgyam ucyate. Vairāgya* means renunciation. We do not require to renounce anything, provided we see everything dovetailed in Kṛṣṇa consciousness. That is required.

(Lecture on *The Nectar of Devotion*, Vṛndāvana. October 29, 1972)

The World is Bhagavān

[T]hose who are highly elevated devotees, they do not see even this material world different from Bhagavān. *Idaṁ hi viśvaṁ bhagavān ivetara.* That is described in the *Śrīmad-Bhāgavatam,* Nārada Muni says. The whole universe is Bhagavān, although it appears different from Him. *Bhagavān ivetara.* So actually, everything is Bhagavān, but it is not this Māyāvāda philosophy, that because everything is Bhagavān, there is no Bhagavān. No. Everything is Bhagavān, and still Bhagavān is there.

(Lecture on *Śrī Caitanya-caritāmṛta, Madhya* 20.395, Hyderabad. August 17, 1976)

The Elements

Actually, there is nothing but Kṛṣṇa all around us. This is explained in the *Bhagavad-Gītā.* He is the taste of water, light of the moon, the fragrance of the flower, light of the sun, sound of the sky, the power of the strong, and so on. So, one who is actually making progress in Kṛṣṇa consciousness, he can see Kṛṣṇa everywhere. At every stage of life, who can avoid the sunlight, the moonlight, the fragrance of the flower, the taste of the water, the sound of the sky, and so on; but one has to learn it, that there is Kṛṣṇa in all these varieties of existence. Without Kṛṣṇa there is nothing. It is simply by the influence of maya that we forget the relationship of Kṛṣṇa with everything that be.

(Letter to Kṛṣṇa Devī, San Francisco, December 21, 1967)

Glossary

Ācārya: A teacher, who teaches by perfect example.

Aghāsura: The snake demon.

Anarthas: sinful attachments.

Ārati: ceremony offering certain items to Śrī Kṛṣṇa.

Arjuna: Kṛṣṇa's best friend to whom He spoke the Bhagavad-Gītā.

Avatāra: A specific form or incarnation of Kṛṣṇa.

Āyurveda: The ancient medical science of ancient India.

Balarāma: Kṛṣṇa's older brother.

Bali Mahārāja: Prahlāda Maharaja's grandson and king of the demons.

Banasura: a demoniac king.

Bhagavad-Gītā: The conversation between Śrī Kṛṣṇa and Arjuna on the battlefield of Kurukṣetra.

bhakti-yogīs: People who practice bhakti, devotional service to Śrī Kṛṣṇa.

Bhīma: Arjuna's older brother.

Bhīṣma: The grandfather of the Kauravas and Pāṇḍavas.

Bhṛgu Muni: a great priest or brāhmaṇa.

Brahmā: The first of all the gods and the creator of the universe. He was directly manifested from Viṣṇu and is thus sometimes called "the unborn."

Brahman: The impersonal effulgence of Śrī Kṛṣṇa.

Burfi: A sweet made from boiled down milk and sugar.

Caitanya Mahāprabhu: The incarnation of Śrī Kṛṣṇa that spread the chanting of the mahā-mantra

around 500 years ago.

Causal Ocean/Universal Ocean: The ocean that separates the material world from the spiritual world.

Dāmodara: a name for Śrī Kṛṣṇa as a baby, when He was tied with a rope around the belly by His mother.

Devas: The demigods.

Devotee: A follower of Śrī Kṛṣṇa.

Dhāma: A holy place, like Vṛndāvana.

Dhenukāsura: A demon in the form of a donkey.

Dhoti: a garment wore traditionally by devotee men, like a pants folded from one long piece of cloth.

Dhṛtarāṣṭra: the blind king of Hastināpura during the time of the war of Kurukṣetra.

Draupadī: the wife of the five Pāṇḍavas.

Durvāsā Muni: a great brāhmaṇa, who was known for his quick anger.

Dvārakā: The city of Kṛṣṇa that was built on the ocean.

Gāndhārī: The wife of Dhṛtarāṣṭra, who voluntarily blindfolded herself because he was blind.

Gāyatrī: is the origin of Vedic knowledge.

Ghee: clarified butter.

Gopāla: a name of Kṛṣṇa as a cowherd boy.

gopīs: the cowherd girls of Vraja.

Govardhana Hill: a sacred Hill in Vraja.

Hiraṇyākṣa: The first demon who fought with Kṛṣṇa in His form of a boar.

Indra: King of the gods, also known as Purandara and Śakra.

Jāmbavān: The bear king that fought alongside Lord Rāma in His fight against Rāvaṇa.

Japa: the process of chanting the Hare Kṛṣṇa mantra on a string of 108 beads.

Jarāsandha: a demoniac king who was killed by Bhīma by being torn in half.

Jīva: the conditioned soul.

Kamsa: the uncle of Kṛṣṇa, who wanted to kill Him since He was a baby.

Karma: the process of cause and effect that cause the conditioned souls to reincarnate birth after birth.

Kauravas: the sons of Dhṛtarāṣṭra, who wanted to steal the kingdom from the Pāṇḍavas.

Kīrtana: the communal singing of the Hare Kṛṣṇa mantra.

Kṣīrodakaśāyī Viṣṇu: The expansion of Viṣṇu as the Supersoul, the form of the Lord in the heart of every living entity.

Kunti: The mother of the Pāṇḍavas.

Kurukṣetra: The name of the place where the Bhagavad-Gītā was spoken by Kṛṣṇa.

Magadhendra: a king and enemy of Kṛṣṇa.

Mahā-mantra: Hare Kṛṣṇa, Hare Kṛṣṇa, Kṛṣṇa Kṛṣṇa, Hare Hare/ Hare Rāma, Hare Rāma, Rāma Rāma, Hare Hare.

Mahārāja Parīkṣit: Arjuna's grandson and the king who heard the Śrīmad-Bhāgavatam Śukadeva Goswāmī.

Mahā-Viṣṇu: The first Viṣṇu (Kāraṇodakaśāyī Viṣṇu) from which all the other Viṣṇus expand. Kāraṇodakaśāyī Viṣṇu enters in every universe as Garbhodakaśāyī Viṣṇu. And this Garbhodakaśāyī Viṣṇu again expands as Kṣīrodakaśāyī Viṣṇu.

Maya: the illusory energy of Kṛṣṇa.

Mithyā: to be false.

Monistic: a system that believes everything is one.

Mother Bhumi: the demigoddess of the Earth planet.

Mother Yaśodā: Kṛṣṇa's adoptive mother.

Nanda Mahārāja: Kṛṣṇa's adoptive father.

Nṛsiṁhadeva: the incarnation of the Lord as a half-man, half-lion

Pāṇḍavas: the five brothers that fought against the Kauravas.

Paneer: cheese made from milk solids hung and pressed in a cheese cloth.

Pārijāta: a flower that originally grew only on the heavenly planets.

Prahlāda: the devotee son of the demon Hiraṇyakaśipu.

Prasādam: Food that is sanctified by offering it to Kṛṣṇa.

Prasena: a prince who was killed while wearing the Syamantaka jewel.

Prema: the nineth stage of bhakti and pure love of God.

Pūtanā: A demoness who tried to kill Kṛṣṇa when He was a small baby.

Rādhā/ Śrīmatī Rādhārāṇī: The eternal consort of Śrī Kṛṣṇa

Rāmacandra: The seventh of the Dasavatāra incarnations of Viṣṇu, who appeared as a king in the solar dynasty (i.e., descending from the sun-god).

Rasa: the mood or flavor of the devotional service being performed.

Rāvaṇa: A powerful leader of the Rākṣasa race who stole Sītā from Lord Rāmacandra.

Rukmiṇī Devī: The principal queen of Śrī Kṛṣṇa in Dvārakā.

Rūpa Gosvāmī: One of the principal followers of Śrī Caitanya Mahāprabhu.

Sādhana: the activities by which we can attain Śrī Kṛṣṇa.

Sannyāsīs: people that have renounced all worldly affairs in favor of focusing only on devotional service.

Śāstra: transcendental literature

Śeṣa: a giant snake on whose head all the planets rest.

Śikṣā guru: a spiritual master that gives the devotee instructions.

Śiśupāla: Kṛṣṇa cut of his head because of his offensive nature.

Sītā: The wife of Lord Rāma

Śiva: He is responsible for the destruction of the material universe at the end of a Yuga.

Śrī Kṛṣṇa: The Supreme Personality of Godhead.

Śrīla Bhaktisiddhānta Sarasvatī Ṭhākura: The spiritual master of Śrīla Prabhupāda.

Śrīla Prabhupāda: The founder Ācārya of the International Society for Kṛṣṇa Consciousness.

Śrīmad-Bhāgavatam: The transcendental literature spoken by Śukadeva Goswāmī.

Subji: a dish made from vegetables.

Sudarśana: the disc weapon of Kṛṣṇa.

Supersoul: The expansion of Kṛṣṇa in the heart of all living entities.

Sūta Gosvāmī: Sūta Gosvāmī was the speaker in a very big meeting at Naimiṣāraṇya forest. He relayed the message of the Śrīmad-Bhāgavatam.

Uddhava: Kṛṣṇa's best friend in Dvārakā.

Vāmanadeva: The dwarf incarnation of Kṛṣṇa.

Vānaprasthas: People who have retired from married life in order to pursue more spiritual activities.

Varāha: the boar incarnation of Kṛṣṇa.

Varuṇa: the demigod of water.

Viśvanātha Cakravartī Ṭhākura: an author who commented on Śrīmad-Bhāgavatam and other holy scriptures.

Vrajarāja Kṛṣṇa: a name for Kṛṣṇa in Vraja meaning the King of Vraja.

Vṛndāvana: The place where Kṛṣṇa appeared on this Earth planet. Also, a place in the spiritual world.

Yajna: fire sacrifice performed at religious ceremonies.

Yamarāja: Demigod of Death.

Yoga-māyā: Kṛṣṇa's illusory energy in the spiritual world.

Yudhiṣṭhira: the oldest brother of Arjuna and the rightful king.

Bibliography

Bhaktivedanta Swami Prabhupāda, A. C. *Bhagavad-Gītā As It Is.* Los Angeles, CA: The Bhaktivedanta Book Trust, 1989

Bhaktivedanta Swami Prabhupāda, A. C. *Śrī Caitanya-caritāmṛta.* Los Angeles, CA: The Bhaktivedanta Book Trust, 1996

Bhaktivedanta Swami Prabhupāda, A. C. *Kṛṣṇa, the Supreme Personality of Godhead [Kṛṣṇa Book].* Los Angeles, CA: The Bhaktivedanta Book Trust, 1997

Bhaktivedanta Swami Prabhupāda, A. C. *The Nectar of Devotion.* Los Angeles, CA: The Bhaktivedanta Book Trust, 1970

Bhaktivedanta Swami Prabhupāda, A. C. *Śrīmad-Bhāgavatam.* Los Angeles, CA: The Bhaktivedanta Book Trust, 1987

Ṭhākura, Bhaktisiddhānta Sarasvatī Gosvāmī. *Śrī Brahma-saṁhitā.* Los Angeles, CA: The Bhaktivedanta Book Trust, 1985